Street by Street

C000072372

STOKE-ON-TRENT

CONGLETON, HANLEY, LEEK, NEWCASTLE-UNDER-LYME, STONE

Alsager, Audley, Barlaston, Biddulph, Cheadle, Endon, Forsbrook, Keele, Kidsgrove, Longton

2nd edition December 2005
© Automobile Association Developments Limited 2005

Original edition printed May 2001

Ordnance Survey® This product includes map data licensed from Ordnance Survey® with the permission of the Controller of Her Majesty's Stationery Office. © Crown copyright 2005. All rights reserved. Licence number 399221.

All rights reserved. No part of this publication may be reproduced, stored in a retrieval system, or transmitted in any form or by any means – electronic, mechanical, photocopying, recording or otherwise – unless the permission of the publisher has been given beforehand.

Published by AA Publishing (a trading name of Automobile Association Developments Limited, whose registered office is Fanum House, Basing View, Basingstoke, Hampshire RG21 4EA. Registered number 1878835).

Mapping produced by the Cartography Department of The Automobile Association. (A02545)

A CIP Catalogue record for this book is available from the British Library.

Printed by Oriental Press in Dubai

The contents of this atlas are believed to be correct at the time of the latest revision. However, the publishers cannot be held responsible or liable for any loss or damage occasioned to any person acting or refraining from action as a result of any use or reliance on any material in this atlas, nor for any errors, omissions or changes in such material. This does not affect your statutory rights. The publishers would welcome information to correct any errors or omissions and to keep this atlas up to date. Please write to Publishing, The Automobile Association, Fanum House (FH12), Basing View, Basingstoke, Hampshire, RG21 4EA.

Ref: ML86z

Key to map pages	ii–iii
Key to map symbols	iv-1
Enlarged map pages	2-5
Main map pages	6-91
Index – towns & villages	92
Index – streets	93-105
Index – featured places	105-106
Acknowledgements	107

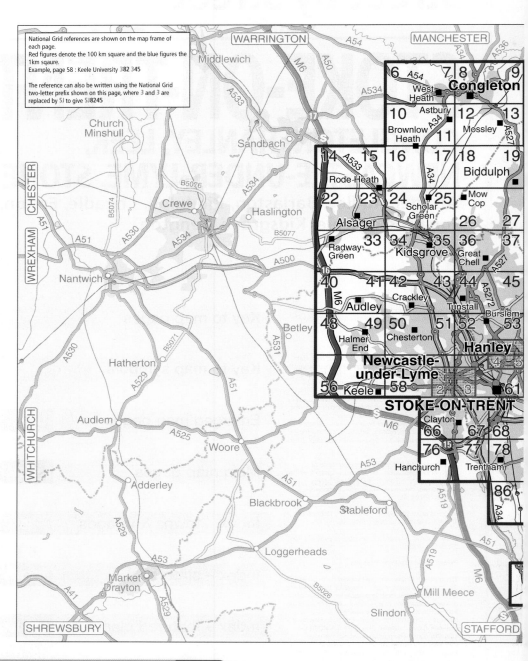

ii

National Grid references are shown on the map frame of each page.
Red figures denote the 100 km square and the blue figures the 1km sqaure.
Example, page 58 : Keele University 3**82** 3**45**

The reference can also be written using the National Grid two-letter prefix shown on this page, where 3 and 3 are replaced by SJ to give SJ**8245**

WARRINGTON

MANCHESTER

Middlewich

A54

A534

6 A54 7 8 9
West Heath Congleton

10 Astbury 12 13
Brownlow Heath 11 Mossley

Church Minshull

Sandbach

14 A533 15 16 17 18 19
Rode Heath Biddulph

22 23 24 25 Mow Cop 26 27
Alsager Scholar Green

Crewe

Haslington

B5077

33 34 35 36 37
Radway Green Kidsgrove Great Chell

40 41 42 43 44 45
A500 Audley Crackley Tunstall Burslem

48 49 50 51 52 53
Halmer End Chesterton Hanley

Nantwich

Betley

56 58 61
Keele

Newcastle-under-Lyme

STOKE-ON-TRENT

Hatherton

Clayton
66 67 68
76 15 77 78
Hanchurch Trentham

Audlem

Woore

Blackbrook

Stableford

86

Adderley

Loggerheads

Market Drayton

Mill Meece

Slindon

SHREWSBURY

STAFFORD

CHESTER
WREXHAM
WHITCHURCH

Scale of enlarged map pages 1:10,000 6.3 inches to 1 mile

0 — 1/4 — miles — 1/2

0 — 1/4 — 1/2 — kilometres — 3/4 — 1

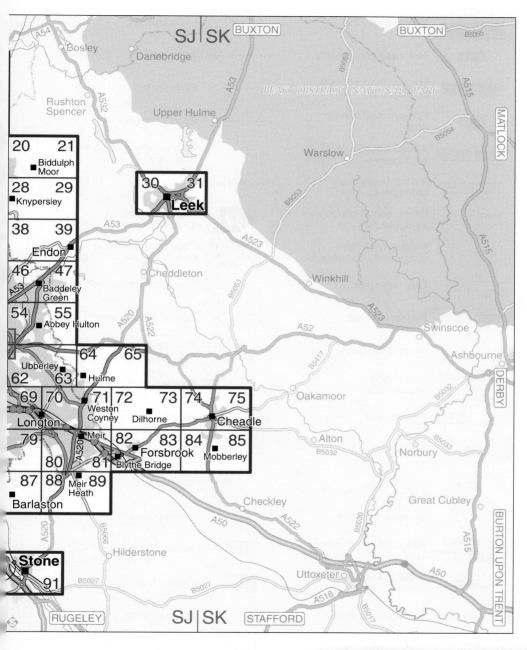

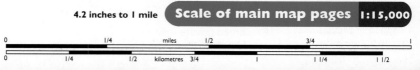

iv

Symbol	Description
Junction 9	Motorway & junction
Services	Motorway service area
	Primary road single/dual carriageway
Services	Primary road service area
	A road single/dual carriageway
	B road single/dual carriageway
	Other road single/dual carriageway
	Minor/private road, access may be restricted
← ←	One-way street
	Pedestrian area
	Track or footpath
	Road under construction
	Road tunnel
P	Parking
P+	Park & Ride
	Bus/coach station
	Railway & main railway station
	Railway & minor railway station
⊖	Underground station
⊖	Light railway & station
+++++++++	Preserved private railway

Symbol	Description
LC	Level crossing
•—•—•—•	Tramway
-----------	Ferry route
....	Airport runway
— · — · — · —	County, administrative boundary
▼▼▼▼▼▼▼▼▼	Mounds
17	Page continuation 1:15,000
3	Page continuation to enlarged scale 1:10,000
	River/canal, lake, pier
	Aqueduct, lock, weir
465 ▲ Winter Hill	Peak (with height in metres)
	Beach
	Woodland
	Park
	Cemetery
	Built-up area
	Industrial building
	Leisure building
	Retail building
	Other building

⠏⠏⠏⠏⠏⠏	City wall	♜	Castle
A&E	Hospital with 24-hour A&E department	🏛	Historic house or building
PO	Post Office	Wakehurst Place NT	National Trust property
📖	Public library	Ⓜ	Museum or art gallery
i	Tourist Information Centre	🏺	Roman antiquity
i	Seasonal Tourist Information Centre	⚱	Ancient site, battlefield or monument
▮ ▮	Petrol station, 24 hour Major suppliers only	⸺	Industrial interest
✝	Church/chapel	❀	Garden
🚻	Public toilets	◉	Garden Centre Garden Centre Association Member
♿	Toilet with disabled facilities	🌱	Garden Centre Wyevale Garden Centre
PH	Public house AA recommended	🌳	Arboretum
🍴	Restaurant AA inspected	🛻	Farm or animal centre
Madeira Hotel ▬	Hotel AA inspected	🦌	Zoological or wildlife collection
🎭	Theatre or performing arts centre	🦜	Bird collection
🎥	Cinema	🐋	Nature reserve
⚑	Golf course	🐟	Aquarium
▲	Camping AA inspected	V	Visitor or heritage centre
🚐	Caravan site AA inspected	♈	Country park
▲🚐	Camping & caravan site AA inspected	⊙	Cave
🎢	Theme park	🌀	Windmill
📖	Abbey, cathedral or priory	🛢	Distillery, brewery or vineyard

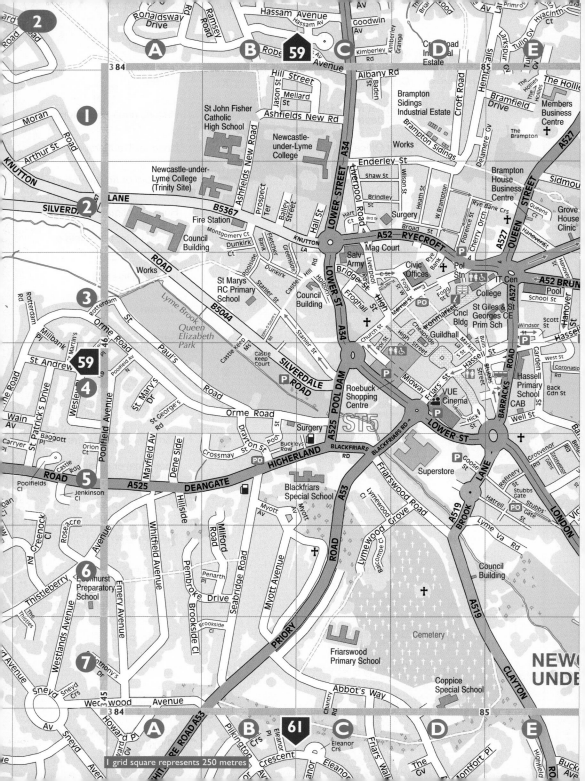

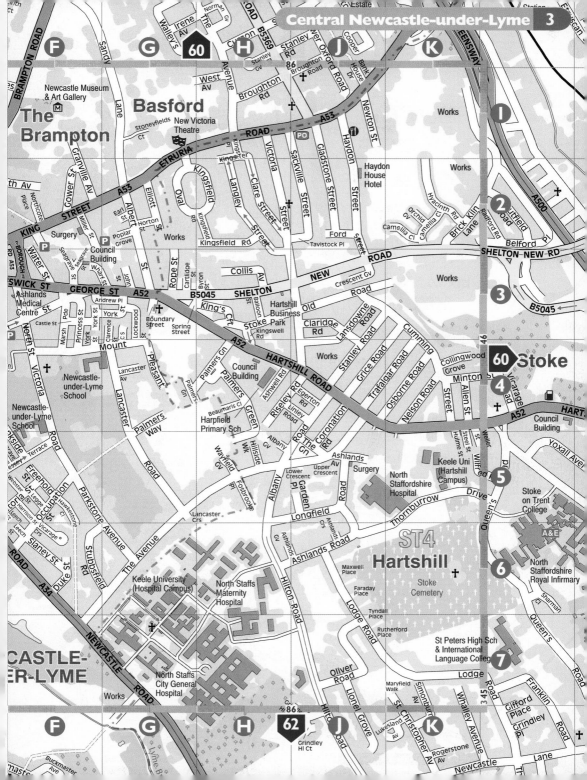

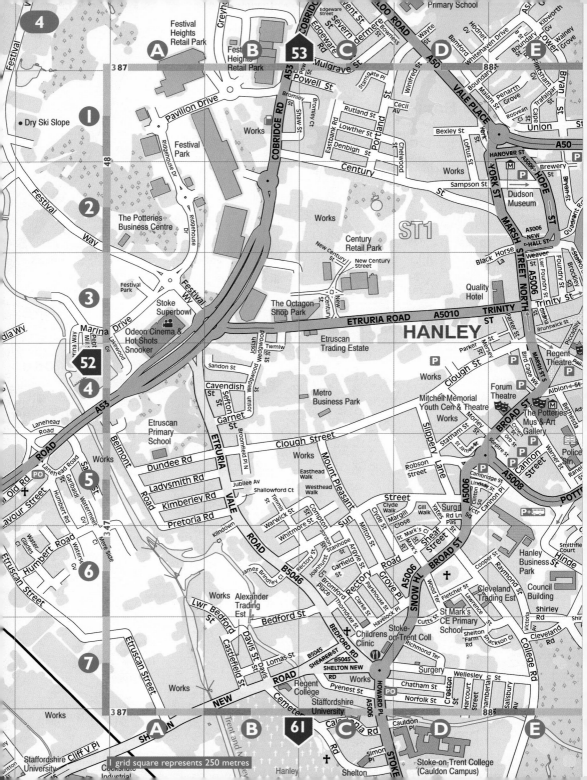

A B C D

Somerford Hall
Farm

Hunters Pointe

81
65
3
82

Hawthorn Lane

Hunters Pointe

I

Holly
Heath

Somerford Park
Farm

Brereton
Court

Moss Lane

2

Moss

Moss Farm

Lane

HOLMES CHAPEL ROAD

64

3

Somerford Farm

Sandy Lane

methwick
reen

4

Lower Medhurst
Green Farm

63
3

A53

5

Road

Upper Medhurst
Green Farm

Handfield Farm

Wallhill Farm

81
3

82

A B 10 C D

Stonyflats

Works

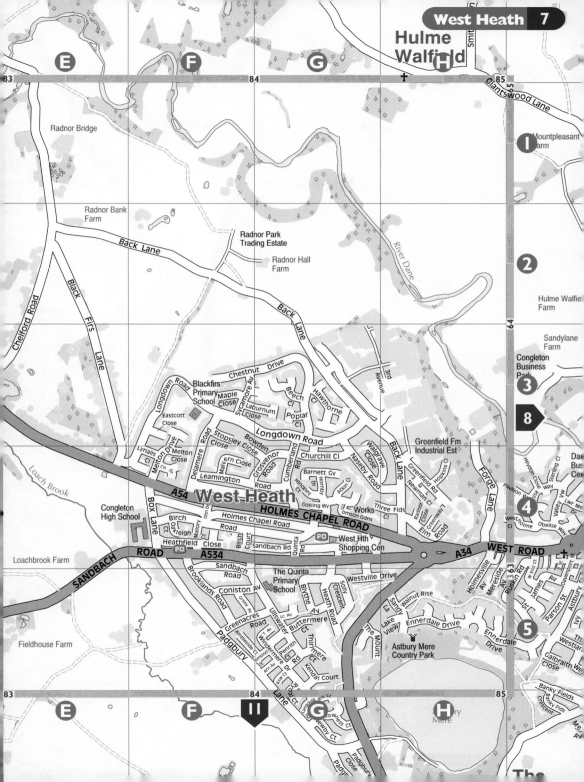

Lighthey

Tanhouse

River Dane

Diglake Farm

Peover Lane

E F G H

87 88 89

65

Macclesfield Canal

Greenhouse Farm

avannah

Buglawton Hall School

Sprink Lane

ah

Malhamdale Road
Gorsdale Cl
Swaledale Av
Harvey
Ribblesdale Av Foster
Road
Lindale
Wharfedale Road
Mardale Close

Buglawton

Bankhouse Drive
Crawford Av
Campbell
St John's Road
Davidson Avenue
Leigh
Dixon Rd
Pirie
Road
Dovd Cl
P Cl

64

A54

Yewtree Farm

Middle Lane

Middle Lane

Ke

High Lowe Av
Tall Ash
Buglawton Prim Sch Bailey
Bailey Crs
Beatty Drive

Crouch Lane

Weathercock Lane

3

Bath Vale

Brookhouse La

Works

Wood Farm

4

Road
Kingsley Rd
Fern Crs
Burns Road
Hutton Drive
Avenue
Cloud View
M Pl

Brook House Farm

Pool Bank

Weathercock

63

Hightown

5

Timbersbro

Jersey Cl

The Parklands

Brookhouse Lane

88 89

Ayrshire Way

E F 13 G H Overedge

Congleton Station

Telford
Brindley View
Worsley Dr

Minton Close

Under Rainow

Sefton Av

Dane in Shaw

10

Upper Medhurst
Green Farm

381
82

Handfield Farm

Wallhill Farm

1

Stonyflats

Works

62

Yewtree Farm

Wallhill Lane

2

Charity Farm

The Cryd

**Brookhouse
Green**

†

Spenmoss

3

Bank
House Lane

61

Spen
Green

Pooles
Lane

**Spen
Green**

Wallhill Lane

4

Bank House

Green

Congleton   Road

Wharams
Bank

Dayhouse Green
Farm

**Brownlo
Heath**

Congleton Road

oss   Lane

5

360

381
82

Alcumlow
Farm

1 grid square represents 500 metres

Fieldhouse Farm

E   F   **7**   G   H

83   84   85

Greenacres Road

Ambleside Av

Windermere Rd

Penrith

Thirlmere Ct

Langdale

BoWdess Ct

Newby Ct

Padgbury Close

Padgbury Lane

Astbury Mere Country Park

Lake View

Ennerdale Dr

The Mount

Buttermere Road

Astbury Mere

Banky Fields
Banky Flds Crescent

Galbraith We

Westian

Me Av

1

The Marsh

62

Fol   Hollow

Bent Farm   Bent Lane

Bent Lane

Astbury

Astbury St Marys CE Prim Sch

School Lane

NEWCASTLE ROAD

2

Cemetery

The Village

Garden Centre

Peel Drive

Peel

3   Dodd's Lane

12

Brownlow

Dubthorn

Watery

Lane

61

4

Child's   Lane

Moreton Cottages

A34

Sandy La

Mill House Farm

Ciss Green

Watery Lane

W

Brook Lane

CONGLETON ROAD

New Road

5

3 60

83   84   85

E   F   **17**   G   H

Home Farm

Oak Farm

9 Canal Walk

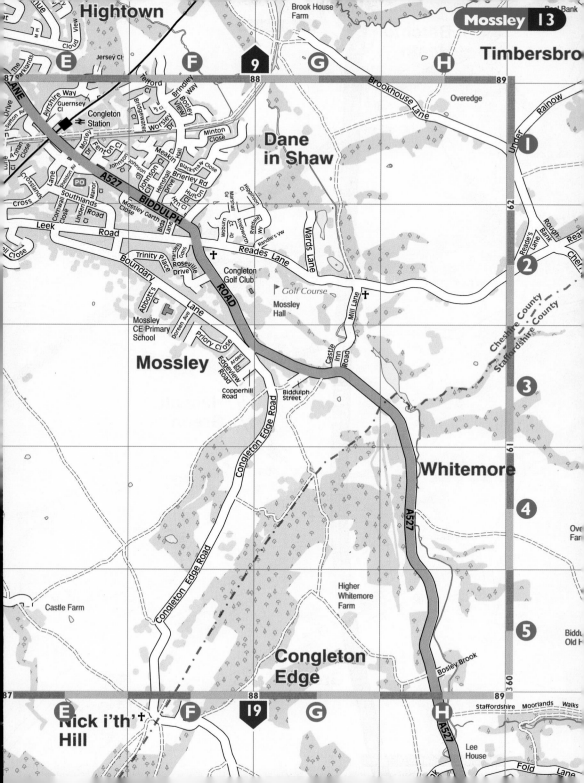

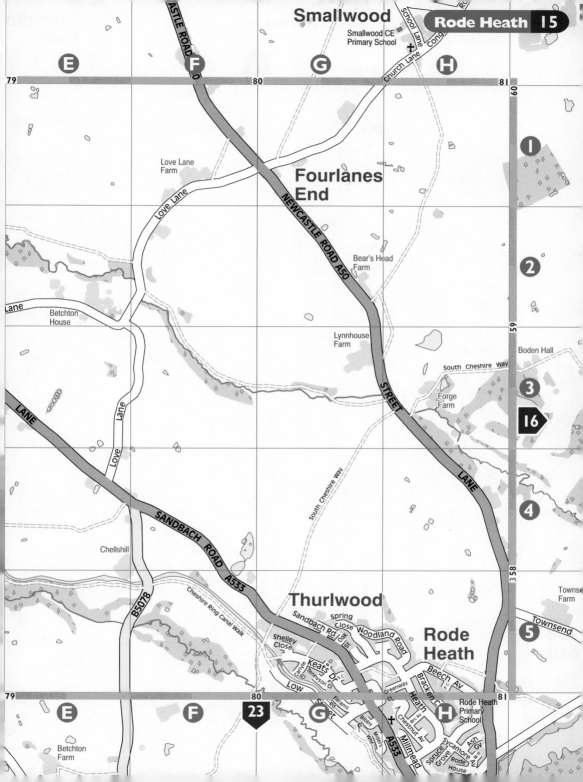

Smallwood

Smallwood CE
Primary School

School Lane

Church Lane

Cong

E 79 **F** 80 **G** **H** 81

60

I

Love Lane
Farm

**Fourlanes
End**

Love Lane

NEWCASTLE ROAD A50

Bear's Head
Farm

2

59

Boden Hall

Lane

Betchton
House

Lynnhouse
Farm

South Cheshire Way

3

Forge
Farm

STREET

16

LANE

Love Lane

South Cheshire Way

LANE

4

58

SANDBACH ROAD A533

Chellshill

Townse
Farm

Townsend

5

B5078

Cheshire Ring Canal Walk

Thurlwood

Sandbach Rd

spring
Close

Woodland Road

**Rode
Heath**

Shelley
Close

Oak

Beech Av

Bracken C

Carlyle Tennyson

Keats D

Greenway

Low

Farms

Heath

Chestnut Av

Rode Heath
Primary School

E 79 **F** 80 **G** **H** 81

23

Betchton
Farm

Bibby

Miller's

Millmead

A533

Spruce Sycamore A

Grove Rode
House

Ash
Gv

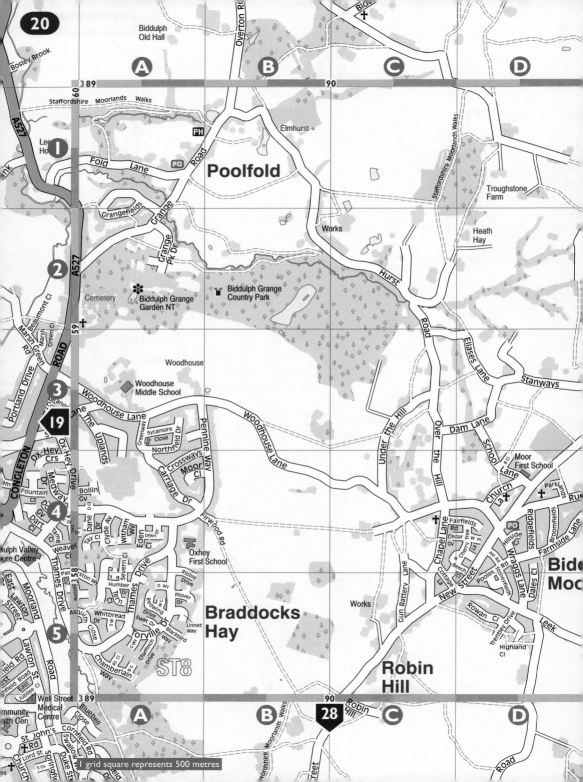

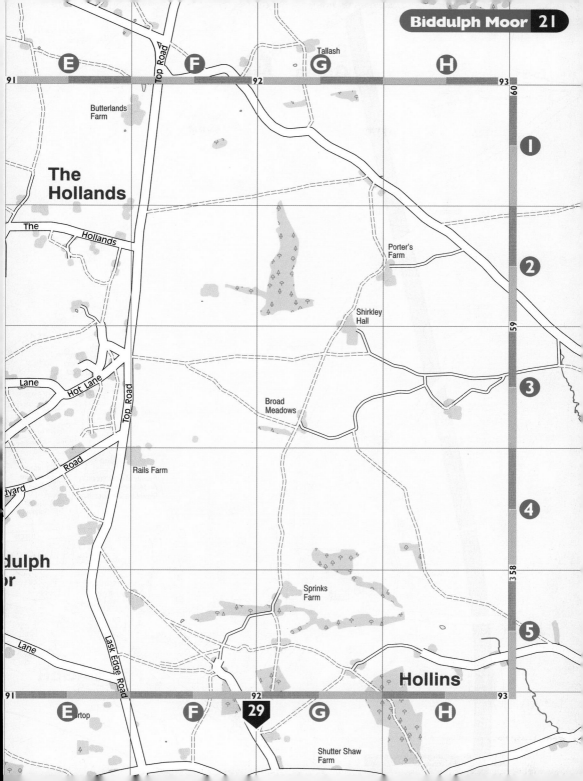

Tallash

E F G H

91 92 93

60

I

Butterlands
Farm

**The
Hollands**

The
Hollands

Porter's
Farm

2

59

Lane Hot Lane

Top Road

Shirkley
Hall

3

Broad
Meadows

Road

Rails Farm

4

58

dulph

or

Sprinks
Farm

5

Lane

Lask Edge Road

Hollins

91 92 93

E rtop F 29 G H

Shutter Shaw
Farm

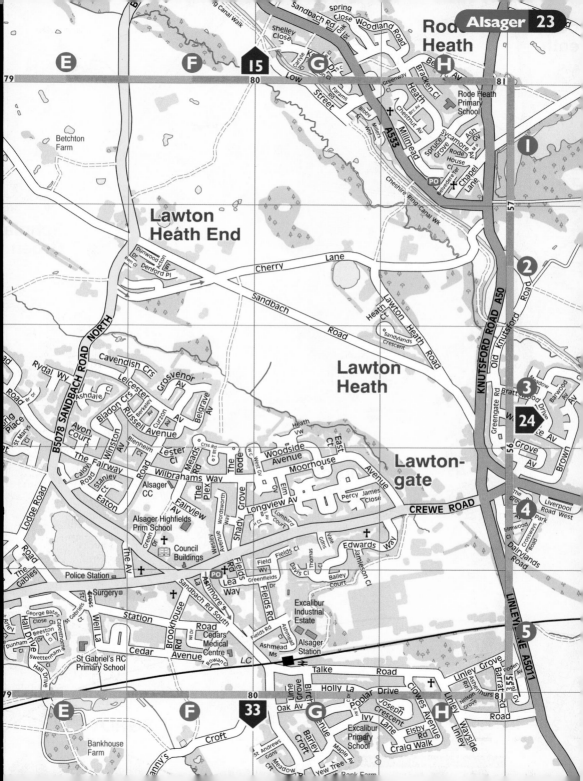

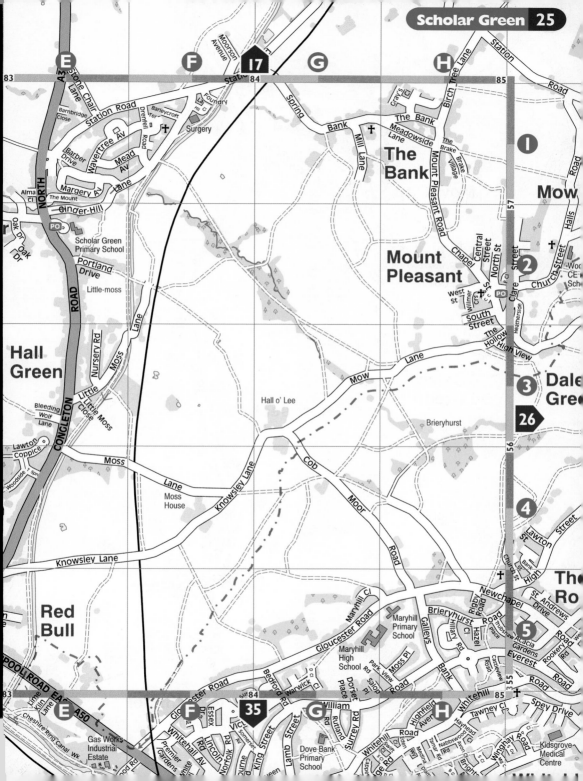

Mow Cop

Dales Green

Harriseahead

The Rookery

Newchapel

1 grid square represents 500 metres

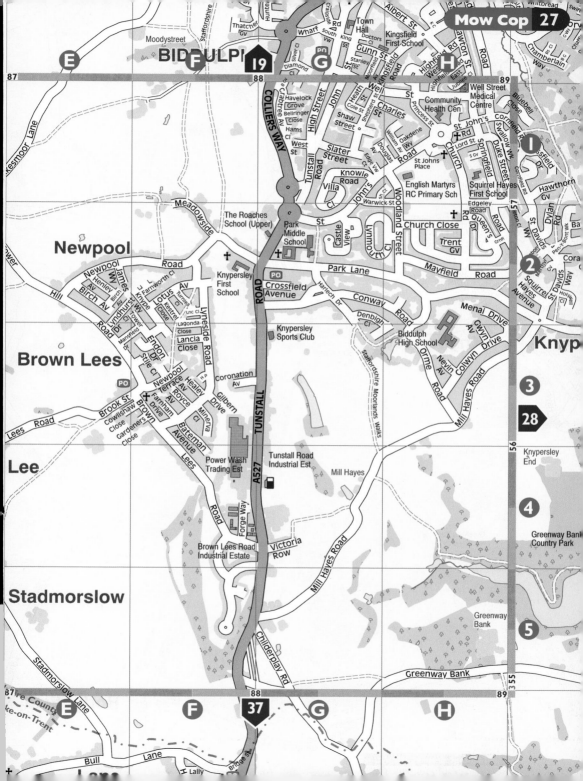

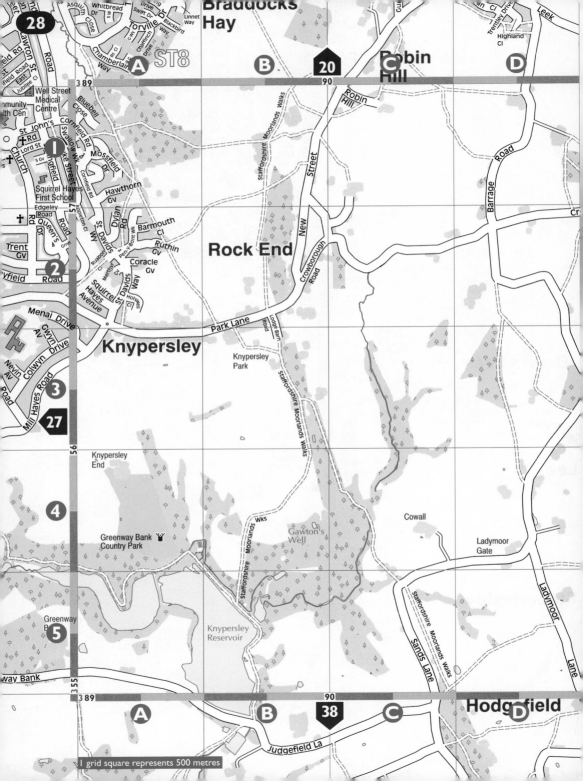

Lane

Lask Edge Road

E

F

21

G

H

Hollins

92

93

Moortop

Shutter Shaw Farm

Lask Edge

Blackwood House

I

57

wporough Road

Greenhouse

The Ashes

2

Damslane

Cowallmoor Lane

3

Char

Moorfields

56

Cowall Moor

Blackwood Hill

4

Fields Farm

Lanehead

5

355

Gratton Lane

E

F

39

G

H

Knowles Fa

92

93

Holehouse Lane

Hollin

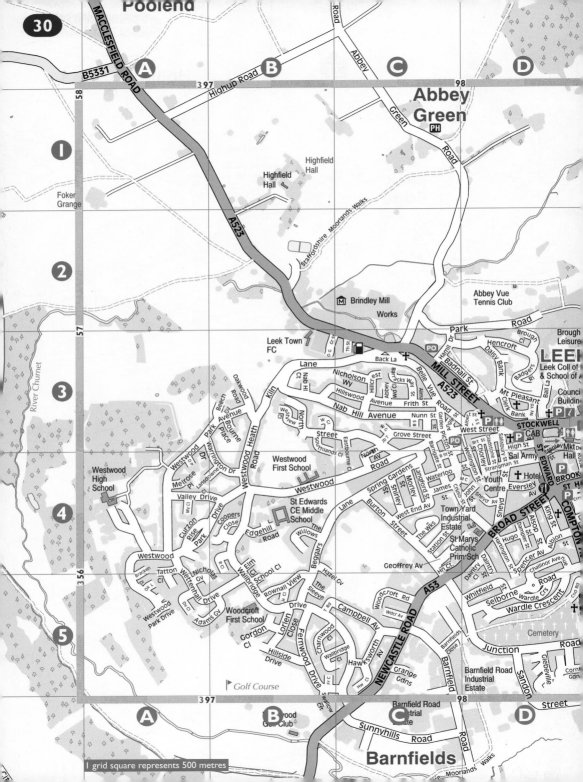

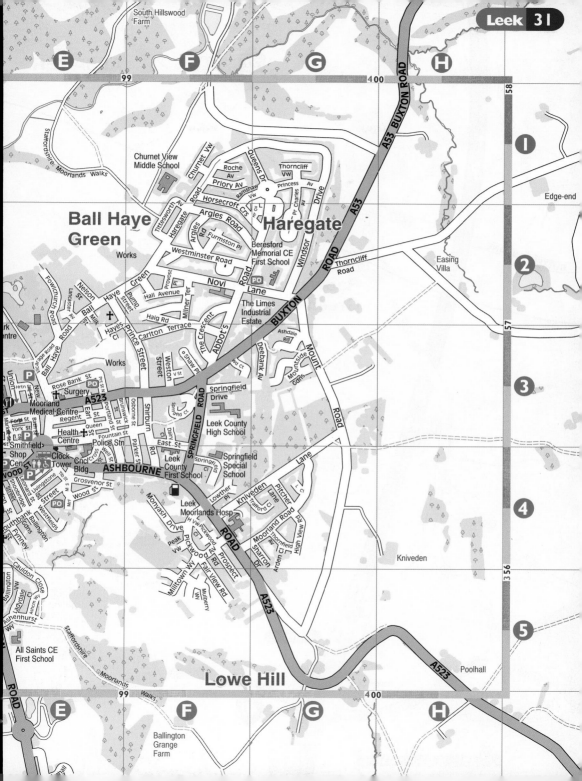

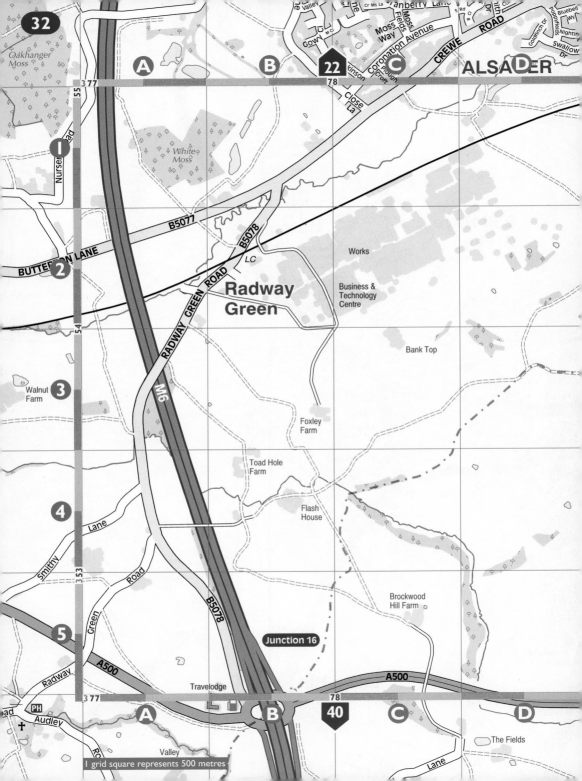

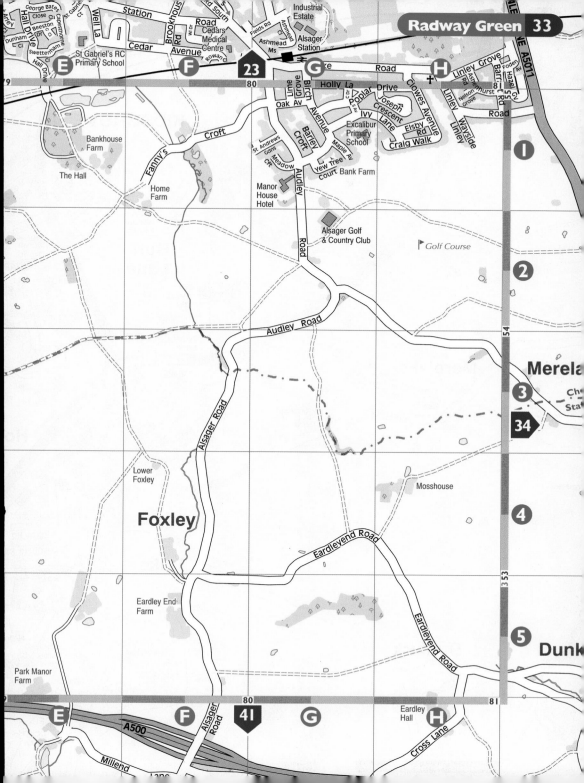

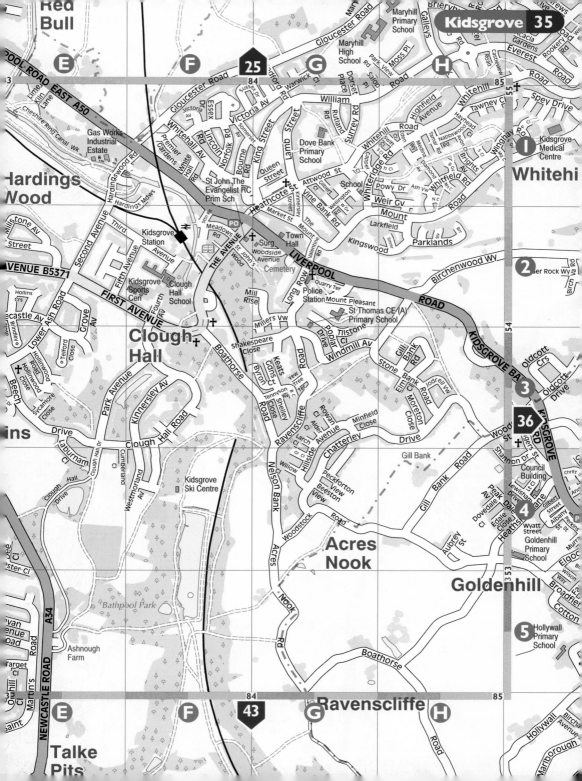

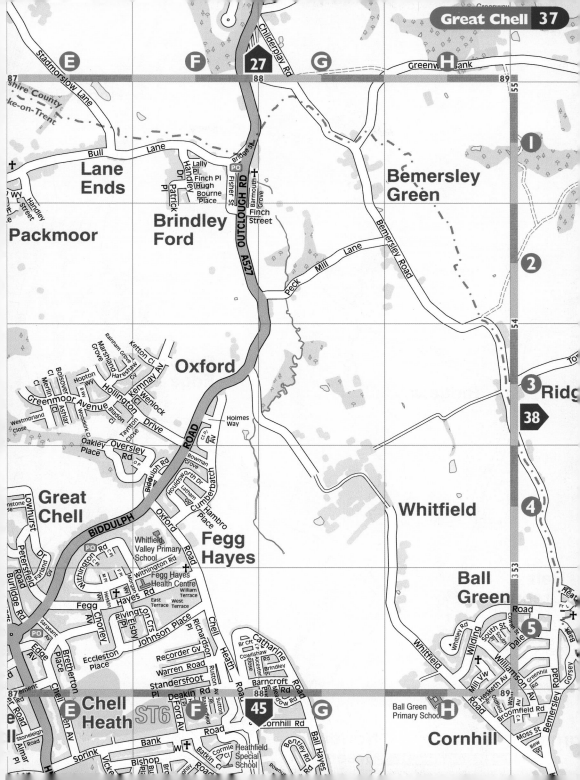

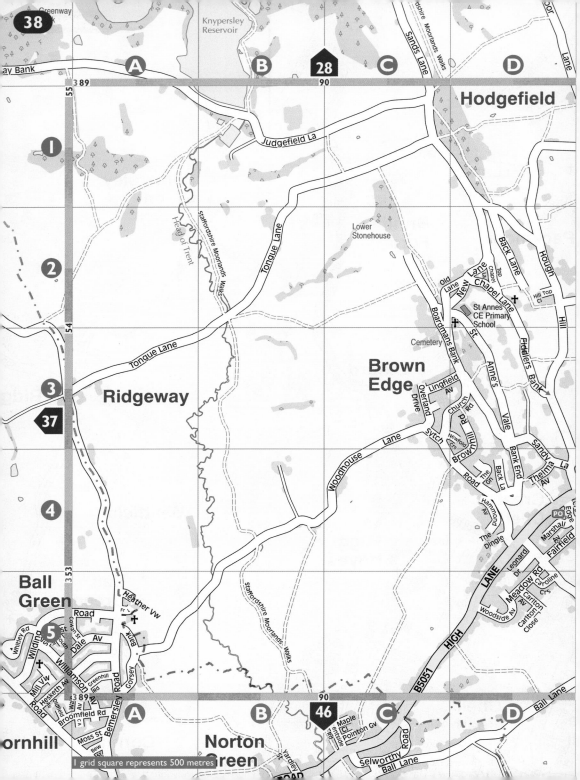

38

A **B** **28** **C** **D**

3 89
90

55

Knypersley
Reservoir

Greenway
Park

ay Bank

Hodgefield

I

Judgefield La

Head of Trent

Staffordshire Moorlands Walks

Sands Lane

Back Lane

Hough

2

54

Tongue Lane

Lower
Stonehouse

Old Lane

New St

Chapel Lane

Top Chapel

St Annes
CE Primary
School

Hill Top Ct

Hill

3

Tongue Lane

Ridgeway

Cemetery

Boardmans Bank

**Brown
Edge**

Fiddlers Bank

37

Overland Drive

Lingfield Av

Church Rd

St Anne's Rd

Vale

Sandy La

4

Woodhouse Lane

Sytch

Newfold Crs

Brownhill Road

The Gn

Back La

Bank End

Thelma Av

Hammond Av

The Dingle

Marshall Av

Fairfield

PO

Edge

**Ball
Green**

Heather Vw

Bank

Staffordshire Moorlands Walks

Leonard Dr

Meadow Rd

Caroline Crs

Woodside Av

Carlton Av

Carlton Close

53

Road

5

Whiteley Rd

Wilding Rd

St Cowan St

Dale Av

Williamson

Corsey Road

Greenhill Rd

Bemersley Road

LANE

HIGH

B5051

Ball Lane

Mill Vw

Hesketh Av

Oldfield Av

Broomfield Rd

3 89

90

Bew Ct

Moss St

ornhill

A

B

46

C

D

**Norton
Green**

Yardley St

Maple Cl

ernside Grp

Pointon Gv

Selworthy
Ball Lane

Road

Ball Lane

I grid square represents 500 metres

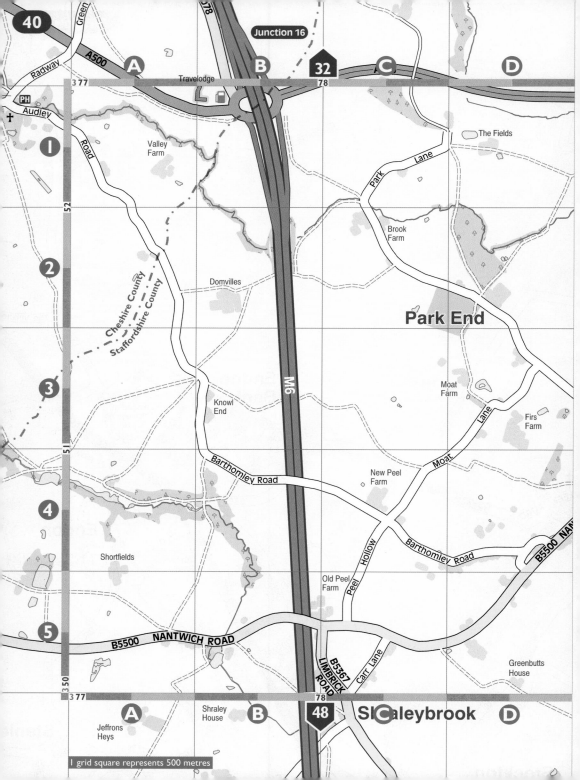

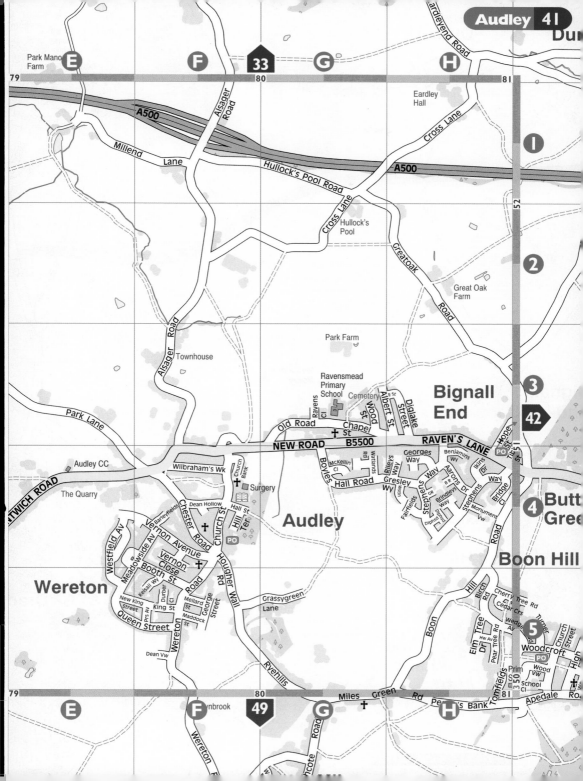

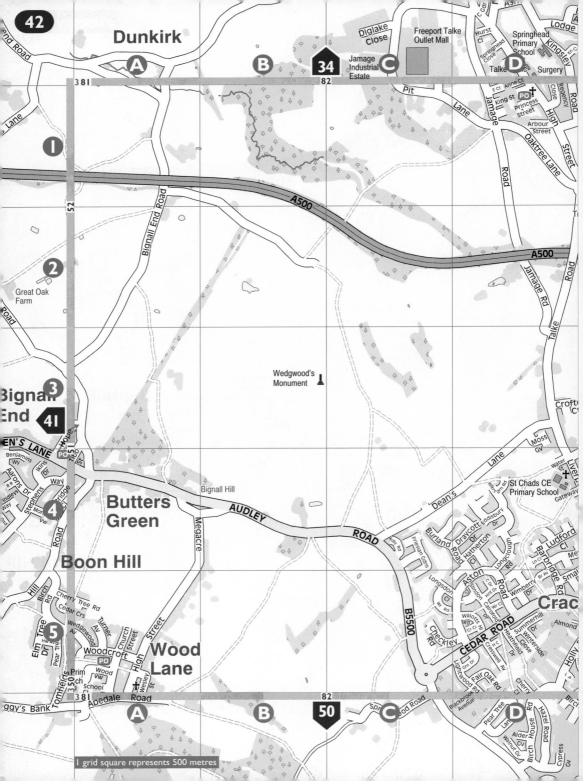

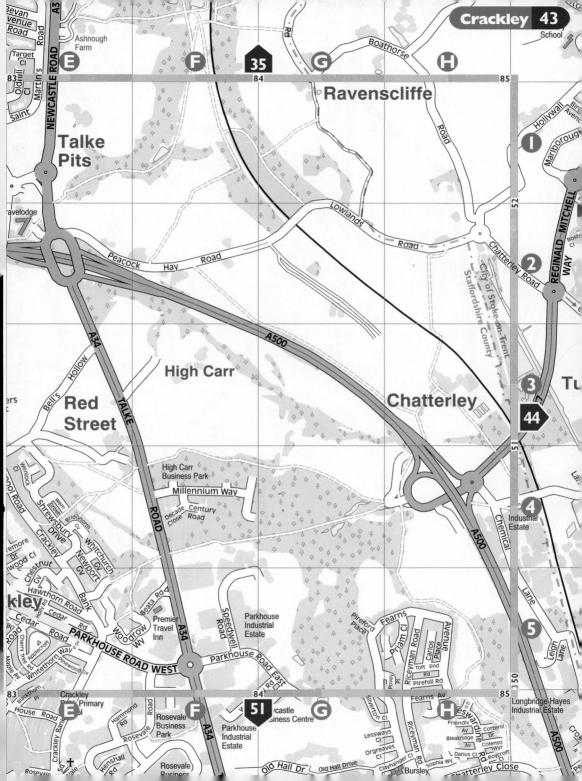

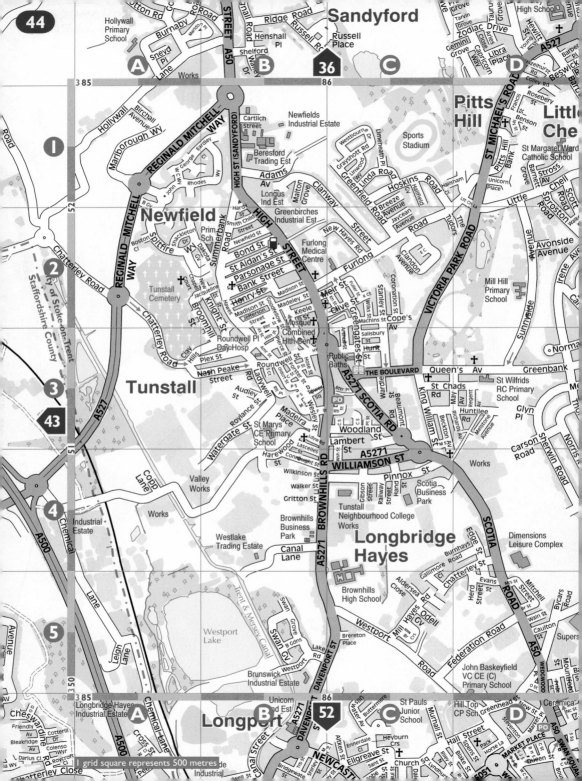

Willfield

Kent Dr

Basnett's Wood Rd

Springbank
Av spencer

Greenmeadow
Grove

LEEK ROAD

A53

39 92

93

Stanley Moss Lane

Lane

E

F

G

H

Stanley
Lane

Stan Bar

I

Edgefield
Lane

Heather Hills

Moss Hill

Amber
Court

Caldon Canal

Stanley Moss Road

Stanley

Puddy Lane

52

**Stockton
Brook**

PO

Stanley Road

2

anley Pool

Staffordshire/County
ity of Stoke-on-Trent

Greenways
Prim Sch

Bunt's Lane

Greenway Hall
Golf Club

Stanley Road

**Stanley
Moor**

Moorhead Dr

The
Avenue

Regency Dr

ROAD

Shaldon Av

Blencarn
Gr

Back Bunt's Lane

Road

Glastonbury Cl

Clewlows

Bank

Surgery

Rosewood

Av

Leighton Cl

Brentwood Gv

Rosy Bank

Hall

Houghwood Lane

3

51

Percival
Drive

Nursery Avenue

Lane

Greenway

Golf Course

Nursery Lane

Roundfields

Green
side Av

Cocks

Brindley
Lane

Leys Lane

Springs B

Baker Crs

North

Brookfield

Quarry Cl

Forresters
Bank

†

PO

A

Bagnall

4

Hillside Rd

Hillside

Malsto

e Av

Baddeley Hall Road

Greenway

Bank

Flash
Lane

Sandy

Red La

Park View
Gv Rd

Edge View

Rd

†

**Baddeley
Edge**

Hillside
Primary
School

Netherton
Grove

Lambourne Dr

Spout Lane

Fowler's
Lane

Light Oaks
Av

Light Oaks

5

Sunnyfield Gv

Wardle La

Rockfield
Av

Bagnall Road

Ingl Pl

Yew Tree
Cl

Light Oaks
Avenue

Newhouse
Farm

Highton
St

man

350

92

93

E

F

55

G

Carmounthead

Jack Hayes

H

Woodhead

Haye

Lane

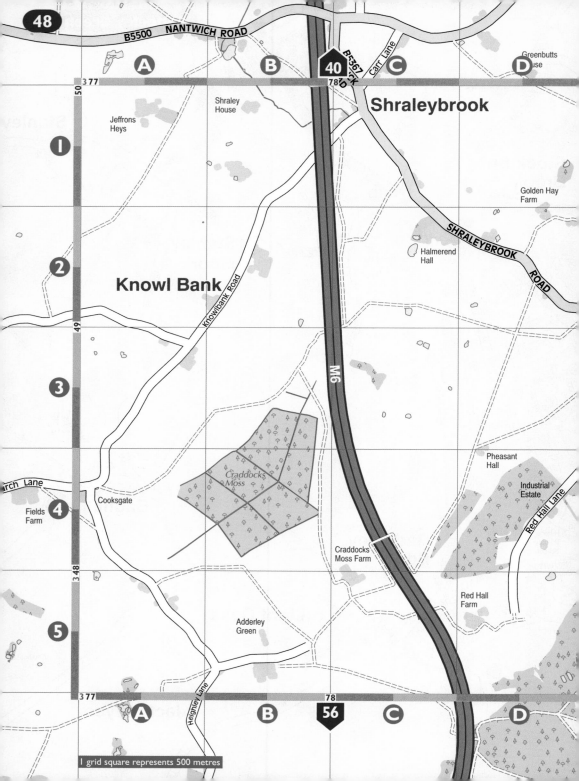

Woodcroft

Apedale Road

Miles Green Rd Peggy's Bank

Wynbrook

Werefon Road

Heathcote Road

Miles Green

Hollins Farm

Wynbrk Cl

Victor Avenue

Station Road

Halmer End

Station Walks

Sir Thomas Boughey High School

B5367 HIGH STREET

Minnie Cl

Lynsey Cl

PO

Minnie Farm

Hy La

Podmore Lane

Podmore Av

Hill Crs

Richard Heathcote Community Prim Sch

PH

PO

HIGH LANE

Alsagers Bank

B5367

Watermills Farm

The Drive

Hay Road

Scot

Leycett Road

Leycett Road

Bankfield Gv

Crackley Lane

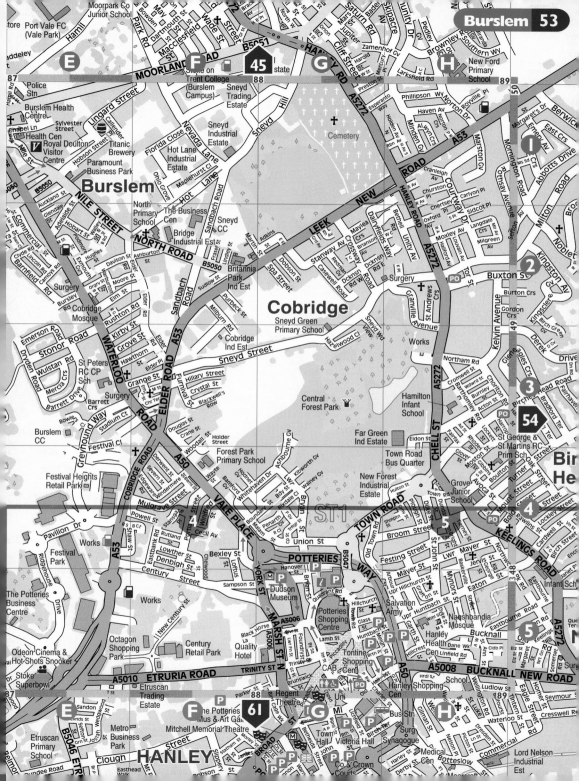

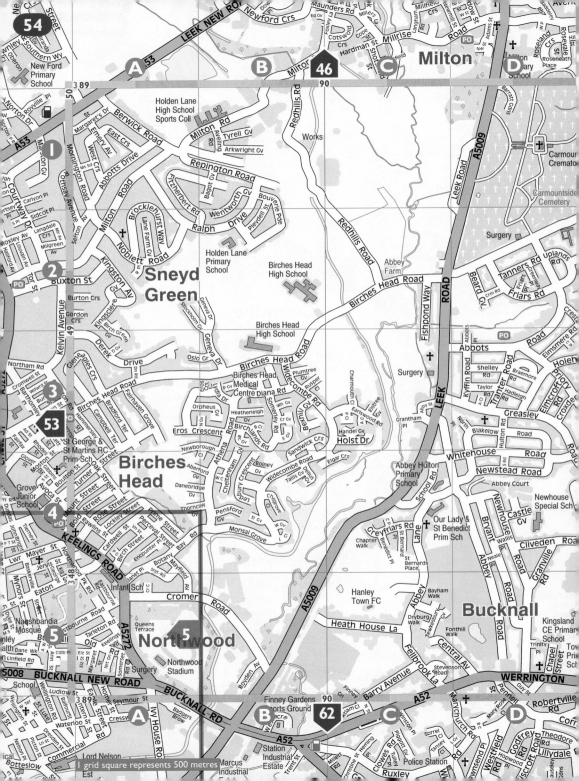

56

A   B   48   C   D

3 77   78

I

47

2

Walton's
Wood

MAIN ROAD

M6

3

Heighley Castle Way

Bowsey Wood Road

46

Woodland Hills

Hidden Hills

Madeley
Manor

P Cl

Cygnet
Close

T Spen

Hillwood Road

**Madeley
Heath**

4

College
Close

Windy
Arbour

KEELE ROAD

A531

Wharf
Terrace

Heath Row

Meadows
Primary
School

Ridge Hl
Drive

A525 KEELE ROAD

Honeywall Lane

Watering Tro

Bank

New Road

Thrn Dr

Holm Oak Drive

C Wk

Beck
Road

Newcastle Road

Woodside

Arbour
Close

Beech Croft

Greenmeadows
Road

Rsd Dr

Salisbury
Cl

Dtn

Kng

**Little
Madeley**

Works

5

Furnace Lane

Apple
Croft

Ht C

Pr Fd

Council
Building

River Lea

Police
Station

PO

Mill Lane

Bevan Place

A525 NEWCASTLE ROAD

**Middle
Madeley**

Pear Tree
Drive

Primrose
Dell

Plover
Field

Cherry Hill

Merlin
Green

The Bridle Path

Moss Lane

Surgery

345

3 77

A

Madeley
High
School

Waterside
Close

B

78

C

D

ower End

1 grid square represents 500 metres

E F ✝ 49 G H

79 80 81

I

cett Road

Bankfield Gv

Crackley Lane

Leycett Lane

Scot Hay

Road

Leycett

Moffatt Way

47

2 Buxton Av

Droitwich

Peebles Road

Bath Road

STT. Rd

Cheddar

Tunbridge

Drive

Ilkley

Pl

Woodhall

M Av

St. Lukes CE
Primary School

Resheat

B5044

Coppice

Road

Silver

Scot Hay

Cheltenham
Gv

**Finney
Green**

Hollywood Lane

Works

STREET

PEPPER

Underwood

3 **Silver**

58

46

Leycett Lane

gger Hill

A525 STATION ROAD

Station Drive

Station
Road

Old
Chapel
Cl

Quarry

Station

Road

Bank

A525

4

Honeywall
Farm

Top
Farm

Station Road

Knights
Cft

Road

Hawthorn

St Johns CE
Primary School

9

Highway Lane

Pump
Bk

Keele

Church
Bank

Church Flds

✝

5

Keele Road

Three Mile Lane

9 Highway Lane 80 81 3 45

E F G H

Moorside
High School

Southlow
Oval
Southlowe
Rd
Av

Wilton Av
Wetley Av

CELLARHEAD ROAD

E   F   G   H

5   96   97

Cellarhead

I

Grove Farm

A52

KINGSLEY

ROAD

LEEK ROAD

Overmoor

Bla
Lar

March
Lane

Windycote   Lane

2

Windycote

Dairyhouse
Lane

nktop

3

46

Cresswell's
Piece

Tickhill Lane

4

Heywood
Grange

Summerhill

5

345

5   96   97

E   F   **72**   G   H

Tickhill

1 grid square represents 500 metres

72

A   B   65   C   D

45 3 95   96

1

Tickhill

Caverswall
Common

Handley Banks

Hardiwick

Tickhill Lane

Foxfield Steam Railway

2

44

3

71

Handley Banks

Stansmore
Hall

Roughcote La

4

Tickhill Lane

Caverswall Road

St Peters CE
(A) Primary
School

Red House
FC

High St

The Hollow

Dilhorne   Lane

LC

Dilhorne Road

PO

The Dams

The Square

Church Ter

St Filumenas RC
Primary School

Caverswall

Field
House

343

5

Blythe

3 95   96   Steam Railway

A   B   82   C   D

Bridge

orne Road

1 grid square represents 500 metres

E F G H

97 98 99 45

I

2

44

Godleybrook

Whitehurst Lane

Works

Godleybarn Lane

Birchenfields Lane

Cartwright's Drumble

Godley Lane

Dilhorne Endowed Primary School

Godley School Lane

Newclosefield

3

74

Adderley

High St

Road

Sarver Lane

Dilhorne

New

Dilhorne Recreation Centre

Callow Hill Lane

The Dale

4

Brookho

343

The Common

DELPHOUSE

A521

5

Callow Hill Farm

Boundary

Little R

CHEADLE ROAD

E **83** F G H

7 98 99

E   F   G   H

Broad Haye

I

Wood House Farm

ROAD A521

Hammersley Hayes Rd
The Crts
Silver St
Foxfield Cl
Dovedale Close
Thorpe Rise
Weaver Close

Donkey Lane

Ayr Road
Wetherby Close
Cheltenham
Sandown Close

Newmarket Way

Cherry Lane

Parkfields

2

Lockwood Road

FROGHALL

Epsom Cl
Ness
Kempton Gv
Haydock Cl
Tay Cl

Churchill Road
Victory Crs
Lomond Gv
Grove
Windermere
Graham Gv
Bala Grove
Coniston Drive

Chasewater Grove

Hales Hall Caravan & Camping Park

ST10

OAKMOOR ROAD

Lower Grange Farm

3

borne Rd
dborne Courts
dy Arbour
King Edward St
Cecily St
Cecily Terrace
Ullswater Drive
Hales Hall Road
Rudyard Wy

B5417

QUEEN STREET

Robina Drive
Keeling Rd
Silverstone Av
Shelsley Rd
Mallory Wy
Goodwood
Oulton Rd
Moor Lane

CHEADLE

Hill Top

4

Hares Lane

Suns St
Well Street
Sunwell Gdns
Well St Medical Centre
Bittern Lane
Hawfinch Rd
Kestrel Lane
Kingfisher Crescent

TAPE STREET
Plant Street
PO
Baddeley St
Surg
Bramshaws Acre
Cheadle Swimming Pool
Dale Cl
Maple Cl
Cedar
Thorney Cl
Elm Dr
Ash Cl
Drive
Beech Close

ASHBOURNE

Lightwood

ROAD B5032

5

Mansion Close
Park Av
Cheadle DC
Mill Road
Bramley Close
Mill Grove
Millbrook Wy
Millstream Close
Millhouse Dr
Millers View
Millwaters

Moss Lane

E   F   **85**   G   H

Barleycroft
Kenzie
Lane
Rakeway Road
Churnet Rd
Dane Gv
Derwent
Avill Dr

Rakeway

I grid square represents 500 metres

E F 79 G H

Crowcrofts

9 90 91 40

Glazeyfield

I

Barlaston

Portland Pl
Flaxman
Ivyhouse Drive
Henley Cl
Ramsay Cl
Jasper
Lakewood Dr
Lime Gv
Etruscan Walk
Bell Lane
Hckw Cl
Lakewood Dr
Wedgwood Lane
Wedgwood Drive
Queen Mary's Drive

Woodeaves

2

Hartw

Hurden Hall

Longton Road

Arderley Pl

Beechfields

Police Station

Blurton Road

Bedcroft

Beechcroft Est

39

3

88

Barlaston

Longton Road

Malthouse La
Barlaston CC

Hartwell Lane

Hartwellhall Farm

Barlaston CE (VC) First School

PO

Vicarage Lane

Broughton Crescent

Cemetery

4

Lower Cullamoor

...tion

Road

Upper House

338

5

Hooks Green

9 90 91

E F G H H

GRINDLE

Stallington

Stallington Rd

Stallington Hospital

Stallington CP School

Meir Heath CP School

Pemberton

Combe

Blythe Av

Birkholme Drive

Hill Top Cl

High Heath Gv

23 High

PO

Hollies Drive

Diamond

Golborn

March

Mrs Av

Willows Drive

Avenue

Fernlea Gv

Golborn

Ht Crs

Blacklake Dr

Birch Gv

Wd Gv

Woodside Dr

Willow Lane

Willow

B5066

Meir Heath CC

eadendale

Idlerocks

Knenhall Lane

Stallington Road

Fulford Dale

Moddershall Grange

Fulford CP School

Baulk Lane

King Cl

Highview Road

Tudor

The Gn

Mk Gv

Fulford Road

F

Crossgate

Moss

St Cl

81

40

39

38

94

95

94

95

E F G H I 2 3 4 5 E F G H

Place	Pg	Ref	Place	Pg	Ref
Abbey Green	30	C1	Butters Green	42	A4
Abbey Hulton	55	E4	Butt Lane	34	C2
Acres Nook	35	G4	Caverswall	72	B5
Adderley Green	70	B1	Cellarhead	65	E1
Alsager	22	D5	Chatterley	43	H5
Alsagers Bank	49	H4	Cheadle	75	F4
Apedale	50	A2	Cheadle Park	74	D3
Ash Bank	63	H2	Chell Heath	45	E1
Astbury	11	H2	Chesterton	50	D2
Audley	41	G4	Church Lawton	24	B4
Baddeley Edge	47	F4	Clayton	67	E2
Baddeley Green	46	C3	Clough Hall	35	F3
Bagnall	47	H4	Coalpit Hill	34	C3
Ball Green	37	H5	Cobridge	53	G2
Ball Haye Green	31	G2	Congleton	12	B1
The Bank	25	H1	Congleton Edge	13	C5
Bank Top	45	F3	Cookshill	71	H4
Barlaston	87	E3	Cornhill	45	H1
Basford	3	G1	Cotwalton	91	H1
Bath Vale	11	F2	Crackley	42	D5
Beasley	51	F2	Cross Heath	59	F1
Bemersley Green	37	H1	Dales Green	26	A3
Bentilee	63	G3	Dane in Shaw	13	C1
Berry Hill	62	D3	Day Green	14	B5
Biddulph	19	F5	Dilhorne	73	F5
Biddulph Moor	20	D1	Dimsdale	51	G4
Bignall End	41	H3	Draycott in the Moors	83	F5
Birches Head	54	A4	Dresden	79	H1
Blackwood Hill	29	H4	Dunkirk	52	A5
Blurton	79	F1	Endon	39	H4
Blythe Bridge	82	A3	Endon Bank	39	G5
Blythe Marsh	82	D3	Etruria	52	D5
Boon Hill	41	H4	Fegg Hayes	37	F4
Boothen	68	A3	Fenton	69	F1
Boundary	73	G5	Fenton Low	62	A5
Braddocks Hay	20	B5	Finney Green	33	F3
Bradeley	45	G3	Florence	80	A1
Bradwell	52	A2	Ford Green	46	A4
The Brampton	3	F1	Forsbrook	82	D2
Brindley Ford	37	F2	Fourlanes End	15	G1
Broad Meadow	51	E3	Foxley	33	F5
Brookhouse Green	10	A3	Freehay	85	F3
Brookhouses	74	A4	Gillow Heath	19	F3
Brown Edge	38	C3	Godleybrook	73	E1
Brown Lees	27	E3	Goldenhill	35	H5
Brownlow	11	E3	Gorstybirch	42	D5
Brownlow Heath	10	D5	Gorstyhill	35	F5
Bucknall	54	D5	Great Chell	37	E4
Buglawton	9	F2	Hall Green	25	E3
Burslem	53	E1	Halmer End	49	E2

Place	Pg	Ref	Place	Pg	Ref
Hanchurch	76	D3	Marsh Green	19	H3
Hanford	67	H5	The Marsh	12	A1
Hanley	4	D3	May Bank	52	A5
Hardings Wood	35	E1	Meir	81	F1
Haregate	31	G2	Meir Hay	70	C5
Harriseahead	26	B3	Meir Heath	88	D1
Hartshill	3	J6	Meir Park	81	F3
Hartwell	88	A2	Merelake	34	A3
Hassall Green	14	C3	Middle Madeley	56	B5
Havannah	8	D1	Middleport	52	B2
Hawthorns	57	H5	Miles Green	49	G1
Hem Heath	78	C3	Milton	46	C5
Heron Cross	68	D2	Mobberley	84	D3
High Carr	43	F3	Moor Green	82	C2
Hightown	21	E5	Mossley	13	F5
Hodgefield	38	D1	Mount Pleasant	25	H2
The Hollands	21	E1	Mount Pleasant	68	D2
Hollins	21	H5	Mow Cop	26	A1
Hollins	34	D3	Newcastle-under-Lyme	2	E7
Hollybush	68	D4	Newchapel	36	C1
Hulme	64	A4	Newfield	44	A2
Huntley	84	C3	Newpool	27	E2
Jack Hayes	55	H1	Newstead	79	E4
Keele	57	H5	Nick I'th' Hill	19	E1
Kerry Hill	55	H2	Normacot	80	C1
Kidsgrove	34	C1	Northwood	5	K2
Knenhall	88	C5	Northwood	67	F5
Knowl Bank	48	A2	Norton Green	46	B1
Knutton	59	E2	Norton-in-the-Moors	46	B3
Knypersley	28	A3	Oak Hill	67	H2
Lane Ends	37	E1	Oulton	36	C1
Lask Edge	29	F1	Oultoncross	91	E1
Lawton-gate	23	H4	Overmoor	65	H1
Lawton Heath	23	G3	Oxford	37	F3
Lawton Heath End	25	F2	Packmoor	37	E2
Leadendale	88	D3	Park End	40	C2
Leek	30	D3	Penkhull	67	G1
Leycett	57	F2	Pitts Hill	44	D1
Light Oaks	47	G5	Poolfold	20	B1
Lightwood	75	F5	Porthill	52	A3
Lightwood	80	C3	Radway Green	32	B2
Little Chell	44	D1	Rakeway	85	G1
Little Madeley	56	B5	Ravenscliffe	43	G5
Little Stoke	91	G5	Red Bull	25	E5
Longbridge Hayes	44	C4	Red Street	43	E3
Longport	52	B1	Ridgeway	58	A3
Longton	69	F3	Robin Hill	20	C5
Lowe Hill	31	F5	Rock End	28	B2
Lower Heath	8	B1	Rode Heath	15	H5
Madeley Heath	56	C4	The Rookery	26	A5
			Rough Close	88	D2

Place	Pg	Ref
Roughcote	71	G1
Sandford Hill	69	H2
Sandyford	36	C5
Scholar Green	24	D2
Scot Hay	57	H2
Seabridge	66	B4
Shelton	61	G3
Shraleybrook	48	C1
Sideway	68	B4
Silverdale	58	A3
Smallthorne	45	H4
Sneyd Green	54	A2
Spen Green	10	B4
Springfields	27	G2
Stadmorslow	27	E5
Stallington	89	H2
Stanfield	45	E3
Stanley Moor	47	G2
Stoke	68	C4
Stoke-on-Trent	61	G4
Stone	91	E3
Stonefield	90	C1
Stonehouses	85	E4
Talke	34	C4
Talke Pits	43	E1
Teanford	84	D4
Thurlwood	15	G5
Timbersbrook	8	H5
Tittensor	86	B4
Townsend	65	E1
Trentham	78	A3
Trent Vale	67	H4
Tunstall	44	A3
Turnhurst	36	D5
Ubberley	63	F3
Wain Lee	26	D4
Walton	90	B4
Wereton	41	E5
Werrington	64	C1
West Heath	7	F4
Westlands	66	B1
Weston Coyney	71	E2
Whitehill	36	A1
Whitemore	13	H4
Whitfield	37	H4
Winnothdale	85	H4
Wolstanton	52	B4
Wood Lane	42	A5

USING THE STREET INDEX

Street names are listed alphabetically. Each street name is followed by its postal town or area locality, the Postcode District, the page number, and the reference to the square in which the name is found.

Standard index entries are shown as follows:

Aarons Dr *ALS/KID* ST7 ....41 H4

Street names and selected addresses not shown on the map due to scale restrictions are shown in the index with an asterisk.

Abercorn St *STOKE* ST4 * 69 F2

GENERAL ABBREVIATIONS

ACC	ACCESS	CUTT	CUTTINGS
ALY	ALLEY	CV	COVE
AP	APPROACH	CYN	CANYON
AR	ARCADE	DEPT	DEPARTMENT
ASS	ASSOCIATION	DL	DALE
AV	AVENUE	DM	DAM
BCH	BEACH	DR	DRIVE
BLDS	BUILDINGS	DRO	DROVE
BND	BEND	DRY	DRIVEWAY
BNK	BANK	DWGS	DWELLINGS
BR	BRIDGE	E	EAST
BRK	BROOK	EMB	EMBANKMENT
BTM	BOTTOM	EMBY	EMBASSY
BUS	BUSINESS	ESP	ESPLANADE
BVD	BOULEVARD	EST	ESTATE
BY	BYPASS	EX	EXCHANGE
CATH	CATHEDRAL	EXPY	EXPRESSWAY
CEM	CEMETERY	EXT	EXTENSION
CEN	CENTRE	F/O	FLYOVER
CFT	CROFT	FC	FOOTBALL CLUB
CH	CHURCH	FK	FORK
CHA	CHASE	FLD	FIELD
CHYD	CHURCHYARD	FLDS	FIELDS
CIR	CIRCLE	FLS	FALLS
CIRC	CIRCUS	FLTS	FLATS
CL	CLOSE	FM	FARM
CLFS	CLIFFS	FT	FORT
CMP	CAMP	FWY	FREEWAY
CNR	CORNER	FY	FERRY
CO	COUNTY	GA	GATE
COLL	COLLEGE	GAL	GALLERY
COM	COMMON	GDN	GARDEN
COMM	COMMISSION	GDNS	GARDENS
CON	CONVENT	GLD	GLADE
COT	COTTAGE	GLN	GLEN
COTS	COTTAGES	GN	GREEN
CP	CAPE	GND	GROUND
CPS	COPSE	GRA	GRANGE
CR	CREEK	GRG	GARAGE
CREM	CREMATORIUM	GT	GREAT
CRS	CRESCENT	GTWY	GATEWAY
CSWY	CAUSEWAY	GV	GROVE
CT	COURT	HGR	HIGHER
CTRL	CENTRAL	HL	HILL
CTS	COURTS	HLS	HILLS
CTYD	COURTYARD	HO	HOUSE

HOL	HOLLOW	NW	NORTH WEST
HOSP	HOSPITAL	O/P	OVERPASS
HRB	HARBOUR	OFF	OFFICE
HTH	HEATH	ORCH	ORCHARD
HTS	HEIGHTS	OV	OVAL
HVN	HAVEN	PAL	PALACE
HWY	HIGHWAY	PAS	PASSAGE
IMP	IMPERIAL	PAV	PAVILION
IN	INLET	PDE	PARADE
IND EST	INDUSTRIAL ESTATE	PH	PUBLIC HOUSE
INF	INFIRMARY	PK	PARK
INFO	INFORMATION	PKWY	PARKWAY
INT	INTERCHANGE	PL	PLACE
IS	ISLAND	PLN	PLAIN
JCT	JUNCTION	PLNS	PLAINS
JTY	JETTY	PLZ	PLAZA
KG	KING	POL	POLICE STATION
KNL	KNOLL	PR	PRINCE
L	LAKE	PREC	PRECINCT
LA	LANE	PREP	PREPARATORY
LDG	LODGE	PRIM	PRIMARY
LGT	LIGHT	PROM	PROMENADE
LK	LOCK	PRS	PRINCESS
LKS	LAKES	PRT	PORT
LNDG	LANDING	PT	POINT
LTL	LITTLE	PTH	PATH
LWR	LOWER	PZ	PIAZZA
MAG	MAGISTRATE	QD	QUADRANT
MAN	MANSIONS	QU	QUEEN
MD	MEAD	QY	QUAY
MDW	MEADOW	R	RIVER
MEM	MEMORIAL	RBT	ROUNDABOUT
MKT	MARKET	RD	ROAD
MKTS	MARKETS	RDG	RIDGE
ML	MALL	REP	REPUBLIC
MNR	MANOR	RES	RESERVOIR
MS	MEWS	RFC	RUGBY FOOTBALL CLUB
MSN	MISSION	RI	RISE
MT	MOUNT	RP	RAMP
MTN	MOUNTAIN	RW	ROW
MTS	MOUNTAINS	S	SOUTH
MUS	MUSEUM	SCH	SCHOOL
MWY	MOTORWAY	SE	SOUTH EAST
N	NORTH	SER	SERVICE AREA
NE	NORTH EAST	SH	SHORE
		SHOP	SHOPPING

SKWY	SKYWAY
SMT	SUMMIT
SOC	SOCIETY
SP	SPUR
SPR	SPRING
SQ	SQUARE
ST	STREET
STN	STATION
STR	STREAM
STRD	STRAND
SW	SOUTH WEST
TDG	TRADING
TER	TERRACE
THWY	THROUGHWAY
TNL	TUNNEL
TOLL	TOLLWAY
TPK	TURNPIKE
TR	TRACK
TRL	TRAIL
TWR	TOWER
U/P	UNDERPASS
UNI	UNIVERSITY
UPR	UPPER
V	VALE
VA	VALLEY
VIAD	VIADUCT
VIL	VILLA
VIS	VISTA
VLG	VILLAGE
VLS	VILLAS
VW	VIEW
W	WEST
WD	WOOD
WHF	WHARF
WK	WALK
WKS	WALKS
WLS	WELLS
WY	WAY
YD	YARD
YHA	YOUTH HOSTEL

POSTCODE TOWNS AND AREA ABBREVIATIONS

ALS/KID	Alsager/Kidsgrove	BIDD	Biddulph	CDLE	Cheadle (Staffs)
AUD/MAD/W	Audlem/Madeley/Woore	BLYBR/FOR	Blythe Bridge/Forsbrook	CONG	Congleton
BARL	Barlaston	BUCK/MIL	Bucknall/Milton	CW/HAS	Crewe/Haslington
		BURS/TUN	Burslem/Tunstall	CW/SHV	Crewe/Shavington

END/WER	Endon/Werrington	NEWUL	Newcastle-under-Lyme
HAN	Hanley	SBCH	Sandbach
LEEK	Leek	STOKE	Stoke-on-Trent
LNGTN	Longton	STONE	Stone

3

3rd Av *CONG* CW12 ....7 H5

A

Aarons Dr *ALS/KID* ST7 ....41 H4
Abbey La *BUCK/MIL* ST2 ....54 C4
Abbey Rd *BUCK/MIL* ST2 ....54 D4
Abbey St *BUCK/MIL* ST2 ....54 D4
Abbey St *BUCK/MIL* ST2 ....54 C4
   NEWUL ST5 ....58 C3
Abbey Wood *LEEK* ST13 ....90 D3
Abbots Dr *BUCK/MIL* ST2 ....54 D3
Abbots PI *BUCK/MIL* ST2 ....54 D3
Abbots St *HAN* ST1 ....31 F3
Abbot's Wy *NEWUL* ST5 ....2 C1
Abbott's CI *CONG* CW12 ....13 F2
Abbotts Dr *HAN* ST1 ....54 A1
Abercorn St *STOKE* ST4 * 69 F2
Aberford Gv *HAN* ST1 ....54 A4
Abingdon Wy *STOKE* ST4 ....78 B3
Acacia Av *NEWUL* ST5 ....59 E2
Acacia Gdns *ALS/KID* ST7 ....26 A5
Acacia Gv *NEWUL* ST5 ....59 E2
Achilles Wy *BUCK/MIL* ST2 ....62 B5
Acorn Ri *LNGTN* ST3 ....80 B2
Acres Nook Rd *BURS/TUN* ST6 ....35 G4
The Acres *NEWUL* ST5 ....58 D5
Acreswood Rd *BURS/TUN* ST6 ....44 B1
Acton St *HAN* ST1 ....53 H3
Acton Wy *ALS/KID* ST7 ....23 F2
Adams Av *BURS/TUN* ST6 ....44 B1
Adams Gv *LEEK* ST13 ....30 A5
Adams St *ALS/KID* ST7 ....46 D5
   NEWUL ST5 ....52 A5
Adamthwaite Dr
   BLYBR/FOR ST11 ....81 H2
Adderley PI *BARL* ST12 ....87 F2
Adderley Rd *BURS/TUN* ST6 ....46 A3
Addington Wy *LNGTN* ST3 ....70 B2
Addison St *HAN* ST1 ....53 H5
Adelaide St *BURS/TUN* ST6 ....53 G2
Adkins St *BURS/TUN* ST6 ....45 F2
Adrian St *STOKE* ST4 ....69 E1
Adventure PI *HAN* ST1 ....4 E4
Aegean CI *STOKE* ST4 ....78 C2
Agger HI *NEWUL* ST5 ....57 E4
Ainsdale CI *LNGTN* ST3 ....80 B1
Ainsley CI *BUCK/MIL* ST2 ....54 C5
Ainsworth St *STOKE* ST4 ....68 C2
Aintree CI *STOKE* ST4 ....78 B3
Airdale Gv *STOKE* ST15 ....91 E1
Airdale Rd *STOKE* ST15 ....91 E1
Airdale Spinney *STOKE* ST15 ....91 E1
Aitken St *BURS/TUN* ST6 ....52 C1
Ajax Wy *BUCK/MIL* ST2 ....62 B5
Akesmoor La *BIDD* ST8 ....26 D1
Alanbrooke Gv *LNGTN* ST3 ....80 B1
Alanley CI *BURS/TUN* ST6 ....43 G5
Alan Rd *BUCK/MIL* ST2 ....63 E1
Alastair Dr *STOKE* ST4 ....67 H3
Albany Gv *STOKE* ST4 ....3 H5
Albany Rd *NEWUL* ST5 ....2 C1
   STOKE ST4 ....3 H5
Albany St *BURS/TUN* ST6 ....36 A4
Albemarle Rd *NEWUL* ST5 ....59 G2
Alberta St *LNGTN* ST3 ....70 A5
Albert Av *LNGTN* ST3 ....70 C4
Albert PI *LNGTN* ST3 ....70 A5
Albert Rd *STOKE* ST4 ....78 B4
Albert St *ALS/KID* ST7 ....41 G3
   BIDD ST8 ....19 G5
   LEEK ST13 ....30 D5
   LNGTN ST3 ....70 A2
   NEWUL ST5 ....5 E2
   NEWUL ST5 ....58 C2
   STONE ST15 ....90 D2
Albert Ter *NEWUL* ST5 ....52 A4
Albion St *HAN* ST1 ....5 F4
   LEEK ST13 ....30 D4
Alcester CI *BURS/TUN* ST6 ....37 F5
Aldbury PI *LNGTN* ST3 ....79 E2
Aldeburgh Dr *NEWUL* ST5 ....66 D5
Alder CI *ALS/KID* ST7 ....25 G2
Alderflat Dr *STOKE* ST4 ....78 D3
Alder Gv *NEWUL* ST5 ....50 D1
Alderhay La *ALS/KID* ST7 ....26 A4
Alderney CI *NEWUL* ST5 ....66 A4
Aldersey Crs *LNGTN* ST3 ....69 F4
Aldersea CI *BURS/TUN* ST6 ....53 E2
Alders Rd *BIDD* ST8 ....20 D4
Alderton Gv *LNGTN* ST3 ....81 F4
Alder Wk *STOKE* ST4 ....67 G3
Aldrin CI *BLYBR/FOR* ST11 ....81 G3
Alexandra Rd *LNGTN* ST3 ....70 C5
   STOKE ST4 ....52 A5
Alexandra St *STONE* ST15 ....90 C2
Alford Dr *END/WER* ST9 ....64 A1
Alfred St *STOKE* ST4 ....62 A5
Alfreton Rd *STOKE* ST4 ....78 A1
Algar Rd *STOKE* ST4 ....67 G1
Alicia Wy *BUCK/MIL* ST2 ....46 C3
Allenby Sq *STOKE* ST4 ....67 G3
Allendale Wk *LNGTN* ST3 ....79 E1
Allensmore Av *STOKE* ST4 ....69 H2
Allen St *CDLE* ST10 ....75 H3
   STOKE ST4 ....3 K4
Allensway *NEWUL* ST5 ....66 A3
Allerton Rd *STOKE* ST4 ....77 H3
All Saints' Rd *STOKE* ST4 ....68 A2
Allthorpe PI *NEWUL* ST5 ....58 B3
Alma CI *ALS/KID* ST7 ....25 E1
Almar PI *BURS/TUN* ST6 ....45 E1
Alma St *LEEK* ST13 ....30 C3
   STOKE ST4 ....68 D1
   STONE ST15 ....90 C2

Almond Gv *LNGTN* ST5 ....69 E4
Almond PI *NEWUL* ST5 ....42 D5
Alsager Rd *ALS/KID* ST7 ....41 F1
   SBCH CW11 ....14 B5
Alsop St *LEEK* ST13 ....30 D4
Alstonfield Av *BUCK/MIL* ST2 ....55 E3
Althrop Gv *LNGTN* ST3 ....70 B4
Altona CI *STOKE* ST15 ....91 E4
Alton CI *NEWUL* ST5 ....58 B5
Alton Gv *BUCK/MIL* ST2 ....63 F5
Alwyn Crs *BURS/TUN* ST6 ....53 H1
Amber Ct *END/WER* ST9 ....47 F1
Amberfield CI *LNGTN* ST3 ....70 C3
Amblecote Dr *LNGTN* ST3 ....70 C5
Ambleside Ct *CONG* CW12 ....7 G5
Ambleside PI *BURS/TUN* ST6 ....45 E5
Ambrose PI *BURS/TUN* ST6 ....36 D4
Amelia CI *BURS/TUN* ST6 ....46 C4
America St *BURS/TUN* ST6 ....44 B3
Amicable St *BURS/TUN* ST6 ....53 E2
Amison St *LNGTN* ST3 ....70 B3
Ampthill PI *STOKE* ST15 ....77 H1
Ancaster St *BURS/TUN* ST6 ....36 B4
Anchor PI *LNGTN* ST3 ....70 A3
Anchor Rd *LNGTN* ST3 ....70 A3
Anchor Ter *LNGTN* ST3 ....70 A3
Anderson PI *BURS/TUN* ST6 ....46 A3
Andrew PI *NEWUL* ST5 ....3 F3
Andrew St *BURS/TUN* ST6 ....36 A4
Anglesey Dr *LNGTN* ST3 ....69 G4
Angle St *LEEK* ST13 ....30 C5
Angus CI *BUCK/MIL* ST2 ....63 E1
Annan CI *CONG* CW12 ....13 E1
Anne Ct *ALS/KID* ST7 ....42 D1
Anne St *BURS/TUN* ST6 ....36 A4
Annette Rd *STOKE* ST4 ....69 H1
Ansmede Gv *LNGTN* ST3 ....79 F1
Anson Rd *STOKE* ST4 ....81 E2
Anthony Gv *LNGTN* ST3 ....88 D1
Anthony PI *LNGTN* ST3 ....70 B3
Antrobus St *CONG* CW12 ....8 B4
Apedale Rd *ALS/KID* ST7 ....50 A1
Apley PI *STOKE* ST4 ....77 H2
Applecroft *NEWUL* ST5 ....43 E5
Appledore Gv *ALS/KID* ST7 ....36 C5
Appleford PI *LNGTN* ST3 ....79 E2
Applegarth CI *STOKE* ST4 ....69 H1
Appleton CI *BIDD* ST8 ....27 H1
Apsley Gv *BARL* ST12 ....86 A4
Aquinas St *STOKE* ST4 ....61 E5
Arbour CI *AUD/MAD/W* CW5 ....56 A5
Arbourfield Dr *BUCK/MIL* ST2 ....62 C2
Arbour St *ALS/KID* ST7 ....42 D1
   HAN ST1 ....5 G2
Arclid Wy *BUCK/MIL* ST2 ....62 D2
Arctic PI *STOKE* ST4 ....77 H2
Arden CI *LEEK* ST13 ....31 G5
Arden Ct *CONG* CW12 ....13 F1
Argles Rd *LEEK* ST13 ....31 F2
Argosy CI *BLYBR/FOR* ST11 ....81 F3
Argyle St *HAN* ST1 ....4 C6
Argyll CI *BLYBR/FOR* ST11 ....82 A4
Argyll Rd *LNGTN* ST3 ....70 B5
Aries CI *BURS/TUN* ST6 ....36 D5
Arkwright Gv *HAN* ST1 ....54 B1
Arley CI *ALS/KID* ST7 ....23 E5
Arlington Wy *LNGTN* ST3 ....80 B1
Arnold Gv *NEWUL* ST5 ....51 H1
Arnside Av *CONG* CW12 ....7 G5
Arran Dr *ALS/KID* ST7 ....36 D3
Arrowsmith Dr *ALS/KID* ST7 ....22 D5
Arthur St *BURS/TUN* ST6 ....44 C2
   NEWUL ST5 ....59 F3
   STONE ST15 ....90 D1
Arundel Wy *LNGTN* ST3 ....70 A1
Ascot CI *CONG* CW12 ....8 B3
Ash Bank Rd *BUCK/MIL* ST2 ....55 E1
Ashbourne Dr *NEWUL* ST5 ....58 B5
Ashbourne Rd *HAN* ST1 ....53 G4
Ashbourne Rd *CDLE* ST10 ....75 F4
   LEEK ST13 ....31 E4
Ashburton St *LNGTN* ST3 ....53 F2
Ashby Crs *LNGTN* ST3 ....80 A1
Ash CI *CDLE* ST10 ....75 F5
Ashcombe Gn *LNGTN* ST3 ....79 F1
Ashcombe Wy *LEEK* ST13 ....31 E5
Ashcroft Av *STOKE* ST4 ....67 G4
Ashcroft CI *NEWUL* ST5 ....51 G3
Ashcroft Gv *NEWUL* ST5 ....51 H3
Ashcroft PI *NEWUL* ST5 ....51 H3
Ashcroft Rd *NEWUL* ST5 * 51 G3
Ashdale CI *ALS/KID* ST7 ....23 E5
Ashdale Ri *NEWUL* ST5 ....66 D4
Ashdale Rd *LEEK* ST13 ....31 G3
   STOKE ST4 ....68 C2
Ashendene Gv *STOKE* ST4 ....77 H2
Ashenhurst Rd *ALS/KID* ST7 ....23 H5
Ashenhurst Wy *LEEK* ST13 ....31 F1
Ashenough Rd *ALS/KID* ST7 ....34 D5
Ashfields Gra *NEWUL* ST5 * 2 B3
Ashfields New Rd *NEWUL* ST5 ....2 B2
Ashfield Sq *BUCK/MIL* ST2 ....62 C2
Ashford St *STOKE* ST4 ....61 F4
Ash Green CI *STOKE* ST4 ....78 A3
Ash Wy *ALS/KID* ST7 ....25 H1
   BARL ST12 ....86 D4
   BLYBR/FOR ST11 ....81 G2
   BUCK/MIL ST2 ....55 E1
   LNGTN ST3 ....69 E5
   NEWUL ST5 ....58 B2

Ash Rd *STONE* ST15 ....91 E3
Ashton CI *CONG* CW12 ....13 F1
Ashton Ct *END/WER* ST9 ....64 A1
   NEWUL ST5 ....67 E5
Ashurst Gv *LNGTN* ST3 ....81 F5
Ash View *ALS/KID* ST7 ....35 H1
Ash Wy *BUCK/MIL* ST2 ....63 H1
   NEWUL ST5 ....66 B3
Ashwood *STOKE* ST4 ....3 H4
Ashwood CI *LNGTN* ST3 ....69 H2
Ashwood Gv *BLYBR/FOR* ST11 ....82 C4
Ashworth St *STOKE* ST4 ....68 D1
Askern CI *LNGTN* ST3 ....80 C1
Aspen CI *ALS/KID* ST7 ....35 H1
Asquith CI *BIDD* ST8 ....19 H5
Astbury CI *ALS/KID* ST7 ....26 A5
Astbury Lane Ends
   CONG CW12 ....12 C2
Astbury St *CONG* CW12 ....8 A5
Aster CI *LNGTN* ST3 ....71 F1
Aston Cha *STONE* ST15 ....91 G5
Aston Lodge Pkwy
   STONE ST15 ....91 G5
Aston Rd *NEWUL* ST5 ....42 D5
Astro Gv *LNGTN* ST3 ....38 D5
Athelstan St *BURS/TUN* ST6 ....44 B5
Athena Rd *HAN* ST1 ....54 B4
Atherstone Rd *STOKE* ST4 ....78 A3
Athlone St *BURS/TUN* ST6 ....45 H4
Atholl Rd *LNGTN* ST3 ....80 A1
Atkin CI *CONG* CW12 ....7 G4
Atlam CI *BUCK/MIL* ST2 ....62 C1
Atlantic Gv *STOKE* ST4 ....78 C2
Atlas St *STOKE* ST4 ....69 E2
Attlee Rd *CDLE* ST10 ....74 D5
Attwood St *ALS/KID* ST7 ....35 G1
Aubrey St *BURS/TUN* ST6 ....35 H4
Auckland St *BURS/TUN* ST6 ....53 E2
Audburn PI *STOKE* ST4 ....70 B4
Audley PI *NEWUL* ST5 ....58 B4
Audley Rd *ALS/KID* ST7 ....33 G5
   ALS/KID ST7 ....42 C4
Audley St *BURS/TUN* ST6 ....44 B3
Augustine St *STOKE* ST15 ....91 H4
Austen CI *CDLE* ST10 ....74 C5
Austin CI *STONE* ST15 ....90 C4
Austin St *HAN* ST1 ....5 H7
Austwick Gv *STOKE* ST4 ....67 G2
Aveling Rd *HAN* ST1 ....54 B2
Avenue Rd *STOKE* ST15 ....61 G5
The Avenue *ALS/KID* ST7 ....23 E4
   ALS/KID ST7 ....35 F2
   BLYBR/FOR ST11 ....82 C4
   END/WER ST9 ....39 G4
   END/WER ST9 ....47 H2
   NEWUL ST5 ....60 B2
   STONE ST15 ....3 G6
   STONE ST15 ....90 D2
Avion CI *BLYBR/FOR* ST11 ....81 H3
Avoca St *HAN* ST1 ....53 H4
Avon CI *ALS/KID* ST7 ....35 H1
   NEWUL ST5 ....66 B3
Avon Ct *ALS/KID* ST7 ....23 E5
Avondale St *BURS/TUN* ST6 ....53 G2
Avon Dr *CONG* CW12 ....12 D1
Avon Gv *CDLE* ST10 ....85 E1
Avonside Av *BURS/TUN* ST6 ....44 D2
Avon Crs *LNGTN* ST3 ....71 F4
Aylesbury Rd *BUCK/MIL* ST2 ....63 E2
Aynsley Av *NEWUL* ST5 * 66 D4
Aynsley CI *CDLE* ST10 ....84 C1
Aynsley Rd *STOKE* ST4 ....61 F5
Aynsley's Dr *BLYBR/FOR* ST11 ....82 A5
Ayr Rd *CDLE* ST10 ....85 E1
Ayrshire Wy *CONG* CW12 ....13 E1
Ayshford St *LNGTN* ST3 ....69 H4

B

Back Bunt's La *END/WER* ST9 ....47 E2
Back Ford Green Rd
   BURS/TUN ST6 ....45 H4
Back Garden St *NEWUL* ST5 ....2 E4
Back Heathcote St
   ALS/KID ST7 * 35 G1
Back La *BURS/TUN* ST6 ....38 D2
   CONG CW12 ....7 E2
   LEEK ST13 ....30 C3
Baddeley Green La
   BUCK/MIL ST2 ....46 D4
Baddeley Hall Rd
   BUCK/MIL ST2 ....47 E4
Baddeley Rd *BUCK/MIL* ST2 ....46 D5
Baddeley St *BURS/TUN* ST6 ....44 D5
   CDLE ST10 ....75 E5
Baden CI *BURS/TUN* ST6 ....45 F1
Baden Gv *BLYBR/FOR* ST11 ....81 G3
Badgers Brow *HAN* ST1 ....5 K4
Badgers Ri *LEEK* ST13 ....30 D3
Badnall St *LEEK* ST13 ....30 D5
Bagnall PI *NEWUL* ST5 ....59 F3
Bagnall Rd *BUCK/MIL* ST2 ....47 F5
Bagnall St *HAN* ST1 ....5 F4
Bagot Gv *HAN* ST1 ....54 B1
Bailey CI *ALS/KID* ST7 ....25 H2
Bailey Rd *CONG* CW12 ....13 F1
Bailey St *NEWUL* ST5 ....69 E3
Bailey's Bank *BIDD* ST8 ....19 H2
Bailey St *NEWUL* ST5 ....58 C3
   STOKE ST4 ....60 D3
Bainbridge Rd *STOKE* ST4 ....78 A3
Bains Gv *NEWUL* ST5 ....59 E2
Baker Crs *BUCK/MIL* ST2 ....46 D5
Baker Cres North *BUCK/MIL* ST2 ....47 E3
Baker Cres South *BUCK/MIL* ST2 ....46 D4
Baker St *STOKE* ST4 ....69 E1
Bakewell CI *NEWUL* ST5 ....58 B3

Bakewell St *STOKE* ST4 ....67 H2
Bala Gv *CDLE* ST10 ....75 F3
Balcombe CI *NEWUL* ST5 ....2 C6
Balfour Gv *BIDD* ST8 ....20 A5
Balfour St *HAN* ST1 ....5 H4
Ball Have Gn *LEEK* ST13 ....31 E3
Ball Haye Rd *LEEK* ST13 ....31 E3
Ball Hayes Rd *LEEK* ST13 ....45 G1
Ballington Gdns *LEEK* ST13 ....31 E4
Ballington St *LEEK* ST13 ....31 E5
Ballinson Rd *LNGTN* ST3 ....79 E1
Balliol St *STOKE* ST4 * 61 E5
Ball La *BURS/TUN* ST6 ....46 C1
   LEEK ST13 ....30 D3
Balloon St *STOKE* ST4 ....3 H3
Balmoral CI *STOKE* ST4 ....68 A5
Balmoral Gdns *CONG* CW12 ....4 D3
Baltic CI *STOKE* ST4 ....78 B3
Bamber PI *NEWUL* ST5 ....51 F3
Bamber St *STOKE* ST4 ....61 F5
Bamford Gv *HAN* ST1 ....53 F4
Banbury Gv *BIDD* ST8 ....19 H5
Banbury St *LNGTN* ST3 ....34 D2
Bancroft La *BLYBR/FOR* ST11 ....82 B4
Bank End *BURS/TUN* ST6 ....38 D5
Bankfield Gv *NEWUL* ST5 ....57 G1
Bankfield Rd *LNGTN* ST3 ....80 D2
Bank Hall *BURS/TUN* ST6 ....45 F4
Bankhouse Dr *CONG* CW12 ....9 E3
Bank House Dr *NEWUL* ST5 ....60 C2
Bank House La *SBCH* CW11 ....10 A5
Bankhouse Rd
   BLYBR/FOR ST11 ....82 D2
   STOKE ST4 ....77 H2
Banks CI *CONG* CW12 ....9 E4
Bankside *NEWUL* ST5 ....2 E4
Bank Side *STONE* ST15 ....90 C5
Banksman Rd *BUCK/MIL* ST2 ....63 F5
Bank St *ALS/KID* ST7 ....44 B2
   BURS/TUN ST6 ....44 B2
   CDLE ST10 ....74 D4
The Bank *ALS/KID* ST7 ....25 H1
Bank Top Av *BURS/TUN* ST6 ....45 E3
Banky Brook CI *HAN* ST1 ....54 A2
Banky Flds *CONG* CW12 ....8 A5
Banky Fields Crs *CONG* CW12 ....12 A1
Bannister CI *STOKE* ST4 ....68 D2
Barber CI *ALS/KID* ST7 ....25 E1
Barber PI *BURS/TUN* ST6 ....36 D5
Barber Rd *BURS/TUN* ST6 ....36 D5
Barber's Sq *NEWUL* ST5 ....52 B5
Barber St *BURS/TUN* ST6 ....45 E3
Barbridge Rd *NEWUL* ST5 ....42 D4
Barbrook Av *LNGTN* ST3 ....70 C3
Barclay St *LNGTN* ST3 ....70 A2
Barford Rd *NEWUL* ST5 ....66 B3
Barford St *BURS/TUN* ST6 ....69 H4
Bargrave St *BUCK/MIL* ST2 ....63 F3
Barker St *LNGTN* ST3 ....70 A4
   NEWUL ST5 ....51 F3
Barks Dr *BURS/TUN* ST6 ....45 H1
Barlaston Old Rd *STOKE* ST4 ....78 B4
Barlaston Rd *LNGTN* ST3 ....79 G4
Barley CPt *ALS/KID* ST7 ....33 G1
Barleycroft *NEWUL* ST5 ....58 E1
Barleycroft Ter *ALS/KID* ST7 ....25 E1
Barleyfields *ALS/KID* ST7 ....41 F4
   BURS/TUN ST6 ....45 F5
Barleyford Dr *LNGTN* ST3 ....70 B1
Barlow St *HAN* ST1 ....5 H5
Barlstone Av *BLYBR/FOR* ST11 ....82 B4
Barmouth CI *BIDD* ST8 ....28 A2
Barmouth Gv *BIDD* ST8 ....37 F2
Barnbridge CI *ALS/KID* ST7 ....25 E1
Barn Ct *NEWUL* ST5 ....67 E4
Barncroft Rd *BURS/TUN* ST6 ....37 F5
Barnes Wy *LNGTN* ST3 ....79 F1
Barnett Gv *BURS/TUN* ST6 ....44 D1
Barn Field *CONG* CW12 ....8 A4
Barnfield Rd *BURS/TUN* ST6 ....53 E2
Barnfields CI *LEEK* ST13 ....30 C5
Barngate St *LEEK* ST13 ....30 C3
Barniea Gv *LNGTN* ST3 ....81 E4
Barn Rd *CONG* CW12 ....8 A3
Barnsdale CI *STOKE* ST4 ....78 B5
Barnwell Gv *STOKE* ST4 ....78 A1
Baron St *STOKE* ST4 ....69 G2
Barracks Rd *NEWUL* ST5 ....2 E4
Barracks Sq *NEWUL* ST5 * 2 E4
Barracks Rd *STOKE* ST4 ....30 C5
Barrage Rd *BIDD* ST8 ....13 H5
Barratt Gdns *BUCK/MIL* ST2 ....54 D1
Barratt Rd *ALS/KID* ST7 ....23 H5
Barrett Crs *BURS/TUN* ST6 ....53 E3
Barrett Dr *BURS/TUN* ST6 ....53 E3
Barrie Gobs *ALS/KID* ST7 ....74 C5
Barrington Ct *NEWUL* ST5 ....60 B1
Barry Av *BUCK/MIL* ST2 ....62 C1
Bartholomew La *BURS/TUN* ST6 ....37 E3
Bartholmey Rd *ALS/KID* ST7 ....40 B4
   HAN ST1 ....54 A1
Bartlem St *LNGTN* ST3 ....70 B2
Barton Crs *BURS/TUN* ST6 ....44 C5
Barton St *STOKE* ST4 ....3 J5
Barwood Av *ALS/KID* ST7 ....24 A3
Basford Park Rd *NEWUL* ST5 ....59 G1
Basford Vw *NEWUL* ST5 * 3 G1
Basildon Gv *LNGTN* ST3 ....70 A5
Baskerville St *HAN* ST1 ....54 A5
Baskeyfield PI *BURS/TUN* ST6 ....45 F1
Basnett's Wood Rd
   NEWUL ST5 ....39 F5
Bassett CI *CDLE* ST10 ....74 C5
Bassilow Rd *STOKE* ST4 ....62 B5
Bateman Av *BIDD* ST8 ....20 A5
Bath Rd *NEWUL* ST5 ....57 H2
Baths Rd *LNGTN* ST3 ....70 A2
Bath St *ALS/KID* ST7 ....35 G2
   LNGTN ST3 ....71 F2
   STOKE ST4 ....60 D4
Bath Ter *STOKE* ST4 ....3 F2
Bathurst St *LNGTN* ST3 ....70 A3

Batkin CI *BURS/TUN* ST6 ....45 F1
Batten CI *BLYBR/FOR* ST11 ....81 G3
Battison Crs *LNGTN* ST3 ....69 H5
Bayham Wk *BUCK/MIL* ST2 ....54 C5
Baytree CI *HAN* ST1 ....54 B3
Beacon Ri *STONE* ST15 ....90 D5
Beaconsfield *NEWUL* ST5 ....52 A2
Beaconsfield Dr *LNGTN* ST3 ....79 E1
Beadnell CI *LNGTN* ST3 ....79 H1
Beard Gv *BUCK/MIL* ST2 ....54 C5
Beasley Av *NEWUL* ST5 ....51 F3
Beasley PI *NEWUL* ST5 ....51 F2
Beata Rd *NEWUL* ST5 ....43 F5
Beatrice Ct *STOKE* ST4 ....68 A5
Beattie Av *NEWUL* ST5 ....59 H1
Beatty Dr *CONG* CW12 ....8 A3
Beaufighter Gv *BURS/TUN* ST6 ....44 B2
Beaufort Av *END/WER* ST9 ....64 A1
Beaufort Rd *LNGTN* ST3 ....70 A5
Beaulieu CI *END/WER* ST9 ....64 A1
Beaumaris CI *STOKE* ST4 ....3 H4
Beaumont CI *BIDD* ST8 ....19 H5
Beaumont Rd *BURS/TUN* ST6 ....44 C3
Beaver Dr *CDLE* ST10 ....74 B4
Beckenham CI *LNGTN* ST3 ....81 G2
Beckett Av *LNGTN* ST3 ....81 F1
Beckfields CI *BIDD* ST8 ....20 A5
Beckford St *HAN* ST1 ....54 B4
Beck Rd *AUD/MAD/W* CW5 ....56 B5
Beckton Av *BURS/TUN* ST6 ....53 G5
Bedale PI *BURS/TUN* ST6 ....79 E1
Bedcroft *BARL* ST12 ....87 E2
Beddow Wy *BURS/TUN* ST6 ....36 D5
Bedford Crs *NEWUL* ST5 ....67 E3
Bedford Gv *ALS/KID* ST7 ....67 E3
Bedford Rd *ALS/KID* ST7 ....25 G5
   HAN ST1 ....4 E7
Bedford St *HAN* ST1 ....4 D7
Beech Av *ALS/KID* ST7 ....15 F1
Beech CI *BIDD* ST8 ....20 C4
   CONG CW12 ....7 G3
Beech Ct *STOKE* ST15 ....91 E3
Beech Cft *AUD/MAD/W* CW5 ....56 B5
Beechcroft Est *BARL* ST12 ....87 F3
Beechfield Gv *STOKE* ST4 ....35 E3
The Beeches *NEWUL* ST5 ....52 B3
Beechfield Rd *STOKE* ST4 ....78 B4
Beechfields *BARL* ST12 ....87 F3
Beech Gv *LEEK* ST13 ....52 A5
   NEWUL ST5 ....52 A5
   STOKE ST4 ....68 A3
Beechmont Gv *HAN* ST1 ....54 B3
Beech Rd *LNGTN* ST3 ....79 F1
Beech St *LNGTN* ST3 ....70 A4
Beechwood CI
   BLYBR/FOR ST11 ....82 B4
   NEWUL ST5 ....77 E1
Beechwood Dr *ALS/KID* ST7 ....42 C5
   STOKE ST15 ....23 E5
Beeston Dr *STOKE* ST4 ....23 E5
Beeston St *LNGTN* ST3 ....70 A2
Beeston Vw *ALS/KID* ST7 ....35 G4
Beggars La *LEEK* ST13 ....30 B4
Belfast CI *BURS/TUN* ST6 ....45 F5
Belfield Av *NEWUL* ST5 ....52 A5
Belford PI *STOKE* ST4 ....67 G4
Belgrave Av *ALS/KID* ST7 ....23 F5
   CONG CW12 ....8 A4
Belgrave Crs *LNGTN* ST3 ....80 A1
Belgrave Rd *LNGTN* ST3 ....80 A1
   NEWUL ST5 ....2 E5
Bell Av *LNGTN* ST3 ....70 B5
Bellefield Vw *NEWUL* ST5 * 58 A3
Bellerton La *BURS/TUN* ST6 ....46 A4
Belle Vue Rd *LEEK* ST13 ....30 C3
Bell La *BARL* ST12 ....87 E1
Bellringer CI *BIDD* ST8 ....27 G1
Bellringer Rd *STOKE* ST4 * 9 F3
   STOKE ST4 ....78 B3
Bell's Hollow *NEWUL* ST5 ....43 E3
Bellwood CI *LNGTN* ST3 ....81 E4
Belmont Rd *HAN* ST1 ....53 G3
Belsay CI *LNGTN* ST3 ....70 A3
Belvedere Rd *STOKE* ST4 ....78 A1
Belvoir Av *STOKE* ST4 ....78 B5
Bemersley Rd *BIDD* ST8 ....37 G2
Benedict PI *BUCK/MIL* ST2 ....54 C4
Bengal Gv *STOKE* ST4 ....78 C2
Bengry Rd *LNGTN* ST3 ....81 F5
Benjamins Wy *ALS/KID* ST7 ....41 H4
Bennett CI *NEWUL* ST5 ....51 H2
Bennett Prec *LNGTN* ST3 * 69 H4
Bennett St *BURS/TUN* ST6 ....52 C2
Benson St *BURS/TUN* ST6 ....70 A4
Benson St *BURS/TUN* ST6 ....44 D1
Bent La *CONG* CW12 ....11 F1
Bentley Av *NEWUL* ST5 ....51 H1
Bentley CI *STONE* ST15 ....90 B5
Bentley Rd *BURS/TUN* ST6 ....45 F1
Berdmore St *STOKE* ST4 ....69 G2
Beresford Crs *NEWUL* ST5 ....58 B5
Beresford St *NEWUL* ST5 ....61 F4
Bergamot Dr *LNGTN* ST3 ....51 E3
Berkeley Av *ALS/KID* ST7 ....23 F3
Berkeley Ct *NEWUL* ST5 ....2 A3
Berkeley St *STOKE* ST4 ....90 C2
Berkshire Dr *CONG* CW12 ....8 B3
Bernard Gv *NEWUL* ST5 * 88 D1
Bernard St *HAN* ST1 ....5 G5
Berne Av *HAN* ST1 ....54 B3
Berryfield Gv *LNGTN* ST3 ....70 A1
Berry Hill Rd *STOKE* ST4 ....61 H5
Berry La *LNGTN* ST3 ....69 H4
Berwick CI *CONG* CW12 ....13 E1
Berwick Rd *ALS/KID* ST7 ....54 A1
Best St *STOKE* ST4 ....69 F1
Beswick CI *CDLE* ST10 ....74 C5
Beswick Rd *BURS/TUN* ST6 ....36 D5
Bethell Rd *HAN* ST1 ....53 H2
Bethesda Rd *HAN* ST1 ....5 F7

Bethesda St HAN ST1 ....4 E4
Betley Pl NEWUL ST5 ....67 E2
Bettany Rd BURS/TUN ST6 ....5 E2
Bevan Av ALS/KID ST7 ....34 D5
Bevandean Cl STOKE ST4 ....78 C5
Beverley Crs BLYBR/FOR ST11 ....82 C2
Beverley Dr BUCK/MIL ST2 ....62 D2
  BUCK/MIL ST2 ....8 C5
Beville St STOKE ST4 ....69 E1
Bewcastle Gv LNGTN ST3 ....81 E3
Bew St BURS/TUN ST6 ....46 A1
Bexhill Gv HAN ST1 ....54 B5
Bexley St HAN ST1 ....54 B4
Bibby St ALS/KID ST7 ....23 G1
Bida La CONG CW12 ....13 F2
Biddulph Rd ALS/KID ST7 ....26 C2
  BURS/TUN ST6 ....37 F4
  CONG CW12 ....13 F1
Biddulph St CONG CW12 ....13 G5
Bignall End Rd ALS/KID ST7 ....42 A2
Billinge St BURS/TUN ST6 * 52 C1
Bilton St STOKE ST4 ....68 A1
Birchall Av BURS/TUN ST6 ....44 A5
Bircham Wk NEWUL ST5 ....66 D5
Birch Av ALS/KID ST7 ....23 C5
  BIDD ST8 ....27 E2
Birch Ct CONG CW12 ....7 F4
Birchdown Av BURS/TUN ST6 ....45 F5
Birchenfields La CDLE ST10 ....73 H2
Birchenwood Rd
  BURS/TUN ST6 ....36 C3
Birchenwood Wy ALS/KID ST7 ....35 H2
Birches Head Rd HAN ST1 ....54 A3
The Birches CDLE ST10 ....75 G4
Birchfield Av ALS/KID ST7 ....23 H1
Birchfield Rd BUCK/MIL ST2 ....55 E4
Birchfields St STONE ST15 ....90 C5
Birchgate Cl STOKE ST4 ....55 E5
Birchgate Gv BUCK/MIL ST2 ....55 E5
Birch Green Gv HAN ST1 ....54 A2
Birch Gv BLYBR/FOR ST11 ....82 C5
  LNGTN ST3 ....89 E1
Birch House Rd NEWUL ST5 ....50 D1
Birchlands Rd HAN ST1 ....54 B5
Birchover Wy BURS/TUN ST6 ....5 E4
Birch Rd ALS/KID ST7 ....41 H5
  CONG CW12 ....7 F4
  STONE ST15 ....91 E4
Birch St HAN ST1 ....5 J1
Birch Ter HAN ST1 ....5 H5
Birch Tree La ALS/KID ST7 ....25 H1
Birch Valley Rd ALS/KID ST7 ....36 A2
Birch Wk LNGTN ST3 ....79 G1
Bird Cage Wk HAN ST1 ....4 E4
Bird Rd LNGTN ST3 ....71 F5
Birkdale Dr ALS/KID ST7 ....26 A5
Birkholme Dr LNGTN ST3 ....81 E5
Birks St STOKE ST4 ....68 B2
Birrell St STOKE ST4 ....69 F2
Biscay Gv STOKE ST4 ....78 C2
Bishop Rd BURS/TUN ST6 ....45 E1
Bishop's Cl ALS/KID ST7 ....34 D3
Bitterne Pl BUCK/MIL ST2 ....63 F4
Bittern La CDLE ST10 ....75 G4
Blackbank Rd NEWUL ST5 ....50 C5
Blackbird Wy ALS/KID ST7 ....36 D2
  BIDD ST8 ....20 A5
Blackbrook Av NEWUL ST5 ....50 C1
Black Firs La CONG CW12 ....7 E2
Blackfriars Rd NEWUL ST5 ....15 H5
Blackheath Cl LNGTN ST3 ....70 B4
Black Horse La HAN ST1 ....4 D3
Blackie's La STONE ST15 ....91 G4
Blacklake Dr LNGTN ST3 ....89 E1
Blackshaw Cl CONG CW12 ....13 G3
Blackthorn Pl NEWUL ST5 ....51 E1
Blackwell's Rw BURS/TUN ST6 ....53 F3
Blackwood Pl LNGTN ST3 ....70 C3
Bladon Av NEWUL ST5 ....66 D5
Bladon Cl BURS/TUN ST6 ....54 D3
Bladon Crs ALS/KID ST7 ....23 E5
Blakelow Rd BUCK/MIL ST2 ....54 D3
Blakeney Av NEWUL ST5 ....66 D4
Blake St BURS/TUN ST6 ....5 H3
  CONG CW12 ....8 A5
Blanchard Cl BLYBR/FOR ST11 ......81 C4
Blandford Cl LNGTN ST3 ....70 A3
Blantyre St LNGTN ST3 ....70 A5
Bleak Pl BURS/TUN ST6 ....53 E2
Bleak St NEWUL ST5 ....60 B1
Bleeding Wolf La ALS/KID ST7 ....25 E3
Blencarn Gv END/WER ST9 ....47 E2
Blenheim Ct ALS/KID ST7 ....23 E3
Blenheim St STOKE ST4 ....68 D2
Blenheim Ter BLYBR/FOR ST11 ......81 C3
Blithfield Cl END/WER ST9 ....44 A2
Bluebell Cl BIDD ST8 ....28 A1
Bluebell Dr NEWUL ST5 ....66 C3
Bluebell Wy ALS/KID ST7 ....22 D5
Bluestone Av BURS/TUN ST6 ....45 F4
Blurton Priory LNGTN ST3 ....79 F2
Blurton Rd BARL ST12 ....87 G3
  LNGTN ST3 ....69 E4
  LNGTN ST3 ....79 G5
Blythe Av CONG CW12 ....7 G5
  LNGTN ST3 ....89 E1
Blythe Bridge Rd
  BLYBR/FOR ST11 ....72 A5
Blythe Cl BLYBR/FOR ST11 ....81 H3
Blythe Gv BLYBR/FOR ST11 * 81 H5
Blythe Mount Pk
  BLYBR/FOR ST11 ....82 C2
Blythe Rd BLYBR/FOR ST11 ....82 C5
Blythe Vw BLYBR/FOR ST11 ....82 B4
Boardmans Bank
  BURS/TUN ST6 ....38 C2
Boathorse Rd ALS/KID ST7 ....35 F3
Bogs La BLYBR/FOR ST11 ....82 B4
Bolberry Cl LNGTN ST3 ....80 C1
Bold St HAN ST1 ....5 H1
Bolina Gv LNGTN ST3 ....69 H1
Bollin Cl ALS/KID ST7 ....34 A5
Bollin Dr CONG CW12 ....12 D1

Bollin Gv BIDD ST8 ....20 A4
Bolney Gv HAN ST1 ....54 B4
Bolsover Cl BURS/TUN ST6 ....37 E5
Bolton Pl LNGTN ST3 ....80 D2
Boma Rd STOKE ST4 ....77 H4
Bondfield Wy LNGTN ST3 ....71 F5
Bond St BURS/TUN ST6 ....44 B2
Bonnard Ct BLYBR/FOR ST11 ....81 G4
Boon Av STOKE ST4 ....68 A1
Boon Hill Rd ALS/KID ST7 ....41 H5
Boothen Cl STOKE ST4 ....68 B3
Boothen Old Rd STOKE ST4 ....68 B3
Boothen Pk STOKE ST4 * 68 B1
Boothen Rd STOKE ST4 ....68 B1
Boothenwood Ter STOKE ST4 ....68 A2
Booth St ALS/KID ST7 ....41 F4
  CONG CW12 ....8 C5
  NEWUL ST5 ....51 F5
  STOKE ST4 ....68 B1
Bordeaux Rd LNGTN ST3 ....81 E2
Bordeaux Wk NEWUL ST5 ....66 B4
Borough Rd CONG CW12 ....8 D4
Borrowdale Rd BURS/TUN ST6 ......46 A3
Boscombe Gv STOKE ST4 ....78 C5
Bosinney Cl STOKE ST4 ....69 H2
Bosley Brook BIDD ST8 ....15 H5
Bosley Gv BURS/TUN ST6 ....36 A4
Bosley Vw CONG CW12 ....13 F1
Boston Cl BURS/TUN ST6 ....44 A2
Boswell St STOKE ST4 ....60 D5
Botany Bay Rd HAN ST1 ....5 K1
Botesworth Gdns
  LNGTN ST6 ....44 B5
Botteslow St HAN ST1 ....5 H5
Boughey Rd ALS/KID ST7 ....41 H4
  STOKE ST4 ....61 G4
Boughey St STOKE ST4 ....68 A1
The Boulevard BURS/TUN ST6 ......44 C5
Boulton St HAN ST1 ....53 H4
  NEWUL ST5 ....52 A3
Boundary La CONG CW12 ....13 F2
Boundary St HAN ST1 ....4 D5
  STOKE ST4 ....5 G3
Boundary Vw CDLE ST10 ....74 B5
Bourne Pl LEEK ST13 ....30 B3
Bourne Rd ALS/KID ST7 ....35 F1
Bournes Bank BURS/TUN ST6 ......52 B1
Bourne St ALS/KID ST7 ....26 A1
  STOKE ST4 ....69 E3
Bouverie Pde HAN ST1 ....54 B1
Bowden Cl CONG CW12 ....7 F5
Bowden St BURS/TUN ST6 ....45 F5
Bowers Ct STONE ST15 ....91 C4
Bower St HAN ST1 ....5 J4
Bowfell Gv STOKE ST4 ....62 D5
Bowland Av NEWUL ST5 ....58 D1
Bowlers Cl BURS/TUN ST6 ....53 E5
Bowman Gv BURS/TUN ST6 ....77 H4
Bowmead Cl STOKE ST4 ....78 C4
Bowness Ct CONG CW12 ....11 C1
Bowness St HAN ST1 ....53 H4
Bowstead St STOKE ST4 * 68 B1
Bowyer Av BURS/TUN ST6 * 46 A1
Box La CONG CW12 ....2 C3
  LNGTN ST3 ....70 D5
Boyles Hall Rd ALS/KID ST7 ....41 C4
Brabazon Cl BLYBR/FOR ST11 ......81 C3
Brackenberry NEWUL ST5 ....5 G1
Bracken Cl ALS/KID ST7 ....15 H5
  BARL ST12 ....86 A4
  LNGTN ST3 ....80 C5
Bracken Dl LEEK ST13 ....30 A5
Brackenfield Av BUCK/MIL ST2 ....63 E3
The Brackens NEWUL ST5 ....66 D5
Bracken St STOKE ST4 ....69 E3
Brackley Av BURS/TUN ST6 ....45 F5
Bradbury Cl BURS/TUN ST6 ....46 A3
Bradbury Gdns CONG CW12 ....12 D2
Bradford Ter HAN ST1 ....53 H4
Bradwell Gra NEWUL ST5 ....51 H5
Bradwell Gv CONG CW12 ....8 D5
Bradwell La NEWUL ST5 ....51 G2
Bradwell St BURS/TUN ST6 ....52 B1
Braemar Cl BUCK/MIL ST2 ....65 E1
Braemore Rd BUCK/MIL ST2 ....54 D5
Braithwell Dr BUCK/MIL ST2 ....46 C4
Brakespeare St BURS/TUN ST6 ....36 A4
The Brake ALS/KID ST7 ....25 H1
Brake Village ALS/KID ST7 ....25 H1
The Brambles NEWUL ST5 ....60 B1
Bramfield Dr NEWUL ST5 ....2 E1
Bramley Cl CDLE ST10 ....75 E5
Bramley Pl STOKE ST4 ....67 G5
Brammall Dr BLYBR/FOR ST11 ....82 A3
Brammer St BURS/TUN ST6 ....69 F5
Brampton Cl END/WER ST9 ....39 H3
Brampton Gdns NEWUL ST5 ....60 A1
Brampton Rd NEWUL ST5 ....2 E1
Brampton Sidings NEWUL ST5 ......2 D1
The Brampton NEWUL ST5 ....2 E1
Brampton Vale Gdns
  BURS/TUN ST6 * 52 C3
Bramshaws Acre CDLE ST10 ....75 E5
Brandon St HAN ST1 ....77 H2
Branston Gv STOKE ST4 ....70 D4
Bransty Gv STOKE ST4 ....78 C5
Brant Av NEWUL ST5 ....51 C5
Brassington Wy
  BUCK/MIL ST2 ....63 E3
Brattice Pl BUCK/MIL ST2 ....63 F5
Brattswood Dr ALS/KID ST7 ....18 H5
Braystones Cl ALS/KID ST7 ....36 C3
Breach La CDLE ST10 ....84 B5
Breach Rd BURS/TUN ST6 ....39 E4
Bream Wy BURS/TUN ST6 ....45 F4
Brecon Wy BURS/TUN ST6 ....59 F1
Breedon Cl NEWUL ST5 ....5 G1
Breeze Av BURS/TUN ST6 ....44 C2
Brendale St STOKE ST4 ....78 A1
Brentnor Cl LNGTN ST3 ....70 D4
Brentwood Gv BUCK/MIL ST2 ......47 E5
Brereton Pl BURS/TUN ST6 ....44 C5
Bretherton Pl BURS/TUN ST6 ......37 E5
Brewery St HAN ST1 ....4 E2

Brewester Rd BUCK/MIL ST2 ....62 B1
Brianson Av BURS/TUN ST6 ....53 G2
Briarbank Cl STOKE ST4 ....59 H1
The Briars NEWUL ST5 ....59 H2
Briarswood ALS/KID ST7 ....35 H2
Briarwood Pl LNGTN ST3 ....70 A7
Brickfield Pl LNGTN ST3 ....70 A2
Brick House St BURS/TUN ST6 ......52 D1
Brick-kiln La NEWUL ST5 ....51 E2
Brick Kiln La STOKE ST4 ....3 K2
Bridestowe Cl LNGTN ST3 ....81 E3
Bridge Cl ALS/KID ST7 ....41 H4
Bridge Ct BLYBR/FOR ST11 ....82 B4
Bridge Crs STOKE ST4 ....90 D4
Bridge Cft BURS/TUN ST6 ....37 F5
Bridge Rd STOKE ST4 ....67 G4
Bridge Rw CONG CW12 ....8 C5
Bridge St BIDD ST8 ....37 F1
  CONG CW12 ....8 B5
  NEWUL ST5 ....2 C3
  NEWUL ST5 ....58 C5
Bridgewater Cl CONG CW12 ....13 F1
Bridgewater St
  BURS/TUN ST6 ....52 B1
Bridgewood St LNGTN ST3 ....70 C3
Bridgnorth Gv NEWUL ST5 ....43 E4
Bridgwood Rd
  BLYBR/FOR ST11 ....82 C3
Bridle Pth BUCK/MIL ST2 ....66 A1
The Bridle Pth NEWUL ST5 ....66 B4
Brierley Rd CONG CW12 ....13 F1
Brierley St BURS/TUN ST6 ....45 E5
Brieryhurst Cl BUCK/MIL ST2 ......55 E4
Brieryhurst Rd ALS/KID ST7 ....25 H5
Brightgreen St LNGTN ST3 ....70 B2
Brighton St BIDD ST8 ....43 E5
Bright St LNGTN ST3 ....81 E1
Brindiwell Gv STOKE ST4 ....78 C3
Brindley Cl ALS/KID ST7 ....35 E2
  STONE ST15 ....90 B1
Brindley La BUCK/MIL ST2 ....45 F4
Brindley Pl BURS/TUN ST6 ....37 C5
Brindley St NEWUL ST5 ....2 C2
Brindleys Wy ALS/KID ST7 ....21 H4
Brindley Wy CONG CW12 ....13 F1
Brindon Cl LNGTN ST3 ....71 F4
Brinsley Av STOKE ST4 ....78 A4
Brisley Hl NEWUL ST5 ....67 H1
Bristol St NEWUL ST5 ....52 B4
Britannia St LEEK ST13 ....30 D5
Brittain Av NEWUL ST5 ....51 F2
Brittle Pl BURS/TUN ST6 ....45 H4
Britton St STOKE ST4 ....60 D5
Brixham Cl BUCK/MIL ST2 ....62 B5
Broadfield Rd BURS/TUN ST6 ......36 A5
Broadhurst La CONG CW12 ....13 F1
Broadhurst St BURS/TUN ST6 * 45 F5
Broad La BURS/TUN ST6 ....42 C4
Broadlawns Dr LNGTN ST3 ....69 H1
Broad Meadow Ct NEWUL ST5 ......51 E3
Broadmine St STOKE ST4 ....68 C3
Broadoak Wy LNGTN ST3 ....79 E1
Broad St HAN ST1 ....30 D4
  LEEK ST13 ....30 D4
  NEWUL ST5 ....2 D2
Broadway LNGTN ST3 ....70 D5
Brockbank Pl BURS/TUN ST6 ....45 F1
Brockiehurst Wy HAN ST1 ....54 A2
Brockley Sq HAN ST1 ....4 E3
Brocksford St STOKE ST4 ....69 G2
Brock Wy NEWUL ST5 ....59 F2
Brogan St STOKE ST4 ....69 F1
Bromfield Ct STOKE ST4 ....90 D2
Bromford Pl HAN ST1 ....4 C6
Bromley Ct HAN ST1 ....4 C1
Bromley Hough STOKE ST4 ....67 H2
Bromley Rd CONG CW12 ....13 F1
Bromley St HAN ST1 ....4 B1
Brompton Dr BUCK/MIL ST2 ....46 D3
Bromsberrow Wy LNGTN ST3 ......81 E3
Bronte Av BUCK/MIL ST2 ....46 C5
Brook Cl BLYBR/FOR ST11 ....81 G4
Brookes Ct STOKE ST4 ....69 E1
Brookfield Av END/WER ST9 ....39 C4
Brookfield Ct STONE ST15 ....91 F5
Brookfield Dr ALS/KID ST7 ....23 E3
Brookfield Rd BUCK/MIL ST2 ......67 E2
Brook Gdns BIDD ST8 ....19 H5
Brookgate BLYBR/FOR ST11 ....82 D2
Brookhouse Dr BARL ST12 ....86 C5
Brookhouse La BUCK/MIL ST2 ....55 G5
  CONG CW12 ....8 A5
Brookhouse Rd ALS/KID ST7 ....23 F5
  CDLE ST10 ....74 A4
  LNGTN ST3 ....71 F5
Brookland Av LNGTN ST3 ....74 B5
Brookland Av LNGTN ST3 ....51 F5
Brookland Rd BURS/TUN ST6 * 44 D1
Brooklands Rd CONG CW12 ....7 F4
Brook La CONG CW12 ....11 F5
  END/WER ST9 ....39 H3
  NEWUL ST5 ....69 H1
Brookmead Gv LNGTN ST3 ....69 H1
Brook Pl NEWUL ST5 ....67 E2
  STOKE ST4 ....60 D3
Brook Rd STOKE ST4 ....78 A3
Brookside Cl NEWUL ST5 ....2 A7
Brookside Ct CDLE ST10 ....74 B4
Brookside Dr LNGTN ST3 ....69 E5
Brookside La STONE ST15 ....90 B4
Brookside Rd CONG CW12 ....8 B4
Brook St BIDD ST8 ....37 F1
  CONG CW12 ....30 D4
  LEEK ST13 ....30 D4
  NEWUL ST5 ....58 C2
  STOKE ST4 ....61 F5
Brookvale Dr LNGTN ST3 ....70 D4
Brook Wk ALS/KID ST7 * 23 G5
Brookwood Cl NEWUL ST5 ....66 C4
Brookwood Dr LNGTN ST3 ....71 H4
  LNGTN ST3 ....81 F1

Broome Hl NEWUL ST5 ....77 E1
Broomfield Pl North HAN ST1 ....4 B4
Broomfield Rd BURS/TUN ST6 ......45 H1
Broomfields BIDD ST8 ....20 D4
Broomhill St BURS/TUN ST6 ....44 B4
Broom St HAN ST1 ....5 G1
Brough Cl LEEK ST13 ....30 D5
Brough La STOKE ST4 ....78 B3
Broughton Crs BARL ST12 ....87 E5
Broughton Rd BUCK/MIL ST2 ......62 B1
  NEWUL ST5 ....2 E5
Brown Av ALS/KID ST7 ....24 A4
Brownhead Rd LNGTN ST3 ....71 E5
Brownhill Rd STOKE ST4 ....38 D4
Brownhills Rd BURS/TUN ST6 ......44 B4
Browning Cl CDLE ST10 ....44 D5
Browning Gv ALS/KID ST7 ....34 C3
Browning Rd LNGTN ST3 ....66 E5
Brown Lees Rd ALS/KID ST7 ....26 D4
  BIDD ST8 ....27 F3
Brownley Rd BURS/TUN ST6 ....45 H5
Brownsea Pl LNGTN ST3 ....69 E5
Brown St BURS/TUN ST6 * 53 E1
  CONG CW12 ....8 C4
Brundall Gv BUCK/MIL ST2 ....63 F2
Brunswick La HAN ST1 ....4 D4
Brunswick St CONG CW12 ....8 C5
  HAN ST1 ....4 D4
  LEEK ST13 ....31 E5
  NEWUL ST5 ....2 E3
Brunt St BURS/TUN ST6 ....52 B2
Brutus Rd NEWUL ST5 ....50 D4
Bryan St HAN ST1 ....4 E2
Bryant Rd BUCK/MIL ST2 ....62 A1
Brymbo Rd NEWUL ST5 ....51 F4
Buccleuch Rd LNGTN ST3 ....70 B5
Buckingham Cl CONG CW12 ....8 D1
Buckingham Crs STOKE ST4 ....78 A4
Buckland Gv STOKE ST4 ....78 C5
Buckley Rd BURS/TUN ST6 ....37 G5
Buckleys Rw NEWUL ST5 ....51 F5
Buckmaster Av NEWUL ST5 ....50 D4
Bucknall New Rd HAN ST1 ....5 H5
Bucknall Old Rd HAN ST1 ....5 G3
Bucknall Rd HAN ST1 ....5 K3
Bude Cl BURS/TUN ST6 ....22 D5
Buller St HAN ST1 ....5 G7
Bull La BIDD ST8 ....37 E1
Bullocks House Rd
  ALS/KID ST7 ....26 C5
Bulstrode St BURS/TUN ST6 ....2 D3
Bunny Hl NEWUL ST5 ....67 E2
Bunts La CONG CW12 ....12 C1
  END/WER ST9 ....47 E2
Burford Av NEWUL ST5 ....2 D3
Burford Wy BUCK/MIL ST2 ....62 C3
Burgess St BURS/TUN ST6 ....52 C2
Burgundy Gv LNGTN ST3 ....81 E2
Burland Rd NEWUL ST5 ....42 C4
Burleigh Gv NEWUL ST5 ....60 B1
Burlidge Rd BURS/TUN ST6 ....53 F5
Burlington Av NEWUL ST5 ....60 B1
Burnaby Rd BURS/TUN ST6 ....36 A5
Burnett Pl BURS/TUN ST6 ....45 H2
Burnham St STOKE ST4 ....69 G2
Burnhays Rd BURS/TUN ST6 ....44 A4
Burnley St HAN ST1 ....53 H5
Burns Ct ALS/KID ST7 ....15 C5
  ALS/KID ST7 ....34 C3
Burnside Cl LNGTN ST3 ....81 F3
Burns Rd CONG CW12 ....8 A5
Burnwood Av ALS/KID ST7 ....35 H1
Burnwood Pl BURS/TUN ST6 ....45 F1
Burrington Dr STOKE ST4 ....78 C4
Burslam St CONG CW12 ....8 C5
Bursley Rd BURS/TUN ST6 ....44 C3
Bursley Wy NEWUL ST5 ....51 G1
Burton Cm HAN ST1 ....5 F3
Burton Pl HAN ST1 ....5 F3
Burton St LEEK ST13 ....30 C4
Burt St NEWUL ST5 ....71 F4
Bushberry Cl STONE ST15 ....90 C5
Bute St STOKE ST4 ....68 B1
Butler St STOKE ST4 ....68 B1
Butterfield Pl BURS/TUN ST6 ......44 C3
Buttermere Cl CONG CW12 ....52 C1
Buttermere Ct CONG CW12 ....7 G5
Butts Gn BUCK/MIL ST2 ....53 F5
The Butts ALS/KID ST7 ....23 F4
Buxton Av NEWUL ST5 ....58 A2
Buxton Old Rd CONG CW12 ....8 D3
Buxton Rd CONG CW12 ....8 D3
  LEEK ST13 ....33 H2
Byatts Gv STOKE ST4 ....53 H2
Byatts Gv LNGTN ST3 ....69 G5
Bycars La BURS/TUN ST6 ....44 D5
Bycars Rd BURS/TUN ST6 ....44 C5
Byland Pl NEWUL ST5 ....66 C3
Byrom St LEEK ST13 ....30 C3
Byron Cl ALS/KID ST7 * 25 C1
  CDLE ST10 ....74 D5
Byron Ct ALS/KID ST7 ....35 E5
Byron St STOKE ST4 ....78 B5
Bywater Dr LNGTN ST3 ....70 B5

C

Cadeby Gv BUCK/MIL ST2 ....46 D4
Cadman Crs BURS/TUN ST6 ....46 A3
Cairn Cl BUCK/MIL ST2 ....63 F1
Caistor Cl BUCK/MIL ST2 ....5 H5
Caldback Pl HAN ST1 ....5 H5
Caldew Gv STOKE ST4 ....78 C5
Caldy Rd ALS/KID ST7 ....23 E4
Caledonia Rd HAN ST1 ....61 F5
California St LNGTN ST3 ....55 E1
Callender Pl BURS/TUN ST6 ....52 C3
Callow Hill La CDLE ST10 ....74 A5
Calrofold Dr NEWUL ST5 ....42 D5
Calvary Crs BUCK/MIL ST2 ....63 F4
Calverley St HAN ST1 ....70 B5

Calver St BURS/TUN ST6 ....44 B3
Calvert Gv NEWUL ST5 ....51 H2
Camberwell Gv STOKE ST4 ....78 C4
Camborne Cl CONG CW12 ....12 C2
Camborne Crs NEWUL ST5 ....66 B2
Cambrian Wy BUCK/MIL ST2 ....55 E5
Cambridge Cl BIDD ST8 ....19 C4
Cambridge Dr NEWUL ST5 ....67 F3
Camden St STOKE ST4 ....69 E3
Camellia Cl STOKE ST4 ....3 J2
Camlet Cl STOKE ST4 ....86 C1
Camillus Rd NEWUL ST5 ....59 E2
Camoys St BURS/TUN ST6 ....53 E2
Campbell Av LEEK ST13 ....30 C5
Campbell Cl CONG CW12 ....8 E5
Campbell Pl STOKE ST4 ....61 F5
Campbell St STOKE ST4 ....68 B3
Campbell Ter HAN ST1 ....54 A3
Campion Av NEWUL ST5 ....60 B1
Canal Arm HAN ST1 * 52 D4
Canal Arm BIDD ST8 ....44 B4
The Canal Ms STOKE ST4 ....78 C4
Canal Rd CONG CW12 ....12 D1
Canal Side BARL ST12 ....86 C4
Canalside Rd STONE ST15 ....90 B1
Canal St BURS/TUN ST6 ....52 B1
  CONG CW12 ....8 C5
Canary Rd BUCK/MIL ST2 ....5 G5
Canberra Crs BLYBR/FOR ST11 ....81 C4
Canning St LNGTN ST3 ....69 F2
Cannon Pl HAN ST1 ....4 E5
Cannon St HAN ST1 ....4 E5
Canterbury Dr BURS/TUN ST6 ......45 F2
Canvey Gv LNGTN ST3 ....81 F3
Capesthorne Cl ALS/KID ST7 ....23 G5
  END/WER ST9 ....64 B1
Cape St HAN ST1 ....4 C5
Capewell St LNGTN ST3 ....70 A3
Capitol Wk CONG CW12 * 8 B5
Cappers Ct ALS/KID ST7 ....35 G1
Cappers La SBCH CW11 ....14 C5
Capper St BURS/TUN ST6 ....44 C3
Capricorn Wy BURS/TUN ST6 ......36 D5
Caraway Cl LNGTN ST3 ....81 E4
Carberry Wy LNGTN ST3 ....70 D3
Cardiff Gv HAN ST1 ....4 E6
Cardigan Gv STOKE ST4 ....78 C4
Cardington Cl NEWUL ST5 ....56 D2
Card St BURS/TUN ST6 ....52 D2
Cardway NEWUL ST5 ....53 H2
Cardwell St HAN ST1 ....5 J1
Carisbrooke Wy STOKE ST4 ....78 C5
Carling Gv STOKE ST4 ....69 G2
Carlisle St LNGTN ST3 ....79 H1
Carlos Cl CDLE ST10 ....74 D4
Carlos Pl NEWUL ST5 ....43 H5
Carlton Av BURS/TUN ST6 ....38 D5
  BURS/TUN ST6 ....45 E1
  NEWUL ST5 ....66 D4
  CDLE ST10 ....84 D1
Carlton House Est
  STOKE ST4 * 61 F4
Carlton Rd BURS/TUN ST6 ....44 D4
Carlton St HAN ST1 ....4 B1
Carlton Ter LEEK ST13 ....31 F5
Carlvle Cl ALS/KID ST7 ....15 C5
Carlyon Pl HAN ST1 ....53 H1
Carmount Rd BUCK/MIL ST2 ......54 D2
Carnation Cl LNGTN ST3 ....71 F1
Carnforth Gv ALS/KID ST7 ....34 C3
Caroline Crs BURS/TUN ST6 ....58 D5
Caroline St LNGTN ST3 ....79 H1
Carpenter Rd LNGTN ST3 ....70 A3
Carriage Dr BIDD ST8 ....20 A4
Carrick Fl STOKE ST4 ....78 A1
Carr La ALS/KID ST7 ....40 C5
Carroll Dr LNGTN ST3 ....70 B3
Carr Rd BURS/TUN ST6 ....56 D3
Carr St ALS/KID ST7 ....36 D2
Carryer Pl NEWUL ST5 ....59 F4
Carson Rd BURS/TUN ST6 ....44 D4
Cartlich St BURS/TUN ST6 ....44 B1
Cartlidge St STOKE ST4 ....3 G3
Cartmel Pl BURS/TUN ST6 ....45 F3
The Cartwright Est
  LNGTN ST3 ....69 H5
Casewell Rd BURS/TUN ST6 ....53 G2
Caspian Gv STOKE ST4 ....78 B3
Castel Cl NEWUL ST5 ....66 A4
Castle Ct STONE ST15 ....91 F5
Castledine Gv LNGTN ST3 ....70 B3
Castlefield St HAN ST1 ....4 A7
Castle Gv BUCK/MIL ST2 ....54 D4
Castle Hill Rd NEWUL ST5 ....2 B3
Castle Keep Ms NEWUL ST5 ....51 E5
Castle Keep Cl NEWUL ST5 ....54 B4
Castle Rdg NEWUL ST5 ....59 F4
Castle Rd ALS/KID ST7 ....26 B1
Castle St NEWUL ST5 ....2 C3
  NEWUL ST5 ....51 E2
Castleton Rd LNGTN ST3 ....80 C2
Castle Vw BIDD ST8 ....27 G2
Castleview Rd ALS/KID ST7 ....25 H5
Caterham Pl
  BLYBR/FOR ST11 ....81 F4
Catharine Rd BURS/TUN ST6 ......37 F5
Caton Crs BURS/TUN ST6 ....46 B4
Cauldon Av NEWUL ST5 ....51 H2
Cauldon Cl LEEK ST13 ....31 E4
Cauldon Pl HAN ST1 ....61 F5
Cauldon Rd STOKE ST4 ....61 F5
Caulton St BURS/TUN ST6 ....44 D5
Causeley Gdns BUCK/MIL ST2 ......62 D1
Cavalier Gv BUCK/MIL ST2 ....63 F4
Cavell Ct BLYBR/FOR ST11 ....89 H2
Cavendish Crs ALS/KID ST7 ....23 E3
Cavendish Gv NEWUL ST5 ....66 D4
Cavendish Rd CDLE ST10 ....85 E5
Cavendish St HAN ST1 ....4 B4

Caverswall La *LNGTN* ST3 ....81 G2
Caverswall Old Rd
   BLYBR/FOR ST11 ....82 B2
Caverswall Rd
   BLYBR/FOR ST11 ....82 B3
   CDLE ST10 ....72 D4
   LNGTN ST3 ....71 F3
Cavour St *HAN* ST1 ....60 D2
Cayley Pl *BLYBR/FOR* ST11 ......81 C4
Cecil Av *HAN* ST1 ....4 C1
Cecilly St *CDLE* ST10 ....75 E3
Cecil Rd *BIDD* ST8 ....19 G5
Cecily Ter *CDLE* ST10 ....75 E3
Cedar Av *ALS/KID* ST7 ....5 J4
   ALS/KID ST7 ....34 D2
   BLYBR/FOR ST11 ....82 C4
Cedar Cl *CDLE* ST10 ....75 E3
Cedar Ct *CONG* CW12 ....12 D2
Cedar Crs *ALS/KID* ST7 ....22 C5
   END/WER ST9 ....59 C5
   LNGTN ST3 ....69 E4
Cedar Pk *STONE* ST15 ....91 E3
Cedar Rd *NEWUL* ST5 ....51 E3
Celandine Cl *BUCK/MIL* ST2 .....46 D5
Celtic Av *ALS/KID* ST7 ....36 D5
Cemetery Av *LNGTN* ST3 ....69 H5
Cemetery Rd *HAN* ST1 ....4 B7
   NEWUL ST5 ....58 D4
Cemetery Vw *LNGTN* ST3 ....69 E4
   NEWUL ST5 ....59 E1
Cemlyn Av *LNGTN* ST3 ....69 E4
Centenary Pl *CONG* CW12 ....8 A7
Central Av *BUCK/MIL* ST2 ....54 C5
Central Ct *BARL* ST12 ....86 C4
Central St *ALS/KID* ST7 ....25 H2
Centre Rd *STONE* ST15 ....90 B1
Century Rd *NEWUL* ST5 ....43 F4
Century St *HAN* ST1 ....5 F4
Chadwell Wy *BUCK/MIL* ST2 .....63 F5
Chadwick St *LNGTN* ST3 ....70 A4
Chadwyn Dr *BUCK/MIL* ST2 ......46 D4
Chaffinch Cl *CONG* CW12 ....12 C1
Chaffinch Dr *BIDD* ST8 ....20 A5
Chain St *BURS/TUN* ST6 ....20 B4
Challenge Cl *BURS/TUN* ST6 * ..45 C3
Challinor Av *LEEK* ST13 ....30 D5
Challinor St *BURS/TUN* ST6 ......44 C3
Chamberlain Av *STOKE* ST4 ......68 A1
Chamberlain St *HAN* ST1 ....4 E5
Chamberlain Wy *BIDD* ST8 ....20 A5
Chance Hall La *ALS/KID* ST7 .....16 B4
Chancery La *ALS/KID* ST7 ....22 D5
   LNGTN ST3 ....70 A4
Chantry Rd *NEWUL* ST5 ....56 E5
Chapel Bank *ALS/KID* ST7 ....26 B1
Chapel Cl *ALS/KID* ST7 ....25 H2
Chapel Ct *BARL* ST12 ....86 C4
Chapel La *ALS/KID* ST7 ....23 H1
   ALS/KID ST7 ....26 C4
   BIDD ST8 ....20 A3
   BURS/TUN ST6 ....38 D2
   NEWUL ST5 ....53 E1
Chapel St *ALS/KID* ST7 ....25 H2
   ALS/KID ST7 ....34 D1
   ALS/KID ST7 ....41 G5
   BLYBR/FOR ST11 ....82 C4
   BUCK/MIL ST2 ....54 D5
   CDLE ST10 ....74 D4
   CONG CW12 ....8 B5
   NEWUL ST5 ....53 E1
   NEWUL ST5 ....59 E1
   NEWUL ST5 ....60 B1
Chaplin Rd *LNGTN* ST3 ....80 A1
Chapter Wk *BUCK/MIL* ST2 ....54 C4
Charles Sq *SBCH* CW11 ....14 B8
Charles St *BIDD* ST8 ....27 C1
   CDLE ST10 ....74 D4
   HAN ST1 ....5 C4
   NEWUL ST5 ....60 B1
Charlestown Gv *LNGTN* ST3 .....81 E5
Charlotte St *BURS/TUN* ST6 .....36 A4
Charlton St *STONE* ST15 ....61 F4
Charminster Rd *LNGTN* ST3 .....81 E5
Charmouth Cl *HAN* ST1 ....54 C3
Charnock Pl *BURS/TUN* ST6 .....37 E4
Charnwood *ALS/KID* ST7 * 34 C3
Charnwood Cl *LEEK* ST13 ....30 E5
Charolais Crs *LNGTN* ST3 ....80 B2
Charter Rd *NEWUL* ST5 ....56 C3
Chartley Cl *BLYBR/FOR* ST11 ...82 A4
Chartwell Cl *END/WER* ST9 ....64 A1
Chase Wk *LNGTN* ST3 ....80 D3
Chasewater Gv *CDLE* ST10 ....75 F5
Chatfield Pl *LNGTN* ST3 ....70 B5
Chatham St *HAN* ST1 ....4 D7
Chatsworth Dr *BURS/TUN* ST6 ..46 A1
   CONG CW12 ....7 F4
   END/WER ST9 ....64 A2
Chatsworth Park Av
   STOKE ST4 ....78 A1
Chatsworth Pl *LNGTN* ST3 ....80 A1
   NEWUL ST5 ....51 G5
Chatteris Cl *BLYBR/FOR* ST11 ..81 F4
Chatterley Cl *NEWUL* ST5 ....51 H1
Chatterley Dr *ALS/KID* ST7 ....35 C4
Chatterley Rd *BURS/TUN* ST6 ...43 H2
Chatterley St *BURS/TUN* ST6 ....44 C5
Chatterley Whitfield
   BURS/TUN ST6 * 37 G3
Chatterton Pl *LNGTN* ST3 ....70 B4
Cheadle Rd *BLYBR/FOR* ST11 ...82 C3
   BLYBR/FOR ST11 ....83 G5
   CDLE ST10 ....84 D5
Cheapside *HAN* ST1 ....4 E5
   NEWUL ST5 ....2 D5
Chebsey Cl *NEWUL* ST5 ....55 E5
Checkley Dr *BIDD* ST8 ....19 H4
Checkley Rd *ALS/KID* ST7 ....36 A3
Cheddleton Rd *LEEK* ST13 ....30 D5
Chelford Rd *BLYBR/FOR* ST11 ...37 H2
Chell Green Av *BURS/TUN* ST6 ..37 G5
Chell Gv *NEWUL* ST5 ....51 G2
Chell Heath Rd *BURS/TUN* ST6 ..37 F5

Chell St *HAN* ST1 ....53 H4
Chelmorton Dr *LNGTN* ST3 ....80 C1
Chelmsford Dr *BUCK/MIL* ST2 ...63 E2
Chelmsford Rd *NEWUL* ST5 ....52 A4
Chelsea Cl *BIDD* ST8 ....19 G3
Chelson St *LNGTN* ST3 ....70 A4
Cheltenham Av *CDLE* ST10 ....75 E2
Cheltenham Gv *HAN* ST1 ....54 B4
   HAN ST1 ....57 H2
Chelwood St *HAN* ST1 ....4 D1
Chemical La *BURS/TUN* ST6 ....43 H4
Chepstow Cl *BIDD* ST8 ....19 G4
Chepstow Pl *LNGTN* ST3 ....70 A1
Cherry Cl *NEWUL* ST5 ....42 D5
Cherry Gv *LNGTN* ST3 ....69 E4
Cherry Hl *NEWUL* ST5 ....59 E2
Cherry Hill Av *LNGTN* ST3 ....71 E5
Cherry Hill La *NEWUL* ST5 ....59 E5
Cherry La *ALS/KID* ST7 ....25 G2
   CDLE ST10 ....75 G2
   STONE ST15 ....91 F4
Cherry Orch *NEWUL* ST5 ....2 D5
Cherry Tree Av *ALS/KID* ST7 ......24 A3
Cherry Tree Cl *STOKE* ST4 ....78 A3
Cherry Tree La *BIDD* ST8 ....20 D4
Cherry Tree Rd *ALS/KID* ST7 ......41 H5
   NEWUL ST5 ....43 E5
Cherry Tree Wy *CONG* CW12 .....42 D5
Cherrywood Gv *LNGTN* ST3 ....80 D4
Chertsey Pl *HAN* ST1 ....53 H2
Chervil Cl *LNGTN* ST3 ....81 E4
Chesham Gv *LNGTN* ST3 ....81 E4
Cheshire Ring Canal Wk
   ALS/KID ST7 ....15 F5
   ALS/KID ST7 ....17 G4
   ALS/KID ST7 ....23 H1
Chessington Crs *STOKE* ST4 ......78 C3
Chester Cl *ALS/KID* ST7 ....34 D4
Chester Crs *NEWUL* ST5 ....66 D2
Chester Rd *ALS/KID* ST7 ....34 D4
   ALS/KID ST7 ....41 F4
Chesterwood Rd
   BURS/TUN ST6 ....45 F5
Chestnut Av *ALS/KID* ST7 ....23 H1
Chestnut Crs *BLYBR/FOR* ST11 ..82 C4
Chestnut Dr *ALS/KID* ST7 ....33 G1
   CONG CW12 ....7 F5
   STONE ST15 ....90 C1
Chestnut Gv *NEWUL* ST5 ....43 E5
Chestnut Rd *BURS/TUN* ST6 ....39 E4
Cheswardine Rd *NEWUL* ST5 .....51 H1
Chetwynd Av *BURS/TUN* ST6 .....46 A1
Chetwynd Rd *NEWUL* ST5 * 51 H1
Chetwynd St *BURS/TUN* ST6 .....45 H4
Cheviot Cl *NEWUL* ST5 ....52 D4
Cheviot Dr *BURS/TUN* ST6 ....59 E1
Childerplay Rd *BIDD* ST8 ....27 F5
Child's La *CONG* CW12 ....11 E4
Chilgrove Cl *HAN* ST1 ....54 B4
Chiltern Pl *NEWUL* ST5 ....59 E1
Chilton St *STOKE* ST4 ....69 F2
Chilworth Gv *LNGTN* ST3 ....79 F1
China St *STOKE* ST4 ....69 F2
Chivelstone Gv *STOKE* ST4 ....78 C4
Cholerton Cl *STOKE* ST4 ....69 E2
Chorley Av *BURS/TUN* ST6 ....37 E5
Chorley St *LEEK* ST13 ....30 D5
Chorlton Rd *HAN* ST1 ....53 H3
Christchurch St *STOKE* ST4 ....69 F2
Christchurch Wy *STONE* ST15 ...90 D3
Christie Pl *LNGTN* ST3 ....70 D2
Christine St *BUCK/MIL* ST2 ....62 C1
Chubb Wy *STOKE* ST4 ....67 G3
Chumleigh Gv *BURS/TUN* ST6 ...45 E4
Church Av *BUCK/MIL* ST2 ....46 D4
Church Bank *ALS/KID* ST7 ....35 H5
   NEWUL ST5 ....57 H5
Church Cl *BIDD* ST8 ....27 H2
   LNGTN ST3 ....80 D5
   STONE ST15 ....91 E3
Churchfield Av *LNGTN* ST3 ....69 E3
Church Flds *NEWUL* ST5 ....57 H5
Churchill Av *STOKE* ST4 ....77 H5
Churchill Cl *BLYBR/FOR* ST11 ...82 A4
   CONG CW12 ....7 G4
Churchill St *STOKE* ST4 ....69 E5
   NEWUL ST5 ....90 C4
Churchill Wy *STOKE* ST4 ....77 H5
Church La *ALS/KID* ST7 ....16 B5
   ALS/KID ST7 ....26 C1
   BIDD ST8 ....20 D4
   BLYBR/FOR ST11 ....82 D2
   END/WER ST9 ....39 H5
   NEWUL ST5 ....52 B5
   NEWUL ST5 ....59 E2
   STOKE ST4 ....67 H5
Church Rd *ALS/KID* ST7 ....22 D4
   BIDD ST8 ....27 G1
   BURS/TUN ST6 ....38 D3
   BURS/TUN ST6 ....79 F1
Church Sq *ALS/KID* ST7 ....52 C1
Church St *ALS/KID* ST7 ....26 A4
   ALS/KID ST7 ....34 D2
   ALS/KID ST7 ....41 F4
   ALS/KID ST7 ....42 A5
   CDLE ST10 ....74 C4
   NEWUL ST5 ....51 G4
   NEWUL ST5 ....51 E2
   NEWUL ST5 ....58 B2
   NEWUL ST5 ....61 F5
   STONE ST15 ....90 D3
Church Ter *BLYBR/FOR* ST11 .....7 J4
   BURS/TUN ST6 ....53 F5
Church Vw *ALS/KID* ST7 ....36 D2
Church Wk *NEWUL* ST5 ....51 E2
   NEWUL ST5 ....59 E2
Churnet Rd *BLYBR/FOR* ST11 ....82 C5
   CDLE ST10 ....75 G5
Churnet Vw *LNGTN* ST3 ....31 F1
Churston Cl *NEWUL* ST5 ....66 D5
Churston Pl *HAN* ST1 ....53 H1
Cinder-Hill La *ALS/KID* ST7 ....25 E2
Cinderhill La *LNGTN* ST3 ....70 B4

Cinder Rock Wy *ALS/KID* ST7 .....36 A2
City Rd *STOKE* ST4 ....68 D1
Clamgoose La *CDLE* ST10 ....74 B1
Clandon Av *BURS/TUN* ST6 ....44 C2
Clanway St *BURS/TUN* ST6 ....44 B5
Clare Av *NEWUL* ST5 ....51 H5
Claremont Cl *NEWUL* ST5 ....52 A2
Clarence Rd *LNGTN* ST3 ....69 H3
Clarence St *NEWUL* ST5 ....5 C4
   NEWUL ST5 ....51 H4
   STOKE ST4 ....62 A5
Clarendon St *STOKE* ST4 ....68 C1
Clare St *ALS/KID* ST7 ....26 A2
   ALS/KID ST7 ....26 C4
   STOKE ST4 ....5 K4
Claridge Rd *STOKE* ST4 ....3 J3
Clarke St *HAN* ST1 ....4 C6
Claud St *STOKE* ST4 ....68 D3
Claydon Crs *LNGTN* ST3 ....66 D5
Clayfield Gv *LNGTN* ST3 ....70 A1
Clayfield Gv West *LNGTN* ST3 ...69 H1
Clayhanger Cl *NEWUL* ST5 ....51 C1
Clayhanger St *BURS/TUN* ST6 ...44 C3
Clay Hills *BURS/TUN* ST6 ....44 A3
Clay Lake *END/WER* ST9 ....39 F3
Clayton Av *CONG* CW12 ....3 D2
Clayton La *NEWUL* ST5 ....67 E3
Clayton Rd *NEWUL* ST5 ....2 E7
Clayton St *HAN* ST1 ....69 H4
Claytonwood Rd *STOKE* ST4 ......67 G4
Cleadon Pl *ALS/KID* ST7 ....35 H5
Clematis Av *HAN* ST1 ....82 B4
Clement Pl *BURS/TUN* ST6 ....46 A3
Clement Rd *BURS/TUN* ST6 ....45 E1
Clerk Bank *LEEK* ST13 ....30 C5
Clermont Av *STONE* ST15 ....68 A5
Cleveland Rd *HAN* ST1 ....4 E7
   NEWUL ST5 ....59 E1
Cleveland St *BURS/TUN* ST6 ......52 D1
Clewlow Pl *LNGTN* ST3 ....70 A2
Clewlows Bank *END/WER* ST9 ...56 E2
Clews St *BURS/TUN* ST6 ....52 C2
Clews Wk *NEWUL* ST5 ....52 A4
Cley Gv *NEWUL* ST5 ....66 D5
Cliffe Pl *BURS/TUN* ST6 ....45 E3
Clifford Av *BURS/TUN* ST6 ....45 E1
Clifford St *HAN* ST1 ....5 G6
Cliff St *BURS/TUN* ST6 ....45 C5
Cliff Vale Pl *STOKE* ST4 ....60 D3
Clifton Gv *STOKE* ST4 ....69 E2
Clifton St *NEWUL* ST5 ....51 H4
   STOKE ST4 ....68 D2
Clinton Sq *HAN* ST1 ....4 D5
Clive Av *BUCK/MIL* ST2 ....46 D3
Cliveden Rd *BUCK/MIL* ST2 ....54 B4
Clive Rd *NEWUL* ST5 ....52 B5
Clive St *BURS/TUN* ST6 ....44 C2
Close La *ALS/KID* ST7 ....22 B4
   ALS/KID ST7 ....26 B1
   ALS/KID ST7 ....32 C1
The Close *ALS/KID* ST7 ....26 B1
   END/WER ST9 ....39 H4
   NEWUL ST5 ....71 F2
Cloud Vw *CONG* CW12 ....9 E5
Clough Hall Dr *ALS/KID* ST7 ......35 E4
Clough Hall Rd *ALS/KID* ST7 ......35 E4
Clough La *END/WER* ST9 ....64 A1
Clough St *HAN* ST1 ....4 B5
Cloverdale Pl *LNGTN* ST3 ....70 D4
Cloverdale Rd *NEWUL* ST5 ....59 H1
Clowes Av *BURS/TUN* ST6 ....53 E5
Clowes Rd *BUCK/MIL* ST2 ....62 C1
Club St *STOKE* ST4 ....68 A1
Clumber Av *NEWUL* ST5 ....67 E1
Clumber Gv *BURS/TUN* ST6 ....67 E2
Clumy Pl *BUCK/MIL* ST2 ....62 E3
Clyde Av *BIDD* ST8 ....20 A4
Clyde Pl *NEWUL* ST5 ....66 C3
Clyde Rd *BURS/TUN* ST6 ....53 E2
Clyde St *HAN* ST1 ....4 C5
Clyne Wk *HAN* ST1 ....4 C4
Clynes Wy *LNGTN* ST3 ....71 F4
Coalpit Hl *ALS/KID* ST7 ....34 D4
Coalport Cl *CDLE* ST10 ....84 C1
Coates Pl *BURS/TUN* ST6 ....37 F3
Cobden St *LNGTN* ST3 ....79 H1
   NEWUL ST5 ....5 H6
Cobham Pl *LNGTN* ST3 ....81 E2
Cob Moor Rd *ALS/KID* ST7 ....25 G4
Cobridge Rd *HAN* ST1 ....4 B1
Cocknage Rd *LNGTN* ST3 ....80 A2
Cocks La *BUCK/MIL* ST2 ....56 C5
Cockster Brook La *LNGTN* ST3 ...69 E5
Cockster Rd *LNGTN* ST3 ....69 F4
Colclough Av *NEWUL* ST5 ....51 C1
Colclough La *BURS/TUN* ST6 .....36 B4
Colclough Rd *LNGTN* ST3 ....81 E1
Colehill Bank *CONG* CW12 ....7 F5
Colenso Wy *NEWUL* ST5 ....51 H1
Coleridge Dr *CDLE* ST10 ....74 C5
Coleridge Rd *NEWUL* ST5 ....69 F5
Cole St *BIDD* ST8 ....27 F1
Colinbourne Cl *STOKE* ST4 ....78 B4
Colin Crs *LNGTN* ST3 ....71 F3
Colindene Gv *LNGTN* ST3 ....67 H1
Collard Av *NEWUL* ST5 ....59 H1
College Rd *ALS/KID* ST7 ....36 A4
College Rd *AUD/MAD/W* CW3 ....56 A4
   HAN ST1 ....4 D7
   STOKE ST4 ....61 F4
Colley Rd *BURS/TUN* ST6 ....36 D5
Colliers Wy *BIDD* ST8 ....27 G1
Collingwood Gv *STOKE* ST4 ....4 A3
Collin Rd *STOKE* ST4 ....67 H2
Collinson Rd *BURS/TUN* ST6 ......36 B4
Collis Av *STOKE* ST4 ....3 H3
Colville St *HAN* ST1 ....69 F1
Colwyn Dr *BIDD* ST8 ....84 C5
Combe Dr *LNGTN* ST3 ....81 E5
Comfrey Cl *LNGTN* ST3 ....81 E4
Commerce St *LNGTN* ST3 ....70 A4
Commercial Rd *HAN* ST1 ....5 H4
Commercial St *BURS/TUN* ST6 ...53 E2
Common La *LNGTN* ST3 ....80 D5

   STONE ST15 ....90 B5
The Common *CDLE* ST10 ....73 F4
Community Dr *ALS/KID* ST7 ....45 H5
Como Pl *NEWUL* ST5 ....66 A1
Compton *LEEK* ST13 ....30 C4
Compton St *HAN* ST1 ....4 C5
Condlyffe Rd *LEEK* ST13 ....30 D5
Conewood Pl *LNGTN* ST3 ....79 E1
Coneygreave Cl *CDLE* ST10 ....84 D1
Conford Cl *BUCK/MIL* ST2 ....62 B2
Congleton Edge Rd
   CONG CW12 ....13 F5
Congleton Rd *ALS/KID* ST7 ....18 C5
   ALS/KID ST7 ....34 D2
   BIDD ST8 ....19 H4
   CONG CW12 ....11 E5
Congleton Rd North
   ALS/KID ST7 ....25 E4
Congleton Rd South
   ALS/KID ST7 ....34 D1
Congreve Rd *LNGTN* ST3 ....69 F5
Conifer Gv *LNGTN* ST3 ....69 F5
The Conifers *ALS/KID* ST7 ....22 D5
Coniston Av *CONG* CW12 ....7 F5
Coniston Cl *CDLE* ST10 ....75 E3
Coniston Gv *NEWUL* ST5 ....51 G5
Coniston Pl *STOKE* ST4 ....77 H5
Connaught Sq *BURS/TUN* ST6 ...44 B4
Conrad Cl *LNGTN* ST3 ....70 B4
Consall Gv *STOKE* ST4 ....78 C4
Consett Rd *LNGTN* ST3 ....70 C2
Consort St *STOKE* ST4 ....61 F5
Constable Av *NEWUL* ST5 ....51 E5
Constable Cl *LNGTN* ST3 ....81 F5
Constance Av *STOKE* ST4 ....74 E2
Convent Court Cl *STOKE* ST4 .....61 F4
Conway Gv *CDLE* ST10 ....85 E1
Conway Rd *BIDD* ST8 ....27 G2
Conway St *STOKE* ST4 ....61 G4
Cookson Av *LNGTN* ST3 ....80 A1
Co-operative La *ALS/KID* ST7 .....49 F2
Cooper Av *NEWUL* ST5 ....60 C1
Cooper Cl *STONE* ST15 ....91 G4
Coopers Cl *STOKE* ST4 ....30 B4
Cooper St *CONG* CW12 ....8 C4
   HAN ST1 ....4 C6
   NEWUL ST5 ....51 E5
Coopers Wy *BIDD* ST8 ....19 F5
Copeland Cl *CDLE* ST10 ....84 D1
Copeland Dr *STOKE* ST4 ....91 G5
Copeland St *STOKE* ST4 ....61 F5
Cope's Av *BURS/TUN* ST6 ....44 C2
Cope St *BUCK/MIL* ST2 ....46 C5
Copperhill Rd *CONG* CW12 ....13 F3
Coppice Av *NEWUL* ST5 ....58 A3
Coppice Cl *BIDD* ST8 * 27 H1
Coppice Gdns *STONE* ST15 ....91 E2
Coppice Gv *LNGTN* ST3 ....70 D4
Coppice Rd *ALS/KID* ST7 ....34 B5
   STONE ST15 ....91 E2
The Coppice *BURS/TUN* ST6 ......53 C2
Coppice Vw *NEWUL* ST5 ....51 C5
Copp La *BURS/TUN* ST6 ....44 A4
Copplestone Gv *LNGTN* ST3 ......70 C4
Coppull Pl *BURS/TUN* ST6 ....59 E1
Copthorne Cl *CONG* CW12 ....8 D5
Coracle Gv *BIDD* ST8 ....28 A2
Coral Gv *STOKE* ST4 ....78 B5
Corfield Pl *BURS/TUN* ST6 ....45 E1
Corina Wy *LNGTN* ST3 ....70 B5
Cornie Cl *BURS/TUN* ST6 ....45 F1
Cornelious St *LNGTN* ST3 ....81 E1
Cornes St *HAN* ST1 ....5 H7
Corneville Rd *BUCK/MIL* ST2 .....62 D1
Cornfield Rd *BIDD* ST8 ....27 F1
Cornhill Cl *NEWUL* ST5 ....51 F5
Cornhill Gdns *LEEK* ST13 ....30 D5
Cornhill Rd *BURS/TUN* ST6 ....45 C1
Cornhill St *LEEK* ST13 ....30 D4
Cornwall Av *NEWUL* ST5 ....60 D4
Cornwall Cl *CONG* CW12 ....13 E2
Cornwallis St *STOKE* ST4 ....68 B1
Cornwall St *LNGTN* ST3 ....70 A3
Cornwood Gv *LNGTN* ST3 ....80 C2
Corona Pk *NEWUL* ST5 * 51 E1
   BIDD ST8 ....27 F5
   LNGTN ST3 ....69 H4
Coronation Rd *CONG* CW12 ....8 D5
   NEWUL ST5 ....2 E5
   STOKE ST4 ....3 J5
Coronation St *BURS/TUN* ST6 ....44 C2
Corporation St *NEWUL* ST5 ....2 C3
   STOKE ST4 ....68 A1
Corranation St *CDLE* ST10 ....74 D4
Corwell Rd *LNGTN* ST3 ....69 F5
Coseley St *BURS/TUN* ST6 ....45 C5
Cotehill Rd *END/WER* ST9 ....64 B1
Cotesheath St *STOKE* ST4 ....61 H5
Coton Ri *BARL* ST12 ....87 E4
Cotswold Crs *BUCK/MIL* ST2 .....46 C5
Cottage Cl *LNGTN* ST3 ....80 C1
Cottage La *BIDD* ST8 ....20 C4
Cotterill Dr *NEWUL* ST5 ....59 H1
Cotterill Gv *NEWUL* ST5 ....51 D2
Cottonwood Cl *ALS/KID* ST7 ......26 C5
Cottonwood Gv *ALS/KID* ST7 .....70 A3
   LNGTN ST3 ....70 A3
Coupe Dr *LNGTN* ST3 ....71 E2
Court La *STOKE* ST4 ....51 H4
Courtney Pl *LNGTN* ST3 ....70 C5
Courtway Dr *HAN* ST1 ....53 H1
The Courtyard *SBCH* CW11 ....10 A2
Coutant St *STONE* ST15 ....3 G4
Covent Gdns *ALS/KID* ST7 ....34 D5
The Covert *NEWUL* ST5 ....58 B5
   NEWUL ST5 ....58 B5
Cowallmoor La *BURS/TUN* ST6 ...29 E3
Cowan St *BURS/TUN* ST6 ....37 H5
Cowley Wy *BUCK/MIL* ST2 ....63 C5
Cowlishaw Rd *BIDD* ST8 ....27 E3

Cowlishaw Rd *BURS/TUN* ST6 ....37 G5
Cowper St *STOKE* ST4 ....69 F1
Coyney Gv *LNGTN* ST3 ....71 E4
Crabtree Av *BIDD* ST8 ....27 G1
Crabtree Cl *STOKE* ST4 ....78 B4
Crackley Bank *NEWUL* ST5 ....43 E4
Crackley La *NEWUL* ST5 ....57 C1
Craig Rd *CONG* CW12 ....85 E3
Craigside *BIDD* ST8 ....19 G5
Craig Wk *ALS/KID* ST7 ....33 H1
Cranberry Dr *NEWUL* ST5 ....42 D5
Cranberry La *ALS/KID* ST7 ....42 D5
Cranberry Moss La
   ALS/KID ST7 ....22 C5
Cranborne Av *BUCK/MIL* ST2 .....22 C5
Cranbrook Cl *STOKE* ST4 ....78 A3
Crane St *HAN* ST1 ....53 F5
Cranfield Cl *BUCK/MIL* ST2 ....22 C5
Cranfield Pl *BUCK/MIL* ST2 ....62 D2
Cranford Ms *ALS/KID* ST7 ....22 C5
Cranford Wy *BUCK/MIL* ST2 ....62 D1
Cranleigh Av *HAN* ST1 ....53 H1
Cranmer St *STOKE* ST4 ....61 F5
Cranswick Gv *BUCK/MIL* ST2 .....63 F3
Cranwell Pl *LNGTN* ST3 ....80 D2
Cranwood Rd *BARL* ST12 ....86 A1
Cranworth Gv *LNGTN* ST3 ....80 C2
Craven Cl *STOKE* ST4 ....78 A2
Crawford St *STOKE* ST4 ....68 D2
Crayford Av *CONG* CW12 ....9 E2
Crediton Av *BURS/TUN* ST6 ....45 E2
Crescent Av *STOKE* ST4 ....3 J5
Crescent Rd *CONG* CW12 ....8 A5
The Crescent *CONG* CW12 ....8 A5
   LEEK ST13 ....31 F5
   NEWUL ST5 ....58 B2
   NEWUL ST5 ....66 C1
   STONE ST15 ....90 D2
Cresswell Av *NEWUL* ST5 ....42 D5
Cresswell La *BLYBR/FOR* ST11 ..83 F5
Cresswellshaw Rd
   ALS/KID ST7 ....5 J4
Crestbrook Rd *BUCK/MIL* ST2 ....23 F3
Crestfield Rd *LNGTN* ST3 ....54 D2
Crestway Rd *BUCK/MIL* ST2 ....80 D2
Crestwood Dr *STONE* ST15 ....22 C5
Crewe Rd *ALS/KID* ST7 ....90 D5
   ALS/KID ST7 ....22 C5
Crick Rd *HAN* ST1 ....23 H4
Critchlow Gv *LNGTN* ST3 ....5 H7
Croft Av *NEWUL* ST5 ....70 B5
Croft Cl *CONG* CW12 ....51 C3
Croft Crs *STOKE* ST4 ....45 C5
Crofter Cl *BIDD* ST8 ....68 A1
Crofters Ct *NEWUL* ST5 ....67 F4
Croftfield St *BUCK/MIL* ST2 ....42 D5
Croft Rd *CDLE* ST10 ....63 F4
   NEWUL ST5 ....74 D4
Croft St *BURS/TUN* ST6 ....2 D1
The Croft *CDLE* ST10 ....52 D1
   STOKE ST4 ....75 E1
Cromartie St *LNGTN* ST3 ....67 H2
Cromer Crs *HAN* ST1 ....70 A5
Cromer Rd *HAN* ST1 ....5 K2
Cromer St *NEWUL* ST5 ....52 B5
Crompton Gv *STOKE* ST4 ....78 C5
Crompton Rd *STONE* ST15 ....91 E4
Cromwell St *BIDD* ST8 ....19 G4
   HAN ST1 ....53 H3
Crosby Rd *STOKE* ST4 ....67 G4
Crossdale Av *BUCK/MIL* ST2 ......46 C4
Cross Edge *BURS/TUN* ST6 ....38 D4
Crossfield Av *BIDD* ST8 ....27 G2
   BLYBR/FOR ST11 ....81 E3
Cross Hi *BURS/TUN* ST6 ....52 D1
Crossland Pl East *LNGTN* ST3 ....81 E2
Crossland Pl West *LNGTN* ST3 ...81 E1
Crosslands *CONG* CW12 ....13 E1
Cross La *ALS/KID* ST7 ....11 E2
   CONG CW12 ....13 E2
Crossley Rd *BURS/TUN* ST6 ....45 E3
Crossmay St *NEWUL* ST5 ....2 B3
Crossmead Gv *HAN* ST1 ....54 B3
Cross St *ALS/KID* ST7 ....19 G5
   BURS/TUN ST6 ....52 A1
   CDLE ST10 ....74 D4
   LEEK ST13 ....31 E4
   LNGTN ST3 ....71 F2
   STONE ST15 ....90 D2
Crossways Rd *BURS/TUN* ST6 ....53 G2
Crossways Rd *ALS/KID* ST7 ....24 A4
The Crossway *NEWUL* ST5 ....60 A1
Croston St *HAN* ST1 ....4 D7
Crouch Av *BURS/TUN* ST6 ....45 E2
Crouch La *CONG* CW12 ....9 H3
Crowborough Rd *BIDD* ST8 ....27 E2
Crowcrofts Rd *STOKE* ST4 ....79 E3
Crown Bank *ALS/KID* ST7 ....34 D4
Crown Bank Crs *ALS/KID* ST7 ....34 D5
Crowndale Pl *BURS/TUN* ST6 .....34 C3
Crown Gdns *ALS/KID* ST7 ....34 D5
Crown St *HAN* ST1 ....4 E4
   STONE ST15 ....90 D5
Crowther St *STOKE* ST4 ....61 G4
Croxden Cl *CDLE* ST10 ....84 D2
Croxden Rd *BUCK/MIL* ST2 ....54 D5
Courtney Pl *LNGTN* ST3 ....81 E4
Cruse St *LEEK* ST13 ....30 C4
Crystal St *BURS/TUN* ST6 ....53 F3
Cumberbatch Av
   BURS/TUN ST6 ....37 F4
Cumberland Rd *ALS/KID* ST7 .....35 E4
Cumberland Rd *CONG* CW12 ......7 G4
Cumberland St *HAN* ST1 ....3 G4
   STOKE ST4 ....62 A5
Cumming St *STOKE* ST4 ....3 K3
Curland Pl *LNGTN* ST3 ....70 D5
Curlew Rd *ALS/KID* ST7 ....36 C2

Curtiss Pl *BLYBR/FOR* ST11 ....81 F4
Curzon Av *ALS/KID* ST7 ....23 F3
Curzon Ri *LEEK* ST13 ....30 A4
Curzon Rd *BURS/TUN* ST6 ....45 E4
Curzon St *NEWUL* ST5 ....60 B2
Cutts St *HAN* ST1 ....4 D7
Cygnet Cl *AUD/MAD/W* CW3 ...56 C4
Cynthia Gv *BURS/TUN* ST6 ....45 E4
Cypress Gv *BLYBR/FOR* ST11 ....82 C4
NEWUL ST5 ....50 D1

D

Dace Gv *BURS/TUN* ST6 ....45 F3
Dahlia Cl *LGNTN* ST3 ....71 F1
Dain Pl *NEWUL* ST5 ....51 H3
Dain St *BURS/TUN* ST6 ....52 C2
Daintry Cl *LEEK* ST13 ....30 D5
Daintry St *LEEK* ST13 ....30 D4
STOKE ST4 ....67 H3
Dairy Cl *LEEK* ST13 ....53 G2
Dairyfields Wy *HAN* ST1 ....53 G2
Dairyhouse La *CDLE* ST10 ....65 H2
Dairylands Rd *ALS/KID* ST7 ....24 A4
Daisy Bank *LEEK* ST13 ....30 D5
Daisybank Dr *CONG* CW12 ....8 B2
Daisy Pl *STOKE* ST4 ....69 E3
Dakota Gv *BURS/TUN* ST6 ....44 A2
Dale Av *BURS/TUN* ST6 ....38 A5
Dale Cl *CDLE* ST10 ....75 E5
Dale Crs *CONG* CW12 ....8 B4
Dalegarth Gv *LGNTN* ST3 ....80 C2
Dale Gv *CONG* CW12 ....9 E5
Daleian Ct *NEWUL* ST5 * 58 C3
Dale Pl *CONG* CW12 ....8 D5
Dales Cl *BIDD* ST8 ....19 E3
Dales Green Rd *ALS/KID* ST7 .....26 A3
Dale St *BURS/TUN* ST6 ....52 C1
Dale Vw *ALS/KID* ST7 ....26 A3
LGNTN ST3 ....71 F4
Daleview Dr *NEWUL* ST5 ....58 C5
Dalewood Rd *NEWUL* ST5 ....5 H4
Dalton Gv *BUCK/MIL* ST2 ....63 F3
Daltry Wy *AUD/MAD/W* CW3 ....56 B5
Daly Crs *NEWUL* ST5 ....58 B5
Dam La *BIDD* ST8 ....30 C3
Dampier St *LEEK* ST13 ....30 C4
The Dams *BLYBR/FOR* ST11 ......71 H5
Dandillion Av *CDLE* ST10 ....84 D2
Dane Bank Av *CONG* CW12 ....8 C3
Danebower Rd *STOKE* ST4 ....79 E4
Danebridge Gv *HAN* ST1 ....54 A4
Dane Cl *ALS/KID* ST7 ....22 C5
Dane Dr *BIDD* ST8 ....20 A4
Dane Gdns *ALS/KID* ST7 ....36 A1
Dane Gv *CDLE* ST10 ....85 E1
Danehill Gv *STOKE* ST4 ....9 F2
Danemead Cl *LGNTN* ST3 ....81 E3
Danes Cft *CONG* CW12 ....78 B3
Dane St *CONG* CW12 ....8 A4
Dane Wk *HAN* ST1 ....5 J3
Darius Cl *NEWUL* ST5 ....51 H1
Darley Gv *CDLE* ST10 ....85 E1
Darnley St *STOKE* ST4 ....61 G4
Darrall Gdns *NEWUL* ST5 ....67 G3
Darsham Gdns *NEWUL* ST5 ......67 E5
Dart Av *BURS/TUN* ST6 ....45 E2
Dart Cl *ALS/KID* ST7 ....22 C4
BIDD ST8 ....19 H4
Dartford Pl *BURS/TUN* ST6 ....45 G2
Dart Gv *CDLE* ST10 ....85 E1
Dartmouth Av *NEWUL* ST5 ....80 D2
Dartmouth Pl *LGNTN* ST3 ....80 D2
Dartmouth St *BURS/TUN* ST6 ...45 F5
Dart Pl *NEWUL* ST5 ....66 C3
Darwin Cl *STOKE* ST15 ....90 B1
Davenport Cl *LEEK* ST13 ....30 A4
Davenport St *BURS/TUN* ST6 ....44 B5
CONG CW12 ....8 A5
Daven Rd *CONG* CW12 ....12 D1
Daventry Cl *BUCK/MIL* ST2 ....62 B2
David Rd *LGNTN* ST3 ....69 E1
Davidson Av *CONG* CW12 ....9 E2
Davis Cl *ALS/KID* ST7 ....23 C4
Davison St *BURS/TUN* ST6 ....53 E2
Davis St *HAN* ST1 ....4 D7
Davy Cl *BUCK/MIL* ST2 ....62 C1
Dawlish Dr *BUCK/MIL* ST2 ....62 D2
Dawn Av *BURS/TUN* ST6............45 E2
Dawn Vw *LGNTN* ST3 ....71 F4
Dayson Pl *NEWUL* ST5 ....51 C2
Deakin Gv *NEWUL* ST5 ....67 E2
Deakin Rd *BURS/TUN* ST6 ....37 E5
Dean Hollow *ALS/KID* ST7 ....41 F4
Dean Pl *HAN* ST1 ....5 H7
Deansberry Cl *STOKE* ST4 ....78 A2
Deanscroft Wy *LGNTN* ST3 ....70 B3
Deansgate *LEEK* ST13 ....53 F1
Dean's La *ALS/KID* ST7 ....42 C4
Dean St *BUCK/MIL* ST2 ....55 E5
Deansway *STOKE* ST4 ....78 B4
Dean Vw *ALS/KID* ST7 ....41 F5
Deaville Rd *BUCK/MIL* ST2 ....63 E1
Debenham Crs *BUCK/MIL* ST2 ..62 C2
Decade Cl *NEWUL* ST5 ....43 F4
Deebank Av *LEEK* ST13 ....31 C3
Dee Cl *ALS/KID* ST7 ....35 E4
HAN ST1 ....5 H4
Dee La *NEWUL* ST5 ....66 D3
Deepdale Cl *BURS/TUN* ST6 ......46 A4
Defoe Dr *LGNTN* ST3 ....70 C3
Delamere Cl *ALS/KID* ST7 ....22 B4
Delamere Gv *NEWUL* ST5 ....5 J3
STOKE ST4 ....78 A3
Delamere Rd *CONG* CW12 ....7 F4
Delaney Dr *LGNTN* ST3 ....70 D3
Delius Gv *HAN* ST1 ....54 B4
Dellwood Gv *LGNTN* ST3 ....70 E1
Delphouse Rd *CDLE* ST10 ....74 D5
Delphside *ALS/KID* ST7 ....41 H4
Delves Pl *NEWUL* ST5 ....66 D2

Denbigh Cl *BIDD* ST8 ....27 G2
NEWUL ST5 ....51 H1
Denbigh St *HAN* ST1 ....4 C1
Denby Av *LGNTN* ST3 ....70 A2
Dency Gv *BURS/TUN* ST6 ....45 E3
Dene Side *NEWUL* ST5 ....2 A5
Denewood Pl *LGNTN* ST3 ....81 F1
Denford Pl *ALS/KID* ST7 ....23 F2
Dennington Crs *LGNTN* ST3 ....79 E1
Dennis St *STOKE* ST4 ....69 F2
Dennis Viollet Av *STOKE* ST4 ....68 C4
Denry Crs *NEWUL* ST5 ....51 G1
Denshaw Wk *LGNTN* ST3 ....70 B3
Denstone Crs *LGNTN* ST3 ....69 F5
Dentdale Cl *LGNTN* ST3 ....81 E3
Denton Cl *NEWUL* ST5 ....66 D4
Denton Gv *LGNTN* ST3 ....70 C4
Derby Pl *NEWUL* ST5 ....67 E3
Derby Rd *ALS/KID* ST7 ....34 D4
Derby St *CONG* CW12 ....8 B4
HAN ST1 ....5 G5
LEEK ST13 ....30 D3
Dereham Wy *BUCK/MIL* ST2 .....43 G3
Derek Dr *HAN* ST1 ....54 A3
Derry St *STOKE* ST4 ....69 E3
Derwent Av *ALS/KID* ST7 ....91 G4
Derwent Cl *ALS/KID* ST7 ....22 C4
Derwent Crs *ALS/KID* ST7 ....36 A1
Derwent Dr *BIDD* ST8 ....20 A4
CDLE ST10 ....85 E1
CONG CW12 ....12 D1
Derwent Pl *NEWUL* ST5 ....59 G1
Derwent St *HAN* ST1 ....53 F4
Devon Cl *NEWUL* ST5 ....67 E3
Devon Gv *BIDD* ST8 ....19 G4
Devon Pl *CONG* CW12 ....8 C3
Devon Wy *LGNTN* ST3 ....80 B1
Dewsbury Rd *STOKE* ST4 ....92 A4
Diamond Av *ALS/KID* ST7 ....35 H1
Diamond Cl *BARL* ST12 ....86 C5
BIDD ST8 ....19 G5
LGNTN ST3 ....89 E1
Diamond Rdg *BARL* ST12 ....86 C1
Diana Rd *HAN* ST1 ....54 B3
Diarmid Rd *STOKE* ST4 ....77 H1
Dickenson Rd East
BURS/TUN ST6 ....53 G2
Dickenson Rd West
BURS/TUN ST6 ....53 G2
Dickens St *BUCK/MIL* ST2 ....55 E5
Dickinson Wy *ALS/KID* ST7 ....41 H3
Diglake Cl *ALS/KID* ST7 ....34 C5
Diglake St *ALS/KID* ST7 ....41 H5
Dilhorne Gv *LGNTN* ST3 ....80 A1
Dilhorne La *BLYBR/FOR* ST11 ...72 B5
Dilhorne Rd *BLYBR/FOR* ST11 ...82 D1
CDLE ST10 ....74 B5
Dilke St *HAN* ST1 ....53 H4
Dill Gv *LGNTN* ST3 ....81 F4
Dimmelow St *LGNTN* ST3 ....71 F2
Dimsdale Pde East *NEWUL* ST5 ...51 H4
Dimsdale Pde West
NEWUL ST5 ....51 H4
Dimsdale St *BURS/TUN* ST6 ......52 C2
Dimsdale Vw East *NEWUL* ST5 ...51 H3
Dimsdale Vw West *NEWUL* ST5 ..51 H3
The Dingle *BURS/TUN* ST6 ....52 C4
Dividy Rd *BUCK/MIL* ST2 ....63 G1
Dixon Cl *STONE* ST15 ....90 B1
Dixon Rd *CONG* CW12 ....9 E2
Dixon's Rw *NEWUL* ST5 ....50 D2
Dobell St *LGNTN* ST3 ....70 B3
Dobson St *BURS/TUN* ST6 ....53 G2
Doctors Cl *BIDD* ST8 ....19 G5
Doddington Pl *NEWUL* ST5 ....66 D1
Dodd's La *CONG* CW12 ....12 A1
Doddswood Dr *CONG* CW12 ....8 D5
Dogcroft Rd *BUCK/MIL* ST2 ......45 G1
Dolesgrind Cl *BLYBR/FOR* ST11 ...82 C2
Dolly's La *BURS/TUN* ST6 ....45 E4
Dominic St *STOKE* ST4 ....61 E4
STONE ST15 * 90 C2
Donald Rd *HAN* ST1 ....54 A3
Doncaster La *STOKE* ST4 ....60 D5
Donkey La *CDLE* ST10 ....75 E2
Dorcas Dr *LGNTN* ST3 ....69 F3
Dixon Rd *CONG* CW12 ....9 E2
Dorchester Dr *ALS/KID* ST7 ....25 C5
Dorchester Wk *BUCK/MIL* ST2 ...63 E2
Doretan Av *CONG* CW12 ....13 F5
Dorian Wy *END/WER* ST9 ....39 H4
Dorking Cl *BUCK/MIL* ST2 ....62 B2
Dorlan Cl *LGNTN* ST3 ....47 E3
Dorridge Gv *NEWUL* ST5 ....52 C5
Dorrington Cl *BUCK/MIL* ST2 .....46 C4
Dorrington Gv *NEWUL* ST5 ....52 A3
Dorset Cl *BUCK/MIL* ST2 ....63 E1
CONG CW12 ....8 C3
Dorset Dr *BIDD* ST8 ....19 G5
Dorset Pl *ALS/KID* ST7 ....25 C5
NEWUL ST5 ....5 J1
Douglas Av *BIDD* ST8 ....27 G1
STOKE ST4 ....67 H3
Douglas Pl *NEWUL* ST5 ....5 H7
Douglas Rd *NEWUL* ST5 ....59 C1
Douglas St *HAN* ST1 ....5 H7
Doulton Cl *CDLE* ST10 ....84 D1
STONE ST15 ....90 B5
Doulton Dr *NEWUL* ST5 ....51 H2
Dovebank Cv *ALS/KID* ST7 ....53 E1
Dovecote Pl *LGNTN* ST3 ....80 D1
Dovedale Cl *BURS/TUN* ST6 ......35 H4
CDLE ST10 ....75 E1
CONG CW12 ....9 E3
Dovedale Pl *NEWUL* ST5 ....58 A3
Dove Gv *BIDD* ST8 ....19 H4
Dove Pl *NEWUL* ST5 ....66 C4
Dove Rd *BLYBR/FOR* ST11 ....82 C3
Downey St *HAN* ST1 ....5 F5
Downfield Pl *BUCK/MIL* ST2 ......46 B5
Downham Rd *NEWUL* ST5 ....52 C2
Downing Av *LGNTN* ST3 ....80 B1
Downsview Gv *LGNTN* ST3 ....69 F4
Dragon Sq *NEWUL* ST5 ....51 E1

Drake Cl *BUCK/MIL* ST2 ....62 B3
Drakeford Gv *BURS/TUN* ST6 .....46 A2
Draycott Cross Rd *CDLE* ST10 ...83 H2
Draycott Cross Rd *CDLE* ST10 ...83 H2
Draycott Dr *CDLE* ST10 ....84 D1
NEWUL ST5 ....42 D4
Draycott Old Rd
BLYBR/FOR ST11 ....82 D3
Drayton Gn *BUCK/MIL* ST2 ....62 C2
Drayton Rd *LGNTN* ST3 ....69 H5
STOKE ST4 ....76 D5
Drayton St *NEWUL* ST5 ....2 B4
Drenfell Rd *ALS/KID* ST7 ....25 F1
Dresden St *HAN* ST1 ....5 H4
The Dreys *NEWUL* ST5 ....78 B3
The Drive *ALS/KID* ST7 ....50 A5
Droitwich Cl *NEWUL* ST5 ....57 H2
Drubbery La *LGNTN* ST3 ....79 C1
Drumber La *ALS/KID* ST7 ....17 H5
Drumburn Cl *NEWUL* ST5 ....36 D4
Drummond St *BURS/TUN* ST6 ...36 A4
Dryburg Wk *BUCK/MIL* ST2 ......54 C5
Dryden Rd *ALS/KID* ST7 ....53 E5
Dryden Wy *CDLE* ST10 ....74 C5
Duddell Rd *STOKE* ST4 ....92 B4
Dudley Pl *LGNTN* ST3 ....81 E2
Duke Bank Ter *BURS/TUN* ST6 ...46 B5
Duke Gdns *NEWUL* ST5 ....58 C5
Duke St *BIDD* ST8 ....27 H1
LEEK ST13 ....30 D4
NEWUL ST5 ....3 F6
Dulverton Av *NEWUL* ST5 ....66 C2
Duncalf Gv *NEWUL* ST5 ....51 H2
Duncalf St *BURS/TUN* ST6 ....52 C4
Duncan St *STOKE* ST4 ....69 E1
Dundas St *HAN* ST1 ....54 C3
Dundee Rd *HAN* ST1 ....4 A5
Dundee St *LGNTN* ST3 ....69 H5
Dunham Cl *ALS/KID* ST7 ....23 E5
Dunkirk *NEWUL* ST5 ....2 B5
Dunkirk Ct *NEWUL* ST5 ....2 B2
Dunning St *BURS/TUN* ST6 ....44 B2
Dunnocksfold Rd *ALS/KID* ST7 ...22 B4
Dunnockswood *ALS/KID* ST7 ......22 C4
Dunnock Wy *BIDD* ST8 ....20 A5
Dunrobin St *LGNTN* ST3 ....70 A5
Dunsany Gv *HAN* ST1 ....54 A3
Dunsford Av *BUCK/MIL* ST2 ......46 C4
Dunster Rd *LGNTN* ST3 ....69 H2
Dunwood Dr *ALS/KID* ST7 ....23 F2
BURS/TUN ST6 * 36 C5
Durber Cl *ALS/KID* ST7 ....41 F5
STOKE ST4 ....67 G5
Durham Dr *LGNTN* ST3 ....80 A2
Durham Gv *NEWUL* ST5 ....67 F5
Durston Pl *LGNTN* ST3 ....70 C4
Dyke St *HAN* ST1 ....5 G2
Dylan Rd *BIDD* ST8 ....20 B4
LGNTN ST3 ....70 B4

E

Eagland Pl *CONG* CW12 ....8 C3
Eagle St *HAN* ST1 ....4 E1
Eamont Av *BURS/TUN* ST6 ....45 E2
Eardley Crs *CONG* CW12 ....7 G2
Eardleyend Rd *ALS/KID* ST7 ....33 G4
Earlsbrook Dr *STOKE* ST4 ....77 H1
Earl's Dr *NEWUL* ST5 ....66 D1
Earls Rd *STOKE* ST4 ....78 B3
East St *LEEK* ST13 ....31 E3
NEWUL ST5 ....3 G2
NEWUL ST5 ....58 C3
Earlswood Rd *HAN* ST1 ....54 C3
Easdale Pl *NEWUL* ST5 ....66 C2
Easedale Cl *BUCK/MIL* ST2 ....46 C4
East Bank Ride
BLYBR/FOR ST11 ....82 C2
Eastbank Rd *HAN* ST1 ....4 C1
Eastbourne Cl *LEEK* ST13 ....30 C5
Eastbourne Rd *HAN* ST1 ....53 H1
Eastbridge Av *HAN* ST1 ....53 H1
Eastcott Cl *CONG* CW12 ....7 F3
East Ct *ALS/KID* ST7 ....23 G3
East Crs *HAN* ST1 ....54 A1
Eastdean Av *BUCK/MIL* ST2 ......62 D1
East Dr *BIDD* ST8 ....19 H5
Easters Cl *BUCK/MIL* ST2 * 46 D5
Eastfield Dr *HAN* ST1 ....5 J3
East Gv *LGNTN* ST3 ....81 E1
Easthead Wk *HAN* ST1 ....4 C5
East Prec *HAN* ST1 * 5 F3
East St *LEEK* ST13 ....71 F1
LGNTN ST3 ....70 B5
East Ter *BURS/TUN* ST6 ....19 F2
East Vw *BURS/TUN* ST6 ....52 C2
Eastwick Crs *STOKE* ST4 ....78 A2
Eastwood Av *BURS/TUN* ST6 .....45 E2
Eastwood Pl *HAN* ST1 ....5 F5
Eastwood Rd *HAN* ST1 ....54 C3
Eaton Bank *CONG* CW12 ....8 D2
Eaton Rd *ALS/KID* ST7 ....23 E4
Eaton St *HAN* ST1 ....5 H2
Eaves La *ALS/KID* ST7 ....55 E5
CDLE ST10 ....51 E1
Ebury Gv *LGNTN* ST3 ....80 D1
Eccleston Pl *BURS/TUN* ST6 ......37 E5
Edale Cl *BURS/TUN* ST6 ....35 H4
NEWUL ST5 ....58 B5
Eddisbury Dr *NEWUL* ST5 ....42 D5
Eden Cl *ALS/KID* ST7 ....35 H1
BIDD ST8 ....20 A4
Eden Gv *CDLE* ST10 ....85 E1
LGNTN ST3 ....80 D1
Edenhurst Av *NEWUL* ST5 ....81 F2
Edensor Rd *LGNTN* ST3 ....69 H5
Edensor St *NEWUL* ST5 ....51 E2
Edensor Ter *LGNTN* ST3 ....69 H5
Edgar Pl *NEWUL* ST5 ....70 A1

Edgbaston Dr *STOKE* ST4 ....78 D2
Edge Av *BURS/TUN* ST6 ....37 E5
Edgefield La *BURS/TUN* ST6 * 47 E4
Edgefield Rd *LGNTN* ST3 ....70 A2
Edgehill Rd *LEEK* ST13 ....30 B4
Edge La *END/WER* ST9 ....39 F4
Edgeley Rd *BIDD* ST8 ....27 H2
Edge St *BURS/TUN* ST6 ....38 A5
Edge View Cl *BUCK/MIL* ST2 .....47 E4
Edge View Ct *BIDD* ST8 ....27 G1
Edge View Rd *BUCK/MIL* ST2 ....47 E4
Edgeview Rd *CONG* CW12 ....13 F5
Edgeware Rd *HAN* ST1 ....53 F4
Edgeware St *HAN* ST1 * 53 F4
Edinburgh Rd *CONG* CW12 ....8 D5
Edison St *STOKE* ST4 ....68 D1
Edmonton Av *BUCK/MIL* ST2 .....46 B5
Ednam Pl *LGNTN* ST3 ....81 E1
Edwal Rd *LGNTN* ST3 ....71 E2
Edward Av *NEWUL* ST5 ....66 D1
STOKE ST4 ....78 B4
Edwards Davies Rd
NEWUL ST5 ....45 G4
Edward Pl *ALS/KID* ST7 ....41 H3
NEWUL ST5 ....52 B5
STOKE ST4 ....62 A5
Edwards Wy *ALS/KID* ST7 ....23 G4
Egerton Cl *BLYBR/FOR* ST11 .....82 C2
Egerton Rd *STOKE* ST4 ....61 H5
Egerton St *STOKE* ST4 ....61 H3
Elaine Av *BURS/TUN* ST6 ....45 F5
Elburton Rd *STOKE* ST4 ....69 G1
Elder Pl *BURS/TUN* ST6 ....53 F3
Elder Rd *BURS/TUN* ST6 ....53 F3
Eldon St *HAN* ST1 ....53 H3
Eleanor Crs *NEWUL* ST5 ....66 D1
Eleanor Pl *NEWUL* ST5 ....66 C1
Eleanor Vw *NEWUL* ST5 ....66 D1
Elenora St *STOKE* ST4 ....61 E4
Elers Gv *BURS/TUN* ST6 ....52 C2
Elgar Crs *HAN* ST1 ....54 C4
Elgin St *STOKE* ST4 ....61 F3
Elgood La *BURS/TUN* ST6 ....36 A4
Eliases La *BIDD* ST8 ....42 D1
Elizabeth Cl *ALS/KID* ST7 ....42 D1
Elizabeth Dr *NEWUL* ST5 ....51 H2
Elizabeth St *CONG* CW12 ....8 A5
HAN ST1 ....5 J5
Elkington Ri *AUD/MAD/W* CW3 ...36 B5
Elkstone Cl *ALS/KID* ST7 ....44 C2
Ellam's Pl *NEWUL* ST5 ....59 E3
Ellastone Gv *STOKE* ST4 ....67 H1
Elldawn Av *BURS/TUN* ST6 ....46 B4
Ellerby Rd *LGNTN* ST3 ....79 E2
Ellgreave St *BURS/TUN* ST6 ......52 C1
Ellington Cl *BUCK/MIL* ST2 ....62 C2
Elliot Rd *STOKE* ST4 ....69 F1
Elliott St *STOKE* ST4 ....3 G2
Ellison St *NEWUL* ST5 ....52 B4
Ellis St *BURS/TUN* ST6 ....53 C2
Elmbrook La *LGNTN* ST3 ....80 C2
Elm Cl *ALS/KID* ST7 ....35 H5
LEEK ST13 ....30 D4
Elmcroft Rd *BUCK/MIL* ST2 ....81 F3
Elmdon Pl *LGNTN* ST3 ....81 F3
Elm Dr *CDLE* ST10 ....75 F5
Elm Gv *ALS/KID* ST7 ....23 G4
Elmhurst Cl *BUCK/MIL* ST2 ....62 B2
Elm Pl *NEWUL* ST5 ....79 F1
Elm Rd *CONG* CW12 ....7 H4
STONE ST15 ....91 E5
Elmsmere Rd *LGNTN* ST3 ....79 G1
Elmsmere Rd *BUCK/MIL* ST2 .....54 D5
Elmstead Cl *STOKE* ST4 ....77 H1
The Elms *NEWUL* ST5 ....52 A2
Elm St *BURS/TUN* ST6 ....53 F4
NEWUL ST5 ....2 B4
Elms Wy *LGNTN* ST3 ....71 E5
Elm Tree Dr *ALS/KID* ST7 ....41 H5
Elmwood Cl *LGNTN* ST3 ....23 H4
Elmwood Dr *BLYBR/FOR* ST11 ...82 C4
Elphinstone Rd *STOKE* ST4 ....67 H4
Elsby Pl *BURS/TUN* ST6 ....33 F3
Elsby Rd *ALS/KID* ST7 ....33 H1
Elsing St *STOKE* ST4 ....68 D1
Elstree Cl *LGNTN* ST3 ....70 D5
Elstree Gv *HAN* ST1 ....54 C3
Elswick Rd *STOKE* ST4 ....69 C1
Eltham Gdns *NEWUL* ST5 ....52 B5
Elton Ter *BURS/TUN* ST6 ....36 A4
Elvington Cl *CONG* CW12 ....13 E1
Emberton St *NEWUL* ST5 ....51 E2
NEWUL ST5 ....66 A4
Emerson Rd *BURS/TUN* ST6 ......53 E3
Emery Av *HAN* ST1 ....54 A1
Emery St *BURS/TUN* ST6 ....53 E3
Empire Pas *STOKE* ST4 ....68 A1
Empire St *STOKE* ST4 ....68 A1
Emsworth Wk *LGNTN* ST3 ....79 E2
Encounter Pl *HAN* ST1 ....5 K1
Enderley St *NEWUL* ST5 ....2 A5
Endon Dr *BIDD* ST8 ....27 F3
Endon Rd *BURS/TUN* ST6 ....46 B1
Engleaav *LGNTN* ST3 ....70 C4
Ennerdale Cl *BURS/TUN* ST6 .....52 C1
Ennerdale Dr *CONG* CW12 ....7 H5
Enoch St *BURS/TUN* ST6 ....52 C1
Enstone Cl *LGNTN* ST3 ....79 F2
Enstone Ct *NEWUL* ST5 ....66 D4
Ephraim St *HAN* ST1 ....5 F6
Epping Rd *STOKE* ST4 ....67 G4
Epsom Cl *CDLE* ST10 ....75 F5
Epworth St *STOKE* ST4 ....61 E5
Ernald Gdns *STONE* ST15 ....90 D4
Eros Crs *HAN* ST1 ....54 B3
Errill Cl *STOKE* ST4 ....68 C1
Erskine St *LGNTN* ST3 ....70 B5
Esdale Pl *NEWUL* ST5 ....66 D2
Esperanto Wy *BURS/TUN* ST6 ....53 G1
Essex Cl *CONG* CW12 ....8 C2
Essex Dr *ALS/KID* ST7 ....35 F1

Essex Pl *NEWUL* ST5 ....66 C1
Eton Av *NEWUL* ST5 ....66 B5
Etruria Old Rd *HAN* ST1 ....60 D1
Etruria Rd *HAN* ST1 ....4 D3
STOKE ST4 ....3 G2
Etruria Vale Rd *HAN* ST1 ....4 B6
Etruria Wy *NEWUL* ST5 ....60 C1
Etruscan St *HAN* ST1 ....60 D2
Etruscan Wk *BARL* ST12 ....87 F1
Eva Gv *NEWUL* ST5 ....77 F2
Evans St *BURS/TUN* ST6 ....44 D5
Evelyn St *STOKE* ST4 ....68 D2
Everest Rd *ALS/KID* ST7 ....26 A5
Eversley Av *LGNTN* ST3 ....70 C5
Eversley Rd *LGNTN* ST3 ....70 C5
Evesham Wy *LGNTN* ST3 ....70 C4
Exmouth Gv *BURS/TUN* ST6 .....53 E2
Eyre St *BURS/TUN* ST6 ....52 C2

F

Faceby Gv *BLYBR/FOR* ST11 .....81 C3
Fairbank Av *STOKE* ST4 ....67 H2
Fairclough Pl *BURS/TUN* ST6 .....45 E3
Fairfax St *HAN* ST1 ....5 H3
Fairfield Av *BURS/TUN* ST6 ....38 C4
LGNTN ST3 ....80 A2
NEWUL ST5 ....52 C5
Fairfields *ALS/KID* ST7 ....41 H4
Fairfields Rd *BIDD* ST8 ....20 C4
Fairhaven Gv *HAN* ST1 ....54 A3
Fairlawn Cl *LGNTN* ST3 ....80 C2
Fairlawns *NEWUL* ST5 ....59 H2
Fairlight Gv *LGNTN* ST3 ....70 C5
Fair Oak Rd *ALS/KID* ST7 ....42 D5
Fairview Av *ALS/KID* ST7 ....23 F4
Fair View Rd *LEEK* ST13 ....31 F4
Fairway *STOKE* ST4 ....77 G2
Fairway Rd *BURS/TUN* ST6 ....45 E3
The Fairway *ALS/KID* ST7 ....41 H4
Falcon Rd *ALS/KID* ST7 ....81 E4
Fallow Fld *LGNTN* ST3 ....79 F2
Fallowfield Cl *STONE* ST15 ....91 F5
Falmouth Rd *CONG* CW12 ....7 F2
Fanny's Cft *ALS/KID* ST7 ....23 G1
Faraday Pl *STOKE* ST4 ....3 J6
Farams Rd *ALS/KID* ST7 ....23 G1
Farcroft Av *NEWUL* ST5 ....51 F2
Fareham Gv *LGNTN* ST3 ....80 C2
Farington Pl *BURS/TUN* ST6 ......37 E5
Farland Gv *BURS/TUN* ST6 ....37 E5
Farleigh Gv *BUCK/MIL* ST2 ....63 E5
Farmadine St *STOKE* ST4 ....78 B5
Farman Cl *BLYBR/FOR* ST11 ......81 C3
Farmers Bank *NEWUL* ST5 ....58 C5
Farmer St *LGNTN* ST3 ....70 A5
Farm Lea *BURS/TUN* ST6 ....38 A5
Farmside La *BIDD* ST8 ....20 D4
Farmwood Cl *LGNTN* ST3 ....81 F1
Farnborough Dr
BLYBR/FOR ST11 ....81 C3
Farndale St *BURS/TUN* ST6 ....44 B3
Farne Gv *LGNTN* ST3 ....69 C4
Farnham Dr *BIDD* ST8 ....27 F3
Farnworth Cl *BIDD* ST8 ....27 F2
Farnworth Rd *LGNTN* ST3 ....70 C4
Farrier Cl *STONE* ST15 ....91 C4
Farrington Cl *BURS/TUN* ST6 .....46 A3
Faulkner Pl *LGNTN* ST3 ....70 D5
Fawcett Wy *HAN* ST1 * 53 H4
Fawfield Dr *BURS/TUN* ST6 ....36 A5
Fawn Cl *LGNTN* ST3 ....81 E2
Fearns Av *NEWUL* ST5 ....43 C5
Featherstone Gv *STOKE* ST4 ......61 E5
Federation Rd *BURS/TUN* ST6 ....14 E5
Fellbrook La *BUCK/MIL* ST2 ....54 C5
Fellgate Ct *NEWUL* ST5 * 45 C5
Fell St *BURS/TUN* ST6 ....46 D3
Felsted St *BUCK/MIL* ST2 ....54 C5
Fence La *CONG* CW12 ....8 B2
Fenlow Av *BUCK/MIL* ST2 ....62 B2
Fennel Gv *LGNTN* ST3 ....81 F4
Fenners Gv *STOKE* ST4 ....78 D2
Fenton Cl *CONG* CW12 ....13 E1
Fenton Pk *STOKE* ST4 ....69 C1
Fenton Rd *BUCK/MIL* ST2 ....62 C1
Fermain Cl *NEWUL* ST5 ....66 A4
Fern Cl *ALS/KID* ST7 ....26 A2
Fern Crs *CONG* CW12 ....9 E5
Ferncroft Cl *STOKE* ST4 ....78 B5
Ferndale *BLYBR/FOR* ST11 ....82 B4
Ferndale Gdns *ALS/KID* ST7 ......26 C5
Ferndown Cl *LGNTN* ST3 ....80 D1
Ferndown Dr *NEWUL* ST5 ....67 E5
Ferndown Dr South
NEWUL ST5 ....77 E1
Ferney Pl *BURS/TUN* ST6 ....36 A5
Fernhurst Cl *STONE* ST15 ....91 F4
Fernhurst Gv *LGNTN* ST3 ....80 C2
Fernie Cl *STONE* ST15 ....91 F5
Fernlea Crs *END/WER* ST9 ....39 H3
Fernleaf Cl *ALS/KID* ST7 ....15 H5
Fernlea Gv *LGNTN* ST3 ....71 F2
LGNTN ST3 ....89 E1
Fern Rd *LGNTN* ST3 ....69 H5
Fernwood Cft *LEEK* ST13 ....30 B5
Fernwood Dr *LEEK* ST13 ....30 B5
Fernwood Gn *STOKE* ST4 ....78 C3
Ferrand Cl *STOKE* ST4 ....68 A5
Festing St *HAN* ST1 ....5 J2
Festival Ct *HAN* ST1 ....53 C4
Festival Hl *CONG* CW12 ....8 D4
Festival Pk *HAN* ST1 ....4 A3
Festival Wy *BURS/TUN* ST6 ....52 D4
HAN ST1 ....4 A3
Fiddlers Bank *BURS/TUN* ST6 ....38 C3
Field Av *BIDD* ST8 ....46 D4
Field Cl *BLYBR/FOR* ST11 ....82 A4
BIDD ST8 ....19 H3
Fielden Cl *BURS/TUN* ST6 ....46 B4

Field End Cl *STONE* ST4 ......78 B3
Field House Ct *STONE* ST15 ......90 C1
Fielding St *STOKE* ST4 ......68 B2
Field Pl *LNGTN* ST3 ......70 A2
Fields Cl *ALS/KID* ST7 ......23 C4
Fields Rd *ALS/KID* ST7 ......23 G5
CONG CW12 ......12 C2
Field St *LEEK* ST13 * 30 D5
Fieldsway *STONE* ST15 ......90 B3
Field Ter *STONE* ST15 ......90 D2
Field Vw *BIDD* ST8 ......19 H4
LNGTN ST3 ......71 F3
Field Wy *ALS/KID* ST7 ......23 G4
Fieldway *BLYBR/FOR* ST11 ......81 H3
BUCK/MIL ST2 ......63 H1
LNGTN ST3 ......69 E4
The Fieldway *STOKE* ST4 ......77 G3
Fife St *STOKE* ST4 ......69 G3
Fifth Av *ALS/KID* ST7 ......35 E2
Fillybrooks Cl *STONE* ST15 ......90 C3
The Fillybrooks *STONE* ST15 ......90 B3
Finchdean Cl *LNGTN* ST3 ......81 E4
Finch Pl *BIDD* ST8 ......37 F1
Finchsmith Pl *LNGTN* ST3 ......69 H5
Finch St *BIDD* ST8 ......37 F2
Finney Gdns *HAN* ST1 * 62 B1
Finney Gn *BUCK/MIL* ST2 ......54 C2
Finstock Av *LNGTN* ST3 ......79 E2
Firbank Pl *LNGTN* ST3 ......70 D3
First Av *ALS/KID* ST7 ......35 E2
BUCK/MIL ST2 ......55 F5
NEWUL ST5 ......52 A2
Fir Tree Rd *LNGTN* ST3 ......79 E2
Firwood Rd *BIDD* ST8 ......20 A4
Fisher St *BIDD* ST8 ......37 F1
Fishpond Wy *BUCK/MIL* ST2 ......54 C3
Fitzgerald Cl *LNGTN* ST3 ......79 E2
Fitzgerald Cl *LNGTN* ST3 ......71 F2
Fitzherbert Rd *HAN* ST1 ......54 A1
Five Oaks Cl *NEWUL* ST5 ......66 A4
Flackett St *LNGTN* ST3 * 70 A2
Flamborough Gv
BURS/TUN ST6 ......52 C2
Flash La *BUCK/MIL* ST2 ......47 E4
STOKE ST4 ......67 G4
Flatts Rd *BURS/TUN* ST6 ......46 A1
Flax Cft *STOKE* ST4 ......91 E4
Flaxman Cl *BARL* ST12 ......87 F3
Flax St *STOKE* ST4 ......68 B1
Fleckney Av *LNGTN* ST3 ......70 C4
Fleming Rd *STOKE* ST4 ......61 F5
Fletcher Bank *NEWUL* ST5 ......2 B2
Fletcher Crs *BUCK/MIL* ST2 ......55 H5
Fletcher Rd *STOKE* ST4 ......68 B2
Fletcher St *HAN* ST1 ......4 D6
Fleur Gv *STOKE* ST4 ......69 H1
Flintsham Gv *HAN* ST1 ......4 E1
Flint St *LNGTN* ST3 ......71 F2
Florence Rd *STOKE* ST4 ......77 H1
Florence St *NEWUL* ST5 ......2 D2
Florida Cl *BURS/TUN* ST6 ......53 F1
Floyd St *STOKE* ST4 ......61 E4
Flynn Rv *STOKE* ST4 ......61 F5
Foden Av *ALS/KID* ST7 ......23 H5
Foden St *STOKE* ST4 ......68 A2
Fogg St East *NEWUL* ST5 ......2 D3
Fogg St *NEWUL* ST5 * 2 D5
Fogg St West *NEWUL* ST5 ......2 D5
Fold La *BIDD* ST8 ......19 H4
Foley Pl *STOKE* ST4 ......69 G3
Foley Rd *LNGTN* ST3 ......69 G4
Foley St *STOKE* ST4 ......69 H3
Fol Hollow *CONG* CW12 ......11 H1
Fontaine Pl *STOKE* ST4 ......69 G3
Fonthill Wk *BUCK/MIL* ST2 ......54 C5
Forber Rd *STOKE* ST4 ......67 H5
Ford Av *BURS/TUN* ST6 ......45 F1
Ford Cl *STONE* ST15 ......90 D4
Ford Green Rd *BURS/TUN* ST6 ......45 F1
Ford Hayes La *BUCK/MIL* ST2 ......63 G3
LNGTN ST3 ......64 A3
Fords La *LEEK* ST13 ......26 B2
Ford St *LEEK* ST13 ......31 E5
NEWUL ST5 ......58 B2
STOKE ST4 ......61 E4
Forest Cl *NEWUL* ST5 ......66 A3
Forest Rd *BURS/TUN* ST6 ......80 D3
Forestside Gv *STOKE* ST4 ......67 H5
Forge La *CONG* CW12 ......7 H4
NEWUL ST5 ......52 C5
Forge Wy *BIDD* ST8 ......20 D1
Forrester Cl *BIDD* ST8 ......19 G5
Forrester Cl *STONE* ST15 ......91 E4
Forresters Bank *BUCK/MIL* ST2 ......47 E3
Forrister St *LNGTN* ST3 ......70 A3
Forster St *BURS/TUN* ST6 ......45 E3
Forsyte Rd *LNGTN* ST3 ......69 H1
Forum Rd *NEWUL* ST5 ......50 D4
Fosbrooke Pl *STONE* ST15 ......3 H5
Foster Ct *LNGTN* ST3 ......69 F5
Foster Rd *CONG* CW12 ......7 H4
Foundry Bank *CONG* CW12 ......8 C4
Foundry La *LNGTN* ST3 ......25 F1
BUCK/MIL ST2 ......62 C1
Foundry St *HAN* ST1 ......4 E1
Fountain Ct *BIDD* ST8 ......19 H4
Fountains Av *NEWUL* ST5 ......66 C5
Fountain Sq *HAN* ST1 ......5 F3
Fountain St *CONG* CW12 ......8 B5
LEEK ST13 ......31 E5
STOKE ST4 ......69 G3
Fourth Av *ALS/KID* ST7 ......35 F2
BUCK/MIL ST2 ......55 F5
Fowlchurch Rd *LEEK* ST13 ......31 E2
Fowler's La *BUCK/MIL* ST2 ......47 F4
Foxfield Cl *CDLE* ST10 ......75 E1
Foxfield Wy *LNGTN* ST3 ......79 E1
Fox Gdns *ALS/KID* ST7 ......34 D3
Foxglove Cl *STOKE* ST4 ......71 F2
Foxglove La *NEWUL* ST5 ......77 E1
Foxlands Cl *ALS/KID* ST7 ......63 F1
Foxley La *BUCK/MIL* ST2 ......46 C4
Foxwood Ct *STONE* ST15 ......90 B3
Frampton Gv *BURS/TUN* ST6 ......36 C5

Francis St *BURS/TUN* ST6 ......44 D1
Franklin Rd *STOKE* ST4 ......60 D5
Franklyn St *HAN* ST1 ......5 H6
Frank St *STOKE* ST4 ......68 A1
Fraser St *BURS/TUN* ST6 ......53 F2
Freckleton Pl *BLYBR/FOR* ST11 ......81 G5
Frederick Av *STOKE* ST4 ......61 E5
Frederick St *STOKE* ST4 ......69 E1
Freebridge Cl *LNGTN* ST3 ......70 C3
Freedom Wk *BURS/TUN* ST6 * 45 G3
Freehold St *NEWUL* ST5 ......3 F5
Free Trade St *HAN* ST1 ......5 G1
Fremantle Rd *STOKE* ST4 ......67 H5
Frenchmore Gv *LNGTN* ST3 ......80 C1
Freshwater Gv *BUCK/MIL* ST2 ......62 B1
Friars Av *STONE* ST15 ......90 D4
Friars Cl *CDLE* ST10 ......74 D5
Friars Ct *CDLE* ST10 * 74 D5
Friars Pl *STOKE* ST4 ......54 D2
Friars Rd *BUCK/MIL* ST2 ......54 D2
Friars' St *NEWUL* ST5 ......2 D4
Friar St *LNGTN* ST3 ......70 A3
Friars Wk *NEWUL* ST5 ......66 D1
Friarswood Rd *NEWUL* ST5 ......2 B3
Friendly Av *NEWUL* ST5 ......51 H1
Friesian Gdns *ALS/KID* ST7 ......42 C4
Frith St *LEEK* ST13 ......30 C5
Frodingham Rd *BUCK/MIL* ST2 ......63 F3
Froghall *NEWUL* ST5 ......2 B2
Froghall Rd *CDLE* ST10 ......75 E2
Frome Wk *BURS/TUN* ST6 ......45 E1
Fulford Rd *STONE* ST15 ......89 H5
Fuller St *BURS/TUN* ST6 ......44 D1
Fulmer Pl *LNGTN* ST3 ......81 F3
Furlong La *BURS/TUN* ST6 ......52 C2
Furlong Pde *BURS/TUN* ST6 ......52 D1
Furlong St *BURS/TUN* ST6 ......44 C2
Furmston Pl *LEEK* ST13 ......31 F2
Furnace Rd *LNGTN* ST3 ......70 B5
Furnival St *BURS/TUN* ST6 ......53 F3
Fynney Gv *LEEK* ST13 ......31 E4

G

The Gables *ALS/KID* ST7 ......23 E5
Gable St *STOKE* ST4 ......68 B1
Gainsborough Rd *LNGTN* ST3 ......79 E2
NEWUL ST5 ......51 E3
Galbraith Cl *CONG* CW12 ......8 A5
Galleys Bank *ALS/KID* ST7 ......23 H5
Gallimore Cl *BURS/TUN* ST6 ......44 C5
Galloway Rd *BUCK/MIL* ST2 ......63 G4
Gallowstree La *NEWUL* ST5 ......59 E5
Galsworthy Rd *LNGTN* ST3 ......69 H1
Garbett St *BURS/TUN* ST6 ......36 A4
Gardeners Cl *BIDD* ST8 ......27 E5
Gardenholm Cl *LNGTN* ST3 ......80 C2
Garden Pl *STOKE* ST4 ......3 J5
Garden St *LEEK* ST13 ......30 C3
NEWUL ST5 ......2 E4
STOKE ST4 ......62 A3
Gardiner Dr *LNGTN* ST3 ......69 G5
Garfield Av *STOKE* ST4 ......77 H1
Garfield Crs *STOKE* ST4 ......77 H1
Garfield St *HAN* ST1 ......4 C6
Garibaldi St *HAN* ST1 ......60 D1
Garlick St *BURS/TUN* ST6 ......45 F5
Garner St *HAN* ST1 ......60 D2
Garners Wk *AUD/MAD/W* CW3 ......56 A5
Garnet St *HAN* ST1 ......30 C4
Garnett Rd East *NEWUL* ST5 ......51 H4
Garnett Rd West *NEWUL* ST5 ......51 H5
Garsdale Crs *LNGTN* ST3 ......79 E2
Garth St *HAN* ST1 ......5 G2
Gaskell Rd *BUCK/MIL* ST2 ......63 F1
Gate St *LNGTN* ST3 ......71 F2
Gateway *NEWUL* ST5 ......2 D4
Gatley Gv *LNGTN* ST3 ......81 F4
Gawsworth Cl *ALS/KID* ST7 ......23 E5
LNGTN ST3 ......70 A1
Gayton Av *BUCK/MIL* ST2 ......46 D4
Gedney Gv *NEWUL* ST5 ......66 B5
Geen St *STOKE* ST4 ......61 F5
Gemini Dr *STOKE* ST4 ......36 C5
Geneva Dr *HAN* ST1 ......54 B3
NEWUL ST5 ......66 A1
Geoffrey Av *LEEK* ST13 ......30 C4
Geoffrey Gv *LNGTN* ST3 ......71 E3
George Av *LNGTN* ST3 ......81 F1
George Bates Cl *ALS/KID* ST7 ......23 E5
George Eardley Cl
BURS/TUN ST6 ......44 A1
George Eastham Av
STOKE ST4 ......68 D4
George La *STONE* ST15 ......91 G4
Georges Cl *LNGTN* ST3 ......69 H3
George St *ALS/KID* ST7 ......41 F5
NEWUL ST5 ......51 E2
NEWUL ST5 * 52 A3
NEWUL ST5 ......58 B3
STOKE ST4 ......62 A5
Georges Wy *ALS/KID* ST7 ......41 H4
Gerrard St *STOKE* ST4 ......61 E4
Gibbins St *HAN* ST1 ......53 H4
Gibson Gv *LNGTN* ST3 ......50 D1
Gibson Pl *LNGTN* ST3 ......71 E5
Gibson St *BURS/TUN* ST6 ......44 C4
Gifford Pl *STOKE* ST4 ......67 H5
Gilbern Dr *BIDD* ST8 ......27 F3
Gilbert Cl *ALS/KID* ST7 ......35 G1
Gilbert St *BURS/TUN* ST6 ......36 A4
Giles Cl *CDLE* ST10 ......74 D4
Giles Vw *HAN* ST1 ......5 K1
Gill Bank Rd *ALS/KID* ST7 ......35 H5
Gill Wk *HAN* ST1 ......4 D5
Gillyflower Cl *BURS/TUN* ST6 ......45 H4
Gilman Av *ALS/KID* ST7 ......46 D4
Gilman Pl *HAN* ST1 ......5 G3
Gilman St *HAN* ST1 ......5 G2
Gimson St *STOKE* ST4 ......69 E1
Girsby Cl *STOKE* ST4 ......78 C5

Gitana St *HAN* ST1 ......4 E3
The Glades *BURS/TUN* ST6 * 52 D4
The Glade *NEWUL* ST5 ......51 E5
Gladstone Dr *BIDD* ST8 ......19 H5
Gladstone Pl *STOKE* ST4 ......67 H2
Gladstone St *LEEK* ST13 ......30 D3
STOKE ST4 ......3 J1
Gladwyn St *BUCK/MIL* ST2 ......55 E5
Glaisher Dr *BLYBR/FOR* ST11 ......81 G5
Glandore Rd *LNGTN* ST3 ......70 D3
Glass St *HAN* ST1 ......5 F2
Glastonbury Cl *END/WER* ST9 ......47 F3
Glebe Cl *BLYBR/FOR* ST11 ......81 G3
Glebe Ct *STONE* ST15 ......61 G5
Glebedale Rd *STOKE* ST4 ......69 E1
Glebe Rd *CDLE* ST10 ......74 B5
Glebe St *ALS/KID* ST7 ......34 D1
HAN ST1 ......61 G5
Glebeville *LEEK* ST13 ......30 D5
Glencastle Wy *STOKE* ST4 ......78 C5
Glencoe St *STOKE* ST4 ......69 H5
Glendale Cl *NEWUL* ST5 ......77 E1
Glendale St *BURS/TUN* ST6 ......53 E3
Glendue Gv *STOKE* ST4 ......78 C4
Gleneagles Crs *HAN* ST1 ......53 H3
Glenfield Wy *BUCK/MIL* ST2 ......63 G5
Glenroyd Av *BUCK/MIL* ST2 ......62 C3
Glenwood Cl *LNGTN* ST3 ......79 E2
NEWUL ST5 ......58 C3
Globe St *BURS/TUN* ST6 ......52 C1
Gloucester Gra *NEWUL* ST5 ......67 E2
Gloucester Rd *ALS/KID* ST7 ......35 F1
Glover St *HAN* ST1 ......61 G5
Glyn Pl *BURS/TUN* ST6 ......44 D3
Goddard St *LNGTN* ST3 ......70 A3
Godfrey Rd *BUCK/MIL* ST2 ......62 D1
Godleybarn La *CDLE* ST10 ......73 C1
Golborn Cl *CDLE* ST10 ......75 E3
Golborn Cl *LNGTN* ST3 ......89 F1
Goldcrest Wy *STOKE* ST4 ......71 F2
Goldenhill Rd *STOKE* ST4 ......69 H3
Golden Cl *CONG* CW12 ......12 C1
Goldfinch Dr *ALS/KID* ST7 ......42 C4
Goldsmith Pl *LNGTN* ST3 ......70 B5
Gold St *LNGTN* ST3 ......69 H4
Golf Links Cl *BURS/TUN* ST6 ......36 A4
Gom's Mill Rd *LNGTN* ST3 ......79 C1
Goodfellow St *BURS/TUN* ST6 ......45 F3
Goodson St *HAN* ST1 ......5 F5
Goodwick St *STOKE* ST4 ......78 C5
Goodwin Av *NEWUL* ST5 ......59 H2
Goodwin Rd *LNGTN* ST3 ......71 H4
Goodwood Av *CDLE* ST10 ......75 E3
Goodwood Pl *STOKE* ST4 ......78 A3
Goosemoor Gv *LNGTN* ST3 ......81 E3
Goose St *NEWUL* ST5 ......2 D5
Gordale Cl *CONG* CW12 ......9 E2
Gordon Av *BURS/TUN* ST6 ......53 G2
CDLE ST10 ......74 B4
Gordon Banks Dr *STOKE* ST4 ......68 D4
Gordon Cl *LEEK* ST13 ......30 B5
Gordon Crs *HAN* ST1 ......53 H2
Gordon Rd *BURS/TUN* ST6 ......75 E3
Gordon St *BURS/TUN* ST6 ......45 F5
NEWUL ST5 ......59 E1
Gorse La *CONG* CW12 ......12 B5
Gorse St *STOKE* ST4 ......69 E3
Gorsey Bank *BURS/TUN* ST6 ......38 A5
Gort Rd *NEWUL* ST5 ......51 F5
Gosforth Gv *BLYBR/FOR* ST11 ......81 C5
Gosling Wy *CONG* CW12 ......7 G4
Govan Av *STOKE* ST4 ......62 A4
Gowan Av *BURS/TUN* ST6 ......45 E2
Gower Rd *STONE* ST15 ......91 F2
Gower St *NEWUL* ST5 ......59 F2
Gowy Cl *ALS/KID* ST7 ......22 B5
Grace St *LEEK* ST13 ......30 B3
Graffam Gv *CDLE* ST10 ......75 E3
Grafton Av *BURS/TUN* ST6 ......45 F4
Grafton Rd *LNGTN* ST3 ......70 A5
Grafton St *HAN* ST1 ......5 G1
Graham St *BUCK/MIL* ST2 ......62 C1
Granchester Cl *LNGTN* ST3 ......81 F4
Grange Ct *BIDD* ST8 ......19 H5
Grangefields *BIDD* ST8 ......19 H5
Grange Gdns *LEEK* ST13 ......30 C5
Grange La *NEWUL* ST5 ......52 B5
Grange Park Dr *BIDD* ST8 ......20 A2
Grange Rd *BIDD* ST8 ......20 A2
LNGTN ST3 ......70 A5
STONE ST15 ......91 F4
Grange St *BURS/TUN* ST6 ......53 E3
The Grange *BURS/TUN* ST6 ......44 B5
Grangewood Av *LNGTN* ST3 ......80 D4
Granite Av *BURS/TUN* ST6 ......53 E2
Granstone Cl *BURS/TUN* ST6 ......36 D4
Grantham Pl *BUCK/MIL* ST2 ......54 C3
Grantley Cl *LNGTN* ST3 ......79 C1
Grant St *STOKE* ST4 * 61 G5
Granville Av *BURS/TUN* ST6 ......53 H2
NEWUL ST5 ......2 E5
Granville Rd *BUCK/MIL* ST2 ......54 D5
Granville Ter *STONE* ST15 ......90 D2
Grasmere Av *CONG* CW12 ......7 F5
NEWUL ST5 ......66 D3
Grasmere Ter *BURS/TUN* ST6 ......53 H2
Grassygreen La *ALS/KID* ST7 ......41 G5
Gratton Rd *BUCK/MIL* ST2 ......63 F1
Grayling Gv *BURS/TUN* ST6 ......45 G4
Gray's Cl *ALS/KID* ST7 ......25 H1
Grayshott Rd *BURS/TUN* ST6 ......44 C1
Greasley Rd *BUCK/MIL* ST2 ......55 F3
Greatbatch Av *STOKE* ST4 ......60 D5
Great Moreton Ter
CONG CW12 * 17 H3
Greatoak Rd *ALS/KID* ST7 ......41 H2
Greenacres Av
BLYBR/FOR ST11 ......81 G2
Greenacres Rd *CONG* CW12 ......7 F5
Greenbank Rd *BURS/TUN* ST6 ......45 E4
NEWUL ST5 ......60 A1
Green Brook Ct *NEWUL* ST5 * 59 H1
Green Cl *BARL* ST12 ......86 D4
Green Cft *ALS/KID* ST7 ......23 H3

Greendale Dr *NEWUL* ST5 ......42 D5
Greendock St *LNGTN* ST3 ......69 H4
Green Dr *ALS/KID* ST7 ......23 F4
Greenfield *BIDD* ST8 ......27 H2
Greenfield Av *BURS/TUN* ST6 ......39 E4
Greenfield Cl *BURS/TUN* ST6 ......39 E4
Greenfield Crs *CDLE* ST10 ......75 E3
Greenfield Rd *BURS/TUN* ST6 ......44 C1
CONG CW12 ......7 H4
Greenfields Rd *END/WER* ST9 ......39 G3
Greengate Rd *ALS/KID* ST7 ......23 H3
Greengates St *BURS/TUN* ST6 ......44 C2
Greenhead St *BURS/TUN* ST6 ......52 D1
Greenhill Rd *BURS/TUN* ST6 ......38 A5
Green La *BLYBR/FOR* ST11 ......82 C4
Greenlea Cl *STOKE* ST4 ......78 C5
Greenmeadow Gv
END/WER ST9 ......39 G5
Greenmeadows Rd
AUD/MAD/W CW3 ......56 A5
Greenmoor Av *BURS/TUN* ST6 ......37 E3
Greenock Cl *NEWUL* ST5 ......59 F5
Greenside Av *BUCK/MIL* ST2 ......47 E3
Greenside *NEWUL* ST5 ......2 B2
Greenside Cl *BUCK/MIL* ST2 ......47 E3
Green's La *BUCK/MIL* ST2 ......63 G1
The Green *BLYBR/FOR* ST11 ......71 H4
BURS/TUN ST6 ......38 D4
CDLE ST10 ......74 B5
CONG CW12 * 8 A4
NEWUL ST5 ......67 E2
Greenway Av *BURS/TUN* ST6 ......46 B3
CONG CW12 ......7 H4
LNGTN ST3 ......81 E4
STOKE ST4 ......77 G3
Greenway Bank *BIDD* ST8 ......27 H5
BUCK/MIL ST2 ......47 E4
Greenway Cl *ALS/KID* ST7 ......23 H1
Greenway Hall Rd
BUCK/MIL ST2 ......47 E4
Greenway Pl *BUCK/MIL* ST2 ......54 D2
Greenway Rd *BIDD* ST8 ......20 A3
Greenways *LNGTN* ST3 ......81 H4
Greenways Gv *CDLE* ST10 ......74 D5
The Greenway *NEWUL* ST5 ......60 A1
Greenwood Av *CONG* CW12 ......8 D4
STOKE ST4 ......69 G3
Greenwood Rd
BLYBR/FOR ST11 ......82 C2
Gregory St *LNGTN* ST3 ......69 G3
Grenadier Cl *STOKE* ST4 ......86 C1
Grenville St *HAN* ST1 ......53 H4
Gresley Wy *STOKE* ST4 ......78 A3
Greyfriars Rd *BUCK/MIL* ST2 ......54 C4
Greyhound Wy *HAN* ST1 ......53 E4
Greysan Av *ALS/KID* ST7 ......36 D3
Greywood Rd *STOKE* ST4 * 67 G4
Grice Rd *STOKE* ST4 ......3 J4
Griffin St *LNGTN* ST3 ......69 H5
Griffiths Wy *STONE* ST15 ......91 G5
Grig Pl *ALS/KID* ST7 ......23 E3
Grindley Hill Ct *STOKE* ST4 ......3 H7
Grindley La *BLYBR/FOR* ST11 ......82 A5
STOKE ST4 ......78 B5
Grindley Pl *STOKE* ST4 ......67 H1
Grisedale Cl *LNGTN* ST3 ......81 E3
Gristhorpe Gv *BUCK/MIL* ST2 ......55 F3
Gritton St *BURS/TUN* ST6 ......44 B4
Grosvenor Av *ALS/KID* ST7 ......35 E3
END/WER ST9 ......39 H5
Grosvenor Cl *STOKE* ST4 ......67 H3
Grosvenor Gdns *NEWUL* ST5 ......2 E5
Grosvenor Pl *BURS/TUN* ST6 * 44 B2
NEWUL ST5 ......52 A4
Grosvenor Rd *CONG* CW12 ......8 D4
LNGTN ST3 ......80 D1
NEWUL ST5 ......2 E5
Grosvenor St *LEEK* ST13 ......31 E4
LNGTN ST3 ......69 G4
Grove Av *ALS/KID* ST7 ......35 E3
STOKE ST4 ......69 E3
Grovebank Rd *STOKE* ST4 * 67 G4
Grove Park Av *STOKE* ST4 ......44 A4
Grove Pl *HAN* ST1 ......54 A1
Grove Rd *STOKE* ST4 ......68 D3
STONE ST15 ......90 B3
Grove St *BURS/TUN* ST6 ......44 B2
LEEK ST13 ......30 C3
NEWUL ST5 ......59 E1
The Grove *ALS/KID* ST7 ......35 E4
BLYBR/FOR ST11 ......82 A4
BURS/TUN ST6 ......44 C1
NEWUL ST5 ......66 D1
Guernsey Cl *CONG* CW12 ......13 E1
Guernsey Dr *NEWUL* ST5 ......66 B5
Guildford St *STOKE* ST4 ......61 G4
Gun Battery La *BIDD* ST8 ......20 C5
Gunn St *BIDD* ST8 ......19 G5
Guy St *BUCK/MIL* ST2 ......55 E5
Gwenys Crs *LNGTN* ST3 ......69 E3
Gwyn Av *BIDD* ST8 ......27 H2

H

Hackwood Cl *BARL* ST12 ......87 E1
Hadden Cl *END/WER* ST9 ......64 B2
Hadden Av *NEWUL* ST5 ......51 F3
Haddon Pl *BUCK/MIL* ST2 ......54 D3
STONE ST15 ......90 A3
Hadleigh Cl *NEWUL* ST5 ......66 D5
Hadleigh Rd *BUCK/MIL* ST2 ......54 D3
Hadrian Wy *NEWUL* ST5 ......50 D3
Haig Rd *LEEK* ST13 ......31 F2
Haig St *LNGTN* ST3 ......70 B5
Hailsham Cl *BURS/TUN* ST6 ......44 C1

Hales Hall Rd *CDLE* ST10 ......75 E3
Hales Pl *LNGTN* ST3 ......80 A1
Halesworth Crs *NEWUL* ST5 ......66 D5
Halfway Pl *NEWUL* ST5 ......59 E2
Halifax Cl *BLYBR/FOR* ST11 ......81 G3
Haliford Av *HAN* ST1 ......53 H2
Hallahan Cl *STONE* ST15 ......91 F5
Hallahan Gv *STOKE* ST4 ......61 E4
Hallam St *STOKE* ST4 ......68 D1
Hall Av *LEEK* ST13 ......31 F2
Halldearn Av *BLYBR/FOR* ST11 ......71 H4
Hall Dr *ALS/KID* ST7 ......23 E5
LNGTN ST3 ......71 F3
Halifield Gv *BURS/TUN* ST6 ......46 A1
Hall Hill Dr *BUCK/MIL* ST2 ......63 H4
Hall Orch *CDLE* ST10 ......74 D4
Hall Rd *ALS/KID* ST7 ......35 E4
STOKE ST4 ......68 D1
Halls Rd *ALS/KID* ST7 ......26 A2
Hall St *ALS/KID* ST7 ......35 E4
BURS/TUN ST6 ......41 F4
NEWUL ST5 ......52 C1
Halton Gn *LNGTN* ST3 ......79 E2
Hambleton Pl *BIDD* ST8 ......27 F3
Hamble Wy *BUCK/MIL* ST2 ......63 F3
Hambro Pl *STOKE* ST4 ......57 F4
Hamil Dr *LEEK* ST13 ......31 E3
Hamil Rd *BURS/TUN* ST6 ......45 E5
Hamilton Rd *ALS/KID* ST7 ......46 D4
Hamilton Rd *LNGTN* ST3 ......70 B5
Hamilton St *STOKE* ST4 ......68 C2
Hamlett Pl *BURS/TUN* ST6 ......46 A3
Hammersley Hayes Rd
CDLE ST10 ......75 E1
Hammersley St *HAN* ST1 ......54 A3
Hammerton Av *BUCK/MIL* ST2 ......62 B2
Hammond Av *BURS/TUN* ST6 ......38 D4
Hammond Rd *NEWUL* ST5 ......51 E1
Hammond Gv *BUCK/MIL* ST2 ......62 D2
Hampshire Cl *CONG* CW12 ......8 D4
Hampshire Crs *LNGTN* ST3 ......81 H4
END/WER ST9 ......39 H4
Hampstead Gv *STOKE* ST4 ......78 C3
Hampton Cl *LEEK* ST13 ......31 F2
Hampton St *HAN* ST1 ......5 G7
Hams Cl *BIDD* ST8 ......27 C1
Hanbridge Av *NEWUL* ST5 ......51 E3
Hanchurch La *STOKE* ST4 ......76 D3
Hancock Rd *CONG* CW12 ......8 D4
Hancock St *STOKE* ST4 ......61 G5
Handel Gv *HAN* ST1 ......54 C3
Handley Banks
BLYBR/FOR ST11 ......72 A4
Handley Bridge *BIDD* ST8 ......37 F1
Handley St *ALS/KID* ST7 ......37 E1
Handsacre Rd *LNGTN* ST3 ......70 B2
Hand St *BURS/TUN* ST6 ......53 G3
Hanley Rd *BURS/TUN* ST6 ......53 C1
Hanover St *HAN* ST1 ......4 E1
NEWUL ST5 ......2 C5
Harber St *LNGTN* ST3 ......70 A4
Harborne Rd *CDLE* ST10 ......75 E3
Harbourne Crs *CDLE* ST10 ......75 E3
Harcourt Av *NEWUL* ST5 ......80 D1
Harcourt St *HAN* ST1 ......53 F1
Hardewick Ct *END/WER* ST9 ......64 B1
Hardinge St *STOKE* ST4 ......68 D1
Harding Rd *HAN* ST1 ......5 F6
Hardings Meadow *ALS/KID* ST7 ......35 E1
Hardingswood Rd *ALS/KID* ST7 ......35 E1
Harding Ter *STOKE* ST4 ......68 D1
Hardman St *BUCK/MIL* ST2 ......46 C5
Hardome Cts *CDLE* ST10 ......74 D3
Hardwick Cl *STOKE* ST4 ......86 B1
Hardy Cl *CDLE* ST10 ......74 C5
Hardy St *BURS/TUN* ST6 ......44 B2
Harecastle Av *ALS/KID* ST7 ......34 C2
Haregate Rd *LEEK* ST13 ......31 F2
Hareshaw Gv *BURS/TUN* ST6 ......37 E3
Harewood Cl *CDLE* ST10 ......74 D3
Harewood St *BURS/TUN* ST6 ......44 B3
Hargreave Cl *BLYBR/FOR* ST11 ......81 G5
Harington Dr *LNGTN* ST3 ......70 C2
Harlech Av *LNGTN* ST3 ......81 F3
Harlech Dr *BIDD* ST8 ......27 G1
Harlequin Dr *BURS/TUN* ST6 ......45 H4
Harley St *HAN* ST1 ......5 G1
Harold St *BURS/TUN* ST6 ......45 G5
Harper Av *ALS/KID* ST7 ......51 H5
Harper Gv *CONG* CW12 ......8 A5
Harper St *BURS/TUN* ST6 ......52 C2
Harpfield Rd *STOKE* ST4 ......67 G1
Harplow La *LNGTN* ST3 ......84 A1
Harpur Crs *ALS/KID* ST7 ......23 D3
Harrier Cl *LNGTN* ST3 ......81 E4
Harrisehead La *ALS/KID* ST7 ......34 C2
Harrison Av *ALS/KID* ST7 ......49 F3
Harrison Rd *BURS/TUN* ST6 ......46 A4
Harrison St *NEWUL* ST5 ......3 G2
Harris St *STOKE* ST4 ......61 E5
Harrogate Gv *NEWUL* ST5 ......57 H2
Harrop Ter *HAN* ST1 ......53 H3
Harrowby Dr *NEWUL* ST5 ......66 B3
Harrowby Rd *LNGTN* ST3 ......69 E3
Harrow Pl *STONE* ST15 ......91 F4
Hart Ct *NEWUL* ST5 ......52 C5
Hartill St *STOKE* ST4 ......61 G4
Hartington St *LEEK* ST13 ......30 C5
NEWUL ST5 ......51 H4
Hartland Av *BURS/TUN* ST6 ......45 G3
Hartley Dr *STOKE* ST4 ......90 B2
Hartley Gdns *CONG* CW12 ......13 F2
Hartshill Av *STOKE* ST4 ......67 H3
Hartwell La *STOKE* ST4 ......87 G3
Hartwell Rd *LNGTN* ST3 ......81 E1
Harvey Rd *CONG* CW12 ......8 A4
LNGTN ST3 ......71 F2
Haslemere Av *BUCK/MIL* ST2 ......46 D5
Haslington Cl *NEWUL* ST5 ......42 D2
Hassall Rd *ALS/KID* ST7 ......22 D2
SBCH CW11 ......15 G4
Hassam Av *NEWUL* ST5 ......59 G2
Hassam Pde *NEWUL* ST5 ......51 H4
Hassell St *NEWUL* ST5 ......2 E5

Hatfield Crs LNGTN ST3.....79 E2
Hathersage Cl LNGTN ST3.....70 A1
Hatherton Cl NEWUL ST5.....42 D4
Hatrell St NEWUL ST5.....2 E5
Havannah La CONG CW12.....8 D1
Havannah St CONG CW12.....8 C1
Havelet Dr NEWUL ST5.....66 B4
Havelock Gv BIDD ST8.....27 C1
Havelock Pl HAN ST1.....4 C7
Haven Av BURS/TUN ST6.....53 H1
Havenside Cl NEWUL ST5.....52 A2
Hawes St BURS/TUN ST6.....44 B2
Hawfinch Rd CDLE ST10.....75 E4
Hawk Cl ALS/KID ST7.....81 E4
Hawkestone Cl NEWUL ST5.....3 F5
Hawkins St STOKE ST4.....68 C1
Hawksdale Cl LNGTN ST3.....81 E3
Hawksmoor Ct LNGTN ST3.....80 C5
Hawksworth Av LEEK ST13.....30 C5
Hawksworth Cl LEEK ST13.....30 C5
Haworth Av CONG CW12.....8 B2
Hawthorne Av ALS/KID ST7.....41 H5
 STOKE ST4.....67 C2
Hawthorne Cl CONG CW12.....7 G3
Hawthorne Ct ALS/KID ST7.....23 C4
Hawthorn Gdns ALS/KID ST7.....34 D5
Hawthorn Gv BIDD ST8.....28 A4
Hawthorn La CONG CW12.....6 B1
Hawthorn Pl LNGTN ST3.....80 D1
Hawthorn Rd NEWUL ST5.....43 E5
Hawthorn St BURS/TUN ST6.....53 E3
Haydock Cl CDLE ST10.....75 E2
Haydon St STOKE ST4.....3 J1
Hayes Cl LEEK ST13.....31 E3
Hayes St BURS/TUN ST6.....45 G4
Hayeswood La ALS/KID ST7.....49 C3
Hayfield Crs STOKE ST4.....62 A5
Hayfield Rd NEWUL ST5.....58 B5
Hayhead Cl ALS/KID ST7.....55 H1
Haymarket BURS/TUN ST6.....44 B5
Hayner Gv LNGTN ST3.....71 F5
Haywood Rd BURS/TUN ST6.....54 A5
Haywood St LEEK ST13.....30 D4
Haywood St STOKE ST4.....61 F5
Hazel Cl ALS/KID ST7.....25 H5
 STOKE ST4.....67 H2
Hazeldene Rd STOKE ST4.....28 A5
Hazel Gv ALS/KID ST7.....24 A5
 BIDD ST8.....20 D4
 LEEK ST13.....30 B4
 LNGTN ST3.....70 D5
Hazelhurst Rd BURS/TUN ST6.....36 D5
Hazelhurst St HAN ST1.....5 H6
Hazel Rd NEWUL ST5.....50 D1
Hazelwood Cl BURS/TUN ST6.....53 C3
Hazelwood Rd END/WER ST9.....39 F5
Hazlitt Wy LNGTN ST3.....74 D3
Headingley Gv STOKE ST4.....70 D3
Heakley Av BURS/TUN ST6.....46 B2
Healey Av BIDD ST8.....27 F3
Heath Av ALS/KID ST7.....23 H1
 NEWUL ST5.....60 A1
Heathcote Rd LNGTN ST3.....69 H1
Heathcote Ri ALS/KID ST7.....49 C1
 LNGTN ST3.....69 H4
Heathcote St ALS/KID ST7.....35 F2
 LNGTN ST3.....69 H1
Heath Cl ALS/KID ST7.....51 E1
 STOKE ST4.....23 C2
Heathdene Cl LNGTN ST3.....69 H5
Heath End Rd ALS/KID ST7.....22 D2
Heather Crs LNGTN ST3.....89 E1
Heather Hills END/WER ST9.....47 F1
Heatherlands Cl LNGTN ST3.....80 D5
Heatherleigh Gv HAN ST1.....54 B3
Heatherside ALS/KID ST7.....26 A3
Heathfield Cl CONG CW12.....7 H3
Heathfield Dr NEWUL ST5.....42 D5
Heathfield Gv STOKE ST4.....80 D4
Heathfield Rd BURS/TUN ST6.....45 C1
Heath Gdns STONE ST15.....90 C5
Heath Gv LNGTN ST3.....81 E5
Heath House La BUCK/MIL ST2.....14 B5
Heath Pl NEWUL ST5.....60 A1
Heath Rd CONG CW12.....7 G5
Heathside La AUD/MAD/W CW3.....56 C4
Heath's Pas LNGTN ST3.....70 B4
Heath St BIDD ST8.....19 H5
 BURS/TUN ST6.....36 A4
 NEWUL ST5.....2 D2
 NEWUL ST5.....51 F3
Heath Vw ALS/KID ST7.....51 H5
Heathwood Dr ALS/KID ST7.....23 D3
Heaton Ter NEWUL ST5.....51 H3
Heber St LNGTN ST3.....70 A3
Hedley Pl NEWUL ST5.....59 F4
Heighley Castle Wy
 AUD/MAD/W ST5.....56 A3
Heighley La AUD/MAD/W CW3.....56 A4
Hellyar-Brook Rd ALS/KID ST7.....22 D3
Helston Av LNGTN ST3.....70 C4
Heming Pl BUCK/MIL ST2.....62 C1
Hemingway Rd LNGTN ST3.....70 D5
Hemlock Rd ALS/KID ST7.....70 A3
The Hempbutts STONE ST15.....91 E3
Hempstalls Gv NEWUL ST5.....60 A1
Hempstalls La NEWUL ST5.....2 D1
Hemsby Wy NEWUL ST5.....66 D5
Hencroft LEEK ST13.....30 C5
Henderson Gv LNGTN ST3.....71 F4
Henley Av BIDD ST8.....27 F2
Henley Cl STOKE ST4.....79 E5
Henry St BURS/TUN ST6.....44 B2
Henshall Hall Dr CONG CW12.....13 F1
Henshall Pl LNGTN ST3.....36 B5
Henshall Rd NEWUL ST5.....51 E1
Herbert St CONG CW12.....8 C4
 STOKE ST4.....68 D1
Herd St BURS/TUN ST6.....36 D5
Hereford Av NEWUL ST5.....67 E5
Hereford Gv BUCK/MIL ST2.....63 F2
Herm Cl NEWUL ST5.....66 A3
Hermes Cl BLYBR/FOR ST11.....81 G1

Heron Cl ALS/KID ST7.....36 D3
 AUD/MAD/W CW3.....56 B5
Heron St STOKE ST4.....69 E2
Hertford Cl CONG CW12.....8 C5
Hertford Gv LNGTN ST3.....69 E3
Hertford St STOKE ST4.....69 E3
Hesketh Av BURS/TUN ST6.....45 H1
Heskin Wy BURS/TUN ST6.....37 E5
Hester Cl ALS/KID ST7.....70 A1
Hethersett Wk BUCK/MIL ST2.....63 F2
Hetts Crs END/WER ST9.....64 B1
Hewitt St BURS/TUN ST6.....36 D5
Heyburn Crs BURS/TUN ST6.....52 C1
Heydon Cl CONG CW12.....8 A4
Heysham Cl LNGTN ST3.....71 F3
Hickman St NEWUL ST5.....2 A3
Hick St NEWUL ST5.....2 D4
Hidden Hills AUD/MAD/W CW3.....56 A4
Hide Pl STOKE ST4 *.....61 E5
Hide St STOKE ST4.....61 G5
Higginson Cl CONG CW12.....13 F1
High Bank Pl BURS/TUN ST6.....45 F5
Highcroft Av CONG CW12.....8 D5
Higher Ash Rd ALS/KID ST7.....34 D5
Higherland NEWUL ST5.....2 B5
Highfield Av ALS/KID ST7.....35 H1
 CDLE ST10.....74 D5
 LNGTN ST3.....80 D1
 NEWUL ST5.....52 B5
Highfield Cl BLYBR/FOR ST11.....81 H5
Highfield Ct NEWUL ST5.....67 E1
Highfield Cl CDLE ST10.....74 D5
Highfield Dr LNGTN ST3.....69 E3
Highfield Gra NEWUL ST5.....52 B5
Highfield Ri STOKE ST4.....77 H2
Highfield Rd CONG CW12.....13 F1
Highfield Rd East BIDD ST8.....27 H1
Highfield Rd West BIDD ST8.....19 H5
Highgate Cl BURS/TUN ST6.....46 A3
Highgrove Rd STOKE ST4.....67 H4
Highland Cl BIDD ST8.....20 D5
 BLYBR/FOR ST11.....82 A4
Highland Dr LNGTN ST3.....80 B2
High La ALS/KID ST7.....44 B4
 BURS/TUN ST6.....38 C5
 BURS/TUN ST6.....51 H5
 BURS/TUN ST6.....50 A5
High Lowe Av CONG CW12.....9 E3
High St ALS/KID ST7.....26 A5
 ALS/KID ST7.....28 B1
 ALS/KID ST7.....33 E1
 ALS/KID ST7.....42 A5
 ALS/KID ST7.....42 D1
 ALS/KID ST7.....49 F2
 BIDD ST8.....27 G1
 BLYBR/FOR ST11.....82 A5
 BURS/TUN ST6.....36 B5
 BURS/TUN ST6.....44 B2
 CDLE ST10.....73 E3
 CDLE ST10.....74 D4
 LEEK ST13.....30 D5
 NEWUL ST5.....51 E2
 NEWUL ST5.....52 B4
 NEWUL ST5.....58 B5
 NEWUL ST5.....90 D5
High St (Sandyford)
 BURS/TUN ST6.....44 B1
Highton St BUCK/MIL ST2.....47 E5
Highup Rd LEEK ST13.....30 B1
High Vw ALS/KID ST7.....25 H5
 LNGTN ST3.....81 E5
High View Rd LEEK ST13.....31 C4
 END/WER ST9.....39 H3
Highway La NEWUL ST5.....57 G5
Higson Av STOKE ST4.....61 C4
Hilderstone Rd LNGTN ST3.....80 D5
Hillary Av CONG CW12.....9 E5
Hillary Cl LNGTN ST3.....25 H5
Hillary St BURS/TUN ST6.....53 F5
Hillberry Cl BUCK/MIL ST2.....62 C2
Hillchurch St HAN ST1.....5 F2
Hill Crs ALS/KID ST7.....49 H3
 STONE ST15.....90 D5
Hillcrest LEEK ST13.....30 C3
Hillcrest St HAN ST1.....5 G3
Hill Dr STONE ST15.....90 D5
Hillesden Ri CONG CW12.....8 A4
Hillfield Av STOKE ST4.....67 C3
Hill Flds CONG CW12.....8 B4
Hillgreen Rd LNGTN ST3.....70 B2
Hillman St BUCK/MIL ST2.....47 H3
Hillport Av NEWUL ST5.....51 H2
Hillside HAN ST1 *.....52 D5
 NEWUL ST5.....2 A5
Hillside Av ALS/KID ST7.....35 G4
 BLYBR/FOR ST11.....82 A3
 END/WER ST9.....39 H4
 LNGTN ST3.....80 D1
Hillside Cl ALS/KID ST7.....26 B1
 BIDD ST8.....20 D4
 BUCK/MIL ST2.....62 D1
Hillside Dr LEEK ST13.....30 B5
Hillside Rd BUCK/MIL ST2.....47 E3
Hillside Wk STOKE ST4.....3 H5
Hill St NEWUL ST5.....2 B1
 STOKE ST4.....68 D1
Hillswood Av LEEK ST13.....30 C3
Hillswood Dr END/WER ST9.....39 G3
Hill Ter ALS/KID ST7.....41 F4
Hilltop Av NEWUL ST5.....60 C2
Hill Top Cl BURS/TUN ST6.....38 D2
Hill Top Crs LNGTN ST3.....80 C1
Hill Vw BUCK/MIL ST2.....46 D4
 LEEK ST13.....31 F4
Hillwood Rd AUD/MAD/W CW3.....56 C4
Hilton Rd STOKE ST4.....3 H6
Hinchco Pl BURS/TUN ST6.....46 A2
Hinckley Cl CONG CW12.....7 H4
Hinckley Gv STOKE ST4.....78 B5
Hinde St HAN ST1.....4 E6
Hines St STOKE ST4.....69 E2
Hitchman St STOKE ST4.....69 E1

Hobart St BURS/TUN ST6.....53 E2
Hobby Cl LNGTN ST3.....81 E3
Hobson St NEWUL ST5.....53 E1
Hodgkinson St NEWUL ST5.....51 F5
Hodnet Gv HAN ST1.....53 F4
Hogarth Pl NEWUL ST5.....51 E3
Holbeach Rd BUCK/MIL ST2.....62 C2
Holborn NEWUL ST5.....2 C3
Holdcroft Rd BUCK/MIL ST2.....54 D4
Holden Av NEWUL ST5.....60 B1
Holden Av North
 BURS/TUN ST6.....53 H1
Holden Av South
 BURS/TUN ST6.....53 H1
Holder St HAN ST1.....53 F5
Holding Crs ALS/KID ST7.....49 F2
Holditch Rd NEWUL ST5.....51 F4
Holehouse La ALS/KID ST7.....16 D5
 END/WER ST9.....39 F1
Holehouse Rd BURS/TUN ST6.....54 D3
Holford St CONG CW12.....8 B4
The Hollands BIDD ST8.....21 E2
Holland St BURS/TUN ST6.....44 B3
Hollies Dr LNGTN ST3.....89 E1
The Hollies NEWUL ST5.....2 E1
Hollings St STOKE ST4.....69 G2
Hollington Dr BURS/TUN ST6.....37 E3
Hollins Crs ALS/KID ST7.....35 E2
Hollins Gra ALS/KID ST7.....34 D3
Hollinshead Av NEWUL ST5.....51 G5
Hollins La ALS/KID ST7.....25 F1
Hollinswood Cl ALS/KID ST7.....35 E3
Hollinwood Cl ALS/KID ST7.....35 E3
Hollinwood Rd ALS/KID ST7.....45 H1
Hollowood Pl BURS/TUN ST6.....45 H1
The Hollow NEWUL ST5.....72 A5
Hollybank Crs ALS/KID ST7.....68 A2
Hollybush Crs LNGTN ST3.....69 E3
Hollybush Rd NEWUL ST5.....69 E4
Holly Cl BUCK/MIL ST2.....63 G5
Holly Dr END/WER ST9.....46 A1
Holly Gv STONE ST15.....91 E4
Holly La ALS/KID ST7.....23 G5
 ALS/KID ST7.....26 C3
Holly Ms NEWUL ST5 *.....59 E3
Holly Pl STOKE ST4.....59 E3
Holly Rd NEWUL ST5.....42 D5
Holly Tree Dr BIDD ST8.....19 G5
Hollywall La ALS/KID ST7.....44 A1
Hollywall La NEWUL ST5.....57 F3
Holm Cl STOKE ST4.....80 B2
Holmes Chapel Rd CONG CW12.....7 H4
Holmesville Av CONG CW12.....7 H5
Holmes Wy BURS/TUN ST6.....44 A1
Holm Oak Dr
 AUD/MAD/W CW3.....56 A5
Holst Dr HAN ST1.....4 E6
Holyhead Crs LNGTN ST3.....71 G3
Holywell Cl BIDD ST8.....28 A2
Homer Pl BURS/TUN ST6.....45 F1
Homer St HAN ST1.....5 J3
Homestead St BUCK/MIL ST2.....63 H4
The Homestead BUCK/MIL ST2.....46 D3
Honeysuckle Av
 BLYBR/FOR ST11.....82 B4
Honeywall LNGTN ST3.....61 E5
Honeywall La
 AUD/MAD/W CW3.....56 D4
Honeywood NEWUL ST5.....59 H1
Hoon Av NEWUL ST5.....51 H5
Hoover St BURS/TUN ST6 *.....44 B3
Hopedale Cl NEWUL ST5.....66 D4
 STOKE ST4.....62 D5
Hope St ALS/KID ST7.....41 H3
 HAN ST1.....4 E2
Hopkins Cl CONG CW12.....7 H4
Hopton Wy BURS/TUN ST6.....37 E5
Hopwood Pl BUCK/MIL ST2.....62 D1
Horatius Rd NEWUL ST5.....50 D3
Hordley St HAN ST1.....5 G4
Hornby Dr CONG CW12.....7 H4
Hornby Rw STOKE ST4.....61 E5
Horsecroft Crs LEEK ST13.....31 F1
Horsecroft Gv HAN ST1.....53 E1
Horsley Gv LNGTN ST3.....79 E2
Horton Dr LNGTN ST3.....71 E3
Horton St LEEK ST13.....31 E3
 HAN ST1.....5 G2
Hose St BURS/TUN ST6.....44 B3
Hoskins Rd BURS/TUN ST6.....44 C1
Hot La BIDD ST8.....19 E3
 BURS/TUN ST6.....53 F2
Hougher Wall Rd ALS/KID ST7.....41 F4
Hough Hill ALS/KID ST7.....38 D2
Houghton St HAN ST1.....5 F6
Houghwood La END/WER ST9.....47 H1
Houldsworth Dr
 BUCK/MIL ST2.....37 F4
Household Rd BUCK/MIL ST2.....63 F4
Houseman Dr LNGTN ST3.....70 C2
Houston Av END/WER ST9.....39 G3
Hoveringham Dr
 BUCK/MIL ST2.....62 C3
Howard Cl LEEK ST13.....30 B5
Howard Crs HAN ST1.....5 K6
Howard Gv NEWUL ST5.....66 B1
Howard Pl HAN ST1.....4 C7
 NEWUL ST5.....66 B1
Howe Gv NEWUL ST5.....70 A5
Howey Gv NEWUL ST5.....59 E2
Howey Hl CONG CW12.....12 B1
Howey La CONG CW12.....8 B5
Howson St HAN ST1.....5 H1
Hugh Bourne Pl BIDD ST8.....37 F1
Hughes Av NEWUL ST5.....59 C2
Hughes St BURS/TUN ST6.....53 E2
Hughson Gv BURS/TUN ST6.....46 A3
Hugo St LEEK ST13.....30 D4
Hulland Cl NEWUL ST5.....66 B3
Hullock's Pool Rd ALS/KID ST7.....41 C1
Hulme Cl NEWUL ST5.....58 B5
Hulme La END/WER ST9.....64 A2
Hulme Rd LNGTN ST3.....70 D1
Hulme St BIDD ST8.....27 C1
 HAN ST1.....5 F4
 LEEK ST13.....30 D4
Hulse St STOKE ST4.....69 G1

Hulton Cl CONG CW12.....13 F1
Hulton Rd BUCK/MIL ST2.....54 D3
Hulton St HAN ST1.....53 H4
Humber Dr BIDD ST8.....20 A5
Humbert Rd HAN ST1.....60 D2
Humber Wy NEWUL ST5.....66 D4
Humbtach St HAN ST1.....5 F3
Hunters Ct BIDD ST8.....19 G5
Hunter St STOKE ST4.....67 H1
Hunters Pointe CONG CW12.....6 C1
Hunters Wy ALS/KID ST7.....34 D3
 STOKE ST4.....67 H1
Huntilee Rd NEWUL ST5.....44 D5
Huntingdon Pl HAN ST1 *.....54 B3
Huntley Av STOKE ST4.....68 A1
Huntley Cl CDLE ST10.....84 D2
Huntley La CDLE ST10.....84 C3
Huntsbank Dr NEWUL ST5.....42 D5
Hunt St BURS/TUN ST6.....44 C3
Huron Gv STOKE ST4.....68 A2
Hurst Cl ALS/KID ST7.....34 D5
Hurst Rd BIDD ST8.....20 C2
Hutton Dr CONG CW12.....9 E5
Hutton St NEWUL ST5.....2 C2
Huxley Pl LNGTN ST3.....89 E1
Hyacinth Ct NEWUL ST5.....60 A2
Hyacinth Rd NEWUL ST5.....3 K2
Hyndley Cl BUCK/MIL ST2.....62 C1
Hyssop Pl BURS/TUN ST6.....45 H4

I

Ian Rd ALS/KID ST7.....36 B1
Ibsen Rd LNGTN ST3.....71 E3
Ikins Dr ALS/KID ST7.....41 H4
Ilam Cl NEWUL ST5.....58 B3
Ilford Side LNGTN ST3.....79 E2
Ilkley Pl NEWUL ST5.....67 E1
Imandra Ct STOKE ST4.....78 A2
Imogen Cl STOKE ST4.....69 H1
Imperial Ct HAN ST1.....5 G6
Ingelow Cl LNGTN ST3.....69 G5
Ingestre Sq LNGTN ST3.....79 E2
Ingleborough Pl BUCK/MIL ST2.....63 E2
Ingleby Rd LNGTN ST3.....79 E2
Inglefield Av BURS/TUN ST6.....45 H1
Ingleton Gv LNGTN ST3.....81 E3
Inglewood Dr NEWUL ST5.....52 A3
Inglewood Gv NEWUL ST5.....52 A3
Inglis St STOKE ST4.....61 G4
Intake Rd ALS/KID ST7.....45 H2
Iona Pl LNGTN ST3.....69 F4
Irene Av BURS/TUN ST6.....36 B2
Iris Cl LNGTN ST3.....71 G2
Ironbridge Dr NEWUL ST5.....59 F2
Ironmarket NEWUL ST5.....2 C2
Isherwood Pl LNGTN ST3.....70 B5
Isis Cl CONG CW12.....12 D1
Island Reach BURS/TUN ST6 *.....52 D4
Ivy Cl BLYBR/FOR ST11.....82 B4
Ivy Gdns CONG CW12.....8 A5
Ivy Gv STONE ST15.....91 H2
Ivyhouse Dr BARL ST12.....87 E1
Ivy House Rd BIDD ST8.....19 G5
Ivy La ALS/KID ST7.....33 G5

J

Jackfield St BURS/TUN ST6.....45 F5
Jack Haye La BUCK/MIL ST2.....55 G1
Jackson Rd CONG CW12.....8 C2
Jackson St BURS/TUN ST6.....53 E1
Jacqueline St HAN ST1.....44 A2
Jade Ct LNGTN ST3.....70 B5
Jamage Rd ALS/KID ST7.....42 D2
James Brindley Cl HAN ST1.....4 B6
James St LEEK ST13.....30 C4
 NEWUL ST5.....52 A4
 STOKE ST4.....68 A2
James Wy BIDD ST8.....27 F2
Jamieson Cl ALS/KID ST7.....23 G4
Janet Pl HAN ST1.....5 J2
Janson St STOKE ST4.....69 F1
Jasmine Cl BLYBR/FOR ST11.....82 B5
Jasmin Wy ALS/KID ST7.....36 D1
Jason St NEWUL ST5.....2 B1
Jasper Cl BARL ST12.....87 E1
Jasper St HAN ST1.....51 H1
Java Crs STOKE ST4.....78 B3
Jaycean Av BURS/TUN ST6.....44 A2
Jean Cl BURS/TUN ST6.....45 E4
Jefferson St ALS/KID ST7.....44 B2
Jenkinson Cl NEWUL ST5.....59 F4
Jenkins St BURS/TUN ST6.....53 F5
Jerbourg Ct NEWUL ST5.....66 A3
Jeremy Cl STOKE ST4.....67 H1
Jersey Cl CONG CW12.....9 E5
 NEWUL ST5.....66 A3
Jersey Crs LNGTN ST3.....80 A1
Jervis St LNGTN ST3.....70 E1
Jervis St HAN ST1.....5 H1
Jesmond Gv LNGTN ST3.....79 E2
Joanhurst Crs HAN ST1.....4 E7
Jodrell Wy ALS/KID ST7.....35 H5
John Bright St HAN ST1.....5 H1
John O'Gaunt's Rd NEWUL ST5.....3 E5
John Rhodes Wy
 BURS/TUN ST6.....44 A1
Johnson Av NEWUL ST5.....51 G5
Johnson Ct CONG CW12.....13 F1
Johnson Pl NEWUL ST5.....3 F5
Johnson St NEWUL ST5.....50 D2
John St BIDD ST8.....27 C1
 HAN ST1.....5 F4
 LEEK ST13.....30 D4

NEWUL ST5.....3 C3
 NEWUL ST5.....59 E2
Jolley St BURS/TUN ST6.....45 G5
Jolliffe St LEEK ST13 *.....30 D4
Jolyon Cl LNGTN ST3.....69 H1
Jonathan Rd STOKE ST4.....78 C5
Jordan Wy STONE ST15.....91 E4
Jordon St HAN ST1.....4 C6
Joseph Crs ALS/KID ST7.....33 G1
Joseph St ALS/KID ST7.....52 C1
Josiah Wedgwood St HAN ST1.....4 B4
Joyce Av BURS/TUN ST6.....45 F4
Jubilee Av HAN ST1.....4 B3
Jubilee Cl BIDD ST8.....27 H1
Jubilee Rd CONG CW12.....8 C5
 NEWUL ST5.....60 B1
 STOKE ST4.....77 H2
Jubilee Ter LEEK ST13.....30 C3
Judgefield La BURS/TUN ST6.....38 B1
Judith Gv STOKE ST4.....68 C2
Junction Rd LEEK ST13.....30 D5
June Rd STOKE ST4.....69 H1
Juniper Cl LNGTN ST3.....81 E4
Jupiter St BURS/TUN ST6.....45 G5
Justin Cl NEWUL ST5.....52 B5

K

Kara Pl STOKE ST4.....78 B2
Kearsley Wy LNGTN ST3.....79 E2
Keary St STOKE ST4.....68 B1
Keates St BURS/TUN ST6 *.....52 D1
Keats Gv ALS/KID ST7.....13 G5
Keats Gdns ALS/KID ST7.....35 G3
Keble Wy LNGTN ST3.....69 G5
Kedleston Rd BURS/TUN ST6.....45 E4
Keele Rd AUD/MAD/W CW3.....56 A5
 NEWUL ST5.....58 A5
Keele St BURS/TUN ST6.....44 B2
Keeling Rd CDLE ST10.....75 E4
Keelings St STOKE ST4.....67 G3
Keelings Rd HAN ST1.....52 A3
Keene Cl BURS/TUN ST6.....46 A3
Kelham Rd STOKE ST4.....69 G1
Kelmore Cl LNGTN ST3.....69 H3
Kelsall St BURS/TUN ST6.....45 G5
 CONG CW12.....8 C4
Kelsall Wy ALS/KID ST7.....41 F5
Kelvin Av HAN ST1.....53 H3
Kelvin St NEWUL ST5.....52 B5
Kemball Rd STOKE ST4.....68 C2
Kemmay Av BURS/TUN ST6.....37 E3
Kempthorne Rd HAN ST1.....5 H7
Kempton Gv CDLE ST10.....75 E2
Kendal Ct CONG CW12.....7 G5
Kendal Gv BUCK/MIL ST2.....63 F2
Kendal Pl NEWUL ST5.....52 B5
Kendrick St STOKE ST4.....70 B4
Kenelyn Crs LNGTN ST3.....69 G5
Kenilworth Gv WK CDLE ST10.....74 B5
Kenley Av END/WER ST9.....39 H3
Kennedy Rd STOKE ST4.....78 B5
Kennermont Rd BUCK/MIL ST2.....55 E4
Kennet Cl NEWUL ST5.....66 D4
Kennet Dr CONG CW12.....12 D1
Kensington Ov STOKE ST4.....78 C5
Kensington Ct ALS/KID ST7.....22 B5
 BURS/TUN ST6.....44 C2
 STOKE ST4.....67 G4
Kensington Dr CONG CW12.....8 D5
Kensworth Cl NEWUL ST5.....66 C4
Kent Dr CONG CW12.....8 B5
 END/WER ST9.....39 G5
 STONE ST15.....90 C1
Kent Gv NEWUL ST5.....50 D1
Kentmere Cl STOKE ST4.....69 H2
Kentmere Pl NEWUL ST5.....66 D1
Kenton St HAN ST1.....5 F4
Kenworthy St BURS/TUN ST6.....44 C2
Kersbrook Ct STOKE ST4.....78 C4
Kervis Gv BLYBR/FOR ST11.....81 H4
Kestrel Av BLYBR/FOR ST11.....81 G1
 CONG CW12.....12 C1
Kestrel La CDLE ST10.....75 E4
Keswick Cl LEEK ST13.....30 B5
Kettering Dr BUCK/MIL ST2.....62 C3
Ketton Cl ALS/KID ST7.....45 H1
Keyworth Wk BUCK/MIL ST2.....62 C2
Kibworth Gv HAN ST1.....53 G4
Kidsgrove Pl BUCK/MIL ST2.....78 D2
Kidsgrove Bank ALS/KID ST7.....33 H5
Kidsgrove Rd BURS/TUN ST6.....36 A3
Kilburn Pl BUCK/MIL ST2.....62 B2
Kildare St ALS/KID ST7.....70 A5
Kilndown Cl HAN ST1.....4 B6
Kiln La LEEK ST13.....30 B5
Kilsby Gv ALS/KID ST7.....45 H1
Kimberley Gra NEWUL ST5.....59 H1
Kimberley Rd HAN ST1.....4 A5
 NEWUL ST5.....59 H2
Kimberley St LNGTN ST3.....80 A1
Kinder Pl NEWUL ST5.....58 B5
King Charles Cl LNGTN ST3.....81 E3
Kingcross St HAN ST1.....5 H1
King Edward St CDLE ST10.....75 E3
Kingfisher Cl
 AUD/MAD/W CW3.....56 B5
 CONG CW12.....12 C1
Kingfisher Crs CDLE ST10.....75 E4
King George St HAN ST1.....53 H3
King's Av NEWUL ST5.....52 A4
 STONE ST15.....90 D2
Kingsbridge Av NEWUL ST5.....54 B3
Kingsbury Dr LNGTN ST3.....54 A2
King's Cft STOKE ST4.....3 H5
King's Gv LNGTN ST3.....81 E3
Kingsdale Cl LNGTN ST3.....81 E3

Kingsfield Crs BIDD ST8 ....19 H5
Kingsfield Ov STOKE ST4 ....3 G2
Kingsfield Rd BIDD ST8 ....27 G1
STOKE ST4 ....3 H2
Kingsford Pl LNGTN ST3 ....81 E2
Kingside Gv STOKE ST4 ....78 C5
Kingsland Av STOKE ST4 ....67 H5
Kingsland Ct STONE ST15 * 91 F4
Kingsland Dr STONE ST15 ....91 F4
Kingsley Rd ALS/KID ST7 ....34 C5
CONG CW12 ....9 E4
END/WER ST9 ....65 G1
Kingsley St LNGTN ST3 ....81 E1
Kingsmead Rd LNGTN ST3 ....80 C5
Kingsnorth Pl BLYBR/FOR ST11 .....81 F4
Kings Pl STOKE ST4 ....3 H1
Kings Rd STOKE ST4 ....78 A1
Kingstable Sq LNGTN ST3 * 69 H5
Kings Ter STOKE ST4 ....3 H2
Kingston Av HAN ST1 ....54 A2
Kingston Dr STONE ST15 ....91 E5
Kingston Pl BIDD ST8 * 20 A5
BURS/TUN ST6 ....46 A5
King St ALS/KID ST7 ....35 G1
ALS/KID ST7 ....41 F5
ALS/KID ST7 ....42 D1
BIDD ST8 ....19 C5
CONG CW12 ....8 D3
LEEK ST13 ....30 D4
NEWUL ST5 ....1 H5
NEWUL ST5 ....51 F2
NEWUL ST5 ....59 C1
STOKE ST4 ....69 E1
Kingsway REast NEWUL ST5 ....61 F5
Kingsway West NEWUL ST5 ....66 C1
Kingswell Rd STOKE ST4 ....3 H5
Kingswinford Pl
BURS/TUN ST6 ....53 H2
Kingswood ALS/KID ST7 ....35 G2
King William St BURS/TUN ST6 .....44 C5
Kinnersley Av ALS/KID ST7 ....35 G1
Kinnersley St ALS/KID ST7 ....35 G1
Kinsey St NEWUL ST5 ....58 B2
Kinver St BURS/TUN ST6 ....45 G5
Kipling Wy BUCK/MIL ST2 ....57 E4
Kirby St BURS/TUN ST6 ....53 E3
Kirkbride Cl LNGTN ST3 ....70 B5
Kirkham St STOKE ST4 ....68 A1
Kirkland La STOKE ST4 ....69 E1
Kirkstall Pl NEWUL ST5 ....66 D5
Kirkstone Ct CONG CW12 ....11 G1
Kirk St ALS/KID ST7 ....45 G5
Kirkwall Gv BUCK/MIL ST2 ....46 D4
Kite Gv ALS/KID ST7 ....35 E3
LNGTN ST3 ....81 E4
Knarsdale Cl LNGTN ST3 ....70 B2
Knebworth Ct CONG CW12 ....13 F2
Knenhall STONE ST15 ....88 B4
Knenhall La STONE ST15 ....89 E4
Knights Cft NEWUL ST5 ....57 H5
Knight St BURS/TUN ST6 ....44 B2
Kniveden La LEEK ST13 ....31 F4
Knowlbank Rd ALS/KID ST7 ....48 B5
Knowle Rd BIDD ST8 ....27 G1
Knowle St STOKE ST4 ....61 E4
Knowle Wood Vw LNGTN ST3 ......69 F4
Knowsley La ALS/KID ST7 ....23 H5
Knutsford Rd ALS/KID ST7 ....23 H5
Knutton La NEWUL ST5 ....2 B1
Knutton Rd NEWUL ST5 ....52 A4
Knypton St NEWUL ST5 ....2 B1
Knypersley Rd BURS/TUN ST6 .....46 A2
NEWUL ST5 ....51 G2
Kyffin Rd BUCK/MIL ST2 ....54 D3

L

Laburnam Cl ALS/KID ST7 ....35 E3
Laburnum Pl BLYBR/FOR ST11 .....82 C4
CONG CW12 ....9 F3
Laburnum Gv LNGTN ST3 ....69 E4
Laburnum Pl LNGTN ST3 * 80 D2
NEWUL ST5 ....66 C3
Ladybank Gv LNGTN ST3 ....79 E2
Ladydale Cl LEEK ST15 ....31 E5
Ladymoor La BURS/TUN ST6 ....28 D5
Ladysmith Rd HAN ST1 ....4 A5
Ladysmith St LNGTN ST3 ....5 F6
Ladywell Rd BURS/TUN ST6 ....44 B5
Lagonda Cl BIDD ST8 ....27 F3
Lakeside BDARL ST12 ....52 D4
Lake Vw CONG CW12 ....7 H5
Lakewood Dr BARL ST12 ....87 E1
Lakewood Ov HAN ST1 ....52 D5
Lally Pl BIDD ST8 ....37 F1
Lambert's La CONG CW12 ....12 D2
Lambert St BURS/TUN ST6 ....44 C5
Lancaster Rd STOKE ST4 ....90 C4
Lambourne Dr BUCK/MIL ST2 ....1 C4
Lambourn Pl LNGTN ST3 ....78 D2
Lamb St ALS/KID ST7 ....35 G1
HAN ST1 ....1 F5
Lamerton Gv LNGTN ST3 ....70 D5
Lamotte Cl STOKE ST4 ....63 H2
Lancaster Av LEEK ST13 ....31 E2
STOKE ST4 ....3 G4
Lancaster Buildings
NEWUL ST5 ....2 D5
Lancaster Crs STOKE ST4 ....3 H2
Lancaster Dr BURS/TUN ST6 ....46 B2
Lancaster Rd STOKE ST4 ....3 G4
Lanchester Cl BIDD ST8 ....27 F2
Lancia Cl BIDD ST8 ....27 F3
Lander Cl STONE ST15 ....91 G4
Lander Pl ALS/KID ST7 ....35 H4
Landrake Cl NEWUL ST5 ....37 H4
Landrake Gv BURS/TUN ST6 ....36 C4
Lane Farm Gv HAN ST1 ....54 A2

Lanehead Rd HAN ST1 ....60 D1
Langdale Ct CONG CW12 ....11 G1
Langdale Crs HAN ST1 ....53 H2
Langdale Rd NEWUL ST5 ....66 D2
Langford Rd BUCK/MIL ST2 ....63 E1
NEWUL ST5 ....1 G4
Langford St LEEK ST13 ....30 C4
Langham Rd ALS/KID ST7 ....46 C5
Langland Dr LNGTN ST3 ....69 G5
Langley Gv NEWUL ST5 ....42 D4
Langley St STOKE ST4 ....4 B3
Lansbury Gv LNGTN ST3 ....71 F4
Lansdell Av NEWUL ST5 ....51 H5
Lansdowne Cl NEWUL ST5 ....30 A4
Lansdowne Rd STOKE ST4 ....3 J4
Lansdowne St LNGTN ST3 ....79 H1
Lapwing Cl ALS/KID ST7 ....36 C2
Lapwing Rd ALS/KID ST7 ....36 B1
Larch Cl ALS/KID ST7 ....35 G3
Larchfields STONE ST15 ....91 E5
Larch Cv LNGTN ST3 ....69 E5
Larchmount Ct STOKE ST4 ....78 B3
Lark Av ALS/KID ST7 ....26 B5
Larkfield ALS/KID ST7 ....35 G2
Larkin Av LNGTN ST3 ....70 B3
Larksfield Rd BURS/TUN ST6 ....65 H3
Larkspur Gv NEWUL ST5 ....62 A5
Lascelles St BURS/TUN ST6 ....44 B3
Lask Edge Rd BIDD ST8 ....21 E5
Laski Crs LNGTN ST3 ....71 F5
Latebrook Cl BURS/TUN ST6 ....36 A4
Latham Gv BURS/TUN ST6 ....37 F4
Latimer Wy BUCK/MIL ST2 ....63 E2
Lauder Pl North BUCK/MIL ST2 ....63 C4
Lauder Pl South BUCK/MIL ST2 ....63 G5
Laurel Crs END/WER ST9 ....64 A1
Laurel Dr ALS/KID ST7 ....35 G5
Laurel St ALS/KID ST7 ....68 D5
Lauren Cl STOKE ST4 ....69 E1
Lavender Av BLYBR/FOR ST11 ....82 B4
Lavender Cl LNGTN ST3 ....71 F2
Lawley St LNGTN ST3 ....70 B4
Lawn Farm Ers BUCK/MIL ST2 * ...1 F4
Lawrence St HAN ST1 ....4 D6
Lawson Ter NEWUL ST5 ....1 H5
Lawton Av ALS/KID ST7 ....24 D5
Lawton Coppice ALS/KID ST7 ......25 E4
Lawton Crs BIDD ST8 ....19 H5
Lawton Heath Rd ALS/KID ST7 .....23 H2
Lawton St ALS/KID ST7 ....26 A4
BIDD ST8 ....19 H5
BURS/TUN ST6 ....44 C5
CONG CW12 ....8 C5
Laxley Rd NEWUL ST5 ....59 C2
Laxton Gv STOKE ST4 ....86 C1
Leacroft STONE ST15 ....91 G4
Leacroft Rd LNGTN ST3 ....70 C3
Leadbeater Av STOKE ST4 ....67 H2
Leadendale La LNGTN ST3 ....88 C2
Leaford Wk BUCK/MIL ST2 ....62 B2
Leaks Aly LNGTN ST3 ....69 H5
Leamington Gdns NEWUL ST5 ......60 C1
Leamington Rd CONG CW12 ....7 F4
Lea Pl LNGTN ST3 ....71 F5
Lea Rd STONE ST15 ....90 C5
Leaside Rd STOKE ST4 ....67 G2
Leason Rd LNGTN ST3 ....71 E5
Leason St STOKE ST4 ....4 D1
Leaswood Cl NEWUL ST5 ....67 E5
Leaswood Pl ALS/KID ST7 ....25 E4
The Lea STOKE ST4 ....78 B3
Lea Wy ALS/KID ST7 ....23 F5
Leawood Rd STOKE ST4 ....42 A3
Ledbury Crs HAN ST1 ....54 B4
Ledstone Wy LNGTN ST3 ....70 C3
Leech Av NEWUL ST5 ....51 F5
Leech St NEWUL ST5 ....3 F6
Leeds St STOKE ST4 ....69 F2
Lee Gv NEWUL ST5 * 66 D3
Leek La BIDD ST8 ....20 D5
Leek New Rd BURS/TUN ST6 ....53 G2
Leek Rd BURS/TUN ST6 ....38 D4
CDLE ST10 ....12 C4
CONG CW12 ....13 E2
END/WER ST9 ....47 G1
HAN ST1 ....5 K5
STOKE ST4 ....64 C5
STOKE ST4 ....61 H3
Leese St STOKE ST4 ....61 F5
Legge St NEWUL ST5 ....3 F5
Leicester Av ALS/KID ST7 ....23 E3
Leicester Cl NEWUL ST5 ....67 E2
Leicester Pl BUCK/MIL ST2 ....63 E2
Leigh La BURS/TUN ST6 ....44 A5
Leigh Rd CONG CW12 ....9 F2
Leigh St BURS/TUN ST6 ....45 E4
Leighton Cl END/WER ST9 ....47 E2
Lennox St LNGTN ST3 ....70 B5
Leonard Av BUCK/MIL ST2 ....46 B5
Leonard Dr BURS/TUN ST6 ....38 D5
Leonard St BURS/TUN ST6 ....45 F5
LEEK ST13 ....31 E4
Leonora St BURS/TUN ST6 ....52 D2
Leopold St STOKE ST4 ....69 E1
Lessways Cl NEWUL ST5 ....1 F5
Lester Cl ALS/KID ST7 ....23 F4
Leveson Rd STOKE ST4 ....77 H1
Leveson St LNGTN ST3 ....70 A5
Levita Rd STOKE ST4 ....67 H3
Lewisham Dr BURS/TUN ST6 ....61 F4
Lewis St STOKE ST4 ....61 H4
Lexham Pl LNGTN ST3 ....70 C5
Leycett Cl NEWUL ST5 ....57 E2
Leycett Rd NEWUL ST5 ....49 C5
Leyfield Rd STOKE ST4 ....78 D4
Ley Gdns LNGTN ST3 ....78 D4
Leys Dr NEWUL ST5 ....66 A3
Leys La BUCK/MIL ST2 ....47 E4
Liberty La BURS/TUN ST6 * 45 G3
Lichfield Cl NEWUL ST5 ....36 D5
Lichfield Pl NEWUL ST5 ....38 C5
Lichfield Rd ALS/KID ST7 ....34 D4
STONE ST15 ....91 F4
Lichfield St STOKE ST4 ....5 G5
STONE ST15 ....90 D3

Liddle St STOKE ST4 ....68 A1
Lidgate Gv LNGTN ST3 ....69 F5
Lidgate Wk NEWUL ST5 ....76 D1
Lid La CDLE ST10 ....74 C5
Light Oaks Av BUCK/MIL ST2 ....47 F5
Lightwater Gv BUCK/MIL ST2 ......46 B5
Lightwood Rd ALS/KID ST7 ....35 G3
NEWUL ST5 ....42 D5
Lilac Cl LNGTN ST3 ....71 G2
Lilac Gv NEWUL ST5 ....69 E4
Lilleshall Rd NEWUL ST5 ....70 A5
Lilleshall St LNGTN ST3 ....70 A5
Lillydale Rd BUCK/MIL ST2 ....62 D1
Lily St NEWUL ST5 ....52 B4
Limbrick Rd ALS/KID ST7 ....40 B5
Lime Cl LNGTN ST3 ....71 G2
Lime Gv ALS/KID ST7 ....25 E4
BARL ST12 ....87 E1
Limeheath Pl BURS/TUN ST6 ....44 C1
Lime Kiln La ALS/KID ST7 ....35 E1
The Limes NEWUL ST5 ....52 B4
Lime St STOKE ST4 ....5 H2
Limewood Cl BLYBR/FOR ST11 ....82 C4
Linacre Wy LNGTN ST3 ....70 C2
Lincoln Av NEWUL ST5 ....67 E2
Lincoln Cl NEWUL ST5 ....67 E2
Lincoln Rd ALS/KID ST7 ....34 D4
BURS/TUN ST6 ....53 E2
Lincoln St HAN ST1 ....5 H4
Lindale Cl CONG CW12 ....9 E2
Lindale St LNGTN ST3 ....81 F3
Linda Rd BUCK/MIL ST2 ....63 E2
Linden Cl CONG CW12 ....15 E2
NEWUL ST5 ....59 H1
Linden Dr BIDD ST8 ....19 G4
Linden Gv BURS/TUN ST6 ....44 B1
Linden Pl LNGTN ST3 ....79 F1
Lindley Pl LNGTN ST3 ....89 E1
Lindley St BURS/TUN ST6 ....53 F2
Lindops La AUD/MAD/W CW3 .....56 B5
Lindum Av STOKE ST4 ....78 C3
Linfield Rd HAN ST1 ....5 H3
Lingard St BURS/TUN ST6 ....45 E4
Lingfield Av BURS/TUN ST6 ....38 C3
Linhope Gv LNGTN ST3 ....81 F3
Linkend Cl HAN ST1 ....54 B4
Links Av NEWUL ST5 ....51 H5
Linksway Cl ALS/KID ST7 ....37 E5
Linksway Ct CONG CW12 ....12 C2
Linley Gv ALS/KID ST7 ....23 H5
Linley La ALS/KID ST7 ....24 A5
Linley Rd ALS/KID ST7 ....33 H1
STOKE ST4 ....3 H4
Linnet Dr LNGTN ST3 ....70 C3
Linnet Wy BURS/TUN ST6 ....20 A5
Linwood Wy BURS/TUN ST6 ....44 C1
Lionel Gv STOKE ST4 ....3 J7
Lion Gv NEWUL ST5 ....51 E1
Lion St CONG CW12 ....8 B5
STOKE ST4 ....61 E5
Lisbon Pl NEWUL ST5 ....59 E5
Liskeard Cl NEWUL ST5 ....62 C3
Litley Dr CDLE ST10 ....84 D2
Little Chell La BURS/TUN ST6 ....44 D1
Little Cliffe Rd LNGTN ST3 ....81 H2
Little Eaves La BURS/TUN ST6 .....55 E3
Little-field LNGTN ST3 ....67 G3
Little La LNGTN ST3 ....88 C1
Little Moss Cl ALS/KID ST7 ....25 E3
Little Moss La ALS/KID ST7 ....25 E4
Little Rd CDLE ST10 ....73 C5
Little Rw ALS/KID ST7 * 35 H1
STOKE ST4 ....62 A4
Little St CONG CW12 ....8 B5
Littondale Cl CONG CW12 ....8 D2
Liverpool Rd East ALS/KID ST7 .....25 G2
Liverpool Rd West ALS/KID ST7 ....24 A4
NEWUL ST5 ....3 G6
NEWUL ST5 ....42 D4
STOKE ST4 ....61 F5
Liverpool Rd East ALS/KID ST7 .....24 D5
Liverpool Rd West ALS/KID ST7 ....24 A4
Livingstone St
BURS/TUN ST6 * 45 G4
LEEK ST13 ....31 E4
Lloyd St STOKE ST4 ....70 A5
Loachbrook Av CONG CW12 ....7 G3
Lockerbie Cl LEEK ST13 ....31 C4
Lockett's La LNGTN ST3 ....70 A5
Lockett St HAN ST1 ....53 H5
Lockington St ALS/KID ST7 ....63 F2
Lockley St HAN ST1 ....4 C1
Lockwood St BUCK/MIL ST2 ....46 D3
STOKE ST4 ....3 J6
Lodge Barn Rd BIDD ST8 ....28 B2
Lodge Rd NEWUL ST5 ....52 A3
Lodge Rd ALS/KID ST7 ....34 D5
ALS/KID ST7 ....35 E5
STOKE ST4 ....3 J6
Loftus St HAN ST1 ....4 D1
Loganbeck Gv LNGTN ST3 ....70 B2
Lomas St HAN ST1 ....4 B2
Lombard Ct ALS/KID ST7 * 23 G4
Lombardy Gv LNGTN ST3 ....71 E5
Lomond Gv CDLE ST10 ....75 E5
London Rd NEWUL ST5 ....2 E5
NEWUL ST5 ....51 E1
STOKE ST4 ....68 A2
London St LEEK ST13 ....30 D4

Longport Rd BURS/TUN ST6 ....52 B2
Long Rw ALS/KID ST7 ....35 G2
Longsdon Cl NEWUL ST5 ....42 C5
Longsdon Gv LNGTN ST3 ....70 C3
Longshaw Av NEWUL ST5 ....51 H2
Longton Hall Rd LNGTN ST3 ....69 G4
Longton Rd BARL ST12 ....87 F2
STOKE ST4 ....78 B4
Longview Av ALS/KID ST7 ....35 G4
Longview Av BARL ST12 ....25 C4
Longview Rd LNGTN ST3 ....70 B2
Lonsdale St NEWUL ST5 ....1 F5
Loomer Rd NEWUL ST5 ....50 D4
Lordship La STOKE ST4 ....68 H5
Lordshire Pl ALS/KID ST7 ....36 D2
Lord St BIDD ST8 ....27 H1
BURS/TUN ST6 ....45 G5
Lorien Cl LEEK ST13 ....30 B5
Loring Rd NEWUL ST5 ....51 H5
Loring Ter South NEWUL ST5 .....51 H5
Lorne St ALS/KID ST7 ....45 E5
Lorraine St ALS/KID ST7 ....36 D2
Lotus Av BIDD ST8 ....27 F2
Lotus Gv ALS/KID ST7 ....45 F5
Loughborough Wk LNGTN ST3 ....70 A3
Louise Dr LNGTN ST3 ....69 F4
Louise St BURS/TUN ST6 ....45 G3
Louvain Av HAN ST1 ....53 H2
Lovage Gv BUCK/MIL ST2 ....63 E2
Lovatt Av NEWUL ST5 ....51 C5
Lovatt St STOKE ST4 ....61 E5
Love La SBCH CW11 ....14 C2
Loveston Gv LNGTN ST3 ....70 C2
Lovell La CONG CW12 ....8 C5
Lowell Dr LNGTN ST3 ....70 C5
Lower Ash Rd ALS/KID ST7 ....35 E3
Lower Bedford St HAN ST1 ....4 A6
Lower Bethesda St HAN ST1 ....5 F5
Lower Bryan St HAN ST1 ....5 G1
Lower Cross St LNGTN ST3 ....70 A3
Lower Foundry St HAN ST1 ....5 H4
Lower Hadderidge
BURS/TUN ST6 ....52 D1
Lower Heath Av CONG CW12 ....8 C5
Lower Heath Av CONG CW12 ....8 C2
Lower High St ALS/KID ST7 ....26 B1
Lower Mayer St HAN ST1 ....5 G1
Lower Meadow Dr CONG CW12 ....8 A4
Lower Milehouse La
NEWUL ST5 ....59 H1
Lower Oxford Rd NEWUL ST5 .....60 C2
Lower Spring Rd LNGTN ST3 ....70 B5
Lower Street Rd NEWUL ST5 ....5 B8
NEWUL ST5 ....1 H5
Lowe St STOKE ST4 ....61 F5
Lowfield Dr BURS/TUN ST6 ....36 C4
Lowhurst Dr BURS/TUN ST6 ....37 E4
Lowlands Rd BURS/TUN ST6 ....43 G2
Lowndes Cl STOKE ST4 ....69 E1
Low St ALS/KID ST7 ....15 C5
Lowther Pl LEEK ST13 ....31 F4
Lowther St HAN ST1 ....4 C1
Lowthorpe Wy BUCK/MIL ST2 .....63 G3
Loxley Pl LNGTN ST3 ....70 B5
Lucas St BURS/TUN ST6 ....52 C2
Lucerne Rd NEWUL ST5 ....58 B2
Ludbrook St STOKE ST4 ....69 H2
Ludford Cl NEWUL ST5 ....42 D4
Ludlow St HAN ST1 ....5 G1
Ludwall Rd LNGTN ST3 ....80 C1
Lugano Cl NEWUL ST5 ....66 A1
Lukesland Av STOKE ST4 * 67 G1
Luke St BURS/TUN ST6 ....52 C2
STOKE ST4 ....5 H4
Lulworth Gv BURS/TUN ST6 ....37 E4
Lundy Rd LNGTN ST3 ....69 G4
Lune Cl CONG CW12 ....13 E1
Lydford Pl LNGTN ST3 ....70 D4
Lydia Dr HAN ST1 ....54 B3
Lyme Brook Pl STOKE ST4 ....68 D5
Lyme Dr STOKE ST4 ....68 D5
Lyme Gv NEWUL ST5 ....60 A1
Lyme Rd LNGTN ST3 ....81 F1
Lymevale Rd STOKE ST4 ....68 C5
Lyme Valley Rd NEWUL ST5 ....59 G4
Lymewood Cl NEWUL ST5 ....2 C5
Lymewood Gv NEWUL ST5 ....2 C6
Lyminster Gv BUCK/MIL ST2 ....46 D5
Lynalls Cl CONG CW12 ....9 E2
Lynam St BURS/TUN ST6 ....45 C5
Lynam Wy AUD/MAD/W CW3 ......56 A5
Lyndhurst Dr BIDD ST8 ....27 E3
Lyndhurst St BURS/TUN ST6 ....45 G5
Lyndhurst St STONE ST15 ....91 G5
Lyneham Cl BUCK/MIL ST2 ....63 G3
Lynmouth Rd BIDD ST8 ....27 F2
Lynmouth Gv BURS/TUN ST6 .....36 C4
Lynn Av ALS/KID ST7 ....34 D4
Lynn St LNGTN ST3 ....71 F2
Lynsey Cl ALS/KID ST7 ....49 C2
Lynton St LNGTN ST3 ....71 F2
Lynton Rd NEWUL ST5 ....66 B2
Lysander Rd LNGTN ST3 ....81 E4

M

Macclesfield Rd CONG CW12 ....8 D1
Macclesfield St BURS/TUN ST6 ....53 H2
Macdonald Crs LNGTN ST3 ....71 E4
Mace St HAN ST1 ....67 H3
Machin Crs NEWUL ST5 ....51 C2
Machin St ALS/KID ST7 ....58 C5
Macintyre St BURS/TUN ST6 ....44 C2
Mackenzie Crs CDLE ST10 ....84 D5
Maclagan St STOKE ST4 ....68 B1
Maddock St ALS/KID ST7 ....41 F5
BURS/TUN ST6 ....52 C2

Madeira Pl BURS/TUN ST6 ....44 B3
Madeley St BURS/TUN ST6 ....44 B2
NEWUL ST5 * 58 B2
Madison St BURS/TUN ST6 ....44 B2
Mafeking St NEWUL ST5 ....69 H5
Magdalen Rd LNGTN ST3 ....79 E2
Magenta Dr NEWUL ST5 ....59 E2
Magnolia Dr BURS/TUN ST6 ....46 B4
Magpie Crs ALS/KID ST7 ....35 H1
Maidstone Gv BUCK/MIL ST2 ....63 E2
Main St LNGTN ST3 ....71 F2
Majors Barn CDLE ST10 ....74 C5
Malam St HAN ST1 ....4 C5
Malcolm Cl BUCK/MIL ST2 ....46 D4
Malcolm Dr BUCK/MIL ST2 ....55 E4
Malhamdale Rd CONG CW12 ....9 E2
Malham Rd NEWUL ST5 ....59 E2
Malkin Wy BURS/TUN ST6 ....52 C3
Mallard Wy ALS/KID ST7 ....35 G3
Mallorie Rd BURS/TUN ST6 ....45 H2
Mallory Ct CONG CW12 ....7 F4
Mallory Wy CDLE ST10 ....7 G3
Mallowdale Cl STOKE ST4 ....78 C4
The Mall NEWUL ST5 * 2 E3
Malstone Av ALS/KID ST7 ....35 E5
Malthouse La BARL ST12 ....87 E3
Malt La LNGTN ST3 ....70 B5
Malton Gv BURS/TUN ST6 ....44 B1
Malvern Av NEWUL ST5 ....57 H2
Malvern Cl LNGTN ST3 ....63 E2
STOKE ST4 ....78 A3
Manchester Rd CONG CW12 ....8 C2
Mandela Wy ALS/KID ST7 ....70 A5
Mandeville Cl BURS/TUN ST6 ....45 G5
Manfold Cl LEEK ST13 ....58 B3
Manifold Dr CDLE ST10 ....85 E1
Manifold Rd BLYBR/FOR ST11 .....58 B3
Mann St LNGTN ST3 ....71 G5
Manor Cl BLYBR/FOR ST11 ....83 E4
Manor Court St STOKE ST4 ....67 H1
Manor Ri STONE ST15 ....90 C4
Manor Rd ALS/KID ST7 ....34 A5
STOKE ST4 ....69 E1
Mansell St ALS/KID ST7 ....35 H5
Mansfield Cl NEWUL ST5 ....67 E5
Mansfield Dr BIDD ST8 ....27 E3
Mansion Cl CDLE ST10 ....85 E1
Maple Av ALS/KID ST7 ....33 G1
STOKE ST4 ....34 D3
NEWUL ST5 ....42 D5
Maple Cl BURS/TUN ST6 ....46 C1
CDLE ST10 ....75 E5
CONG CW12 ....7 F3
Maple Gdns CONG CW12 ....90 D5
Maplehurst Cl BURS/TUN ST6 .....53 F1
Maple Pl ALS/KID ST7 ....23 H1
LNGTN ST3 ....71 F5
Marcel Cl LNGTN ST3 ....68 A5
March La END/WER ST9 ....65 H5
Marchwood Ct ALS/KID ST7 ....67 G1
Mardale Cl CONG CW12 ....9 E2
Margaret Av STOKE ST4 ....77 H2
Margaret St HAN ST1 ....5 G3
STONE ST15 ....90 C2
Margery Av ALS/KID ST7 ....25 E1
Maries Wy NEWUL ST5 ....58 D3
Marina Dr HAN ST1 ....54 C3
NEWUL ST5 ....58 D3
Marina Wy HAN ST1 ....60 D1
Market La NEWUL ST5 ....1 F5
Market Pl BURS/TUN ST6 ....52 D1
NEWUL ST5 ....1 F5
Market Sq HAN ST1 * 5 F3
Market Square Ar HAN ST1 * 5 F3
Market St ALS/KID ST7 ....35 G2
CONG CW12 ....8 B5
LEEK ST13 ....31 E3
STOKE ST4 ....5 F6
Marlborough Cl END/WER ST9 .....39 G5
Marlborough St STOKE ST4 ....68 D2
Marlborough Wy
BURS/TUN ST6 ....44 A1
Marlow Cl BURS/TUN ST6 ....45 F5
Marlow Ct LNGTN ST3 ....70 B2
Marlow Rd LNGTN ST3 ....70 B2
Marriott St STOKE ST4 ....69 G2
Marsden St HAN ST1 ....5 G3
Marshall Av BURS/TUN ST6 ....53 H4
Marshall Gv CONG CW12 ....13 F1
Marshall St NEWUL ST5 ....44 C5
Marsh Av ALS/KID ST7 ....75 E4
BURS/TUN ST6 ....45 F5
NEWUL ST5 ....52 A4
Marsh Cl ALS/KID ST7 ....22 C5
Marshfield La BIDD ST8 ....19 G5
Marsh Green Cl BIDD ST8 ....19 H3
Marsh Green Rd BIDD ST8 ....19 H3
Marsh Gv BIDD ST8 ....19 H2
Marshland Gv BURS/TUN ST6 .....37 E3
Marsh La ALS/KID ST7 ....22 C5
Marsh Pde NEWUL ST5 ....3 F4
Marsh St North HAN ST1 ....5 F1
Marsh St South HAN ST1 ....5 F3
Marsh Vw LNGTN ST3 ....81 E5
Marsh Wy LNGTN ST3 ....52 A4
Mars St BURS/TUN ST6 ....52 C3
Marston Gv HAN ST1 ....53 H1
Martindale Cl LNGTN ST3 ....80 D2
Martin St STOKE ST4 ....53 H2
Marton Cl CONG CW12 ....7 F4
Marychurch Rd BUCK/MIL ST2 ....62 C1
Mayfield Wk STOKE ST4 ....3 J7
Maryhill Cl ALS/KID ST7 ....39 H5
Mary Rose Ct BUCK/MIL ST2 ......3 F5
Mary Rose Cl CDLE ST10 ....74 D2
Masefield Rd LNGTN ST3 ....69 G5
Maskery Pl CONG CW12 ....8 B4
Mason Dr BIDD ST8 ....19 G5
Mason St STOKE ST4 ....69 F2

Masterson St STOKE ST4 .....68 D1
Matlock St HAN ST1 .....5 F7
Matthews Pl CONG CW12 .....9 E5
Matthews Wk HAN ST1 .....5 G5
Maud St STOKE ST4 .....62 A5
Maunders Rd BUCK/MIL ST2 .....46 B5
Maureen Av BUCK/MIL ST2 .....36 B5
Maureen Gv NEWUL ST5 .....60 A1
Mawdesley St BURS/TUN ST6 .....53 F3
Mawdsley Cl ALS/KID ST7 .....22 B5
Mawson Gv STOKE ST4 .....61 H3
Maxton Wy LNGTN ST3 .....71 F5
Maxwell Pl STOKE ST4 .....3 J6
May Av BURS/TUN ST6 .....44 D5
    NEWUL ST5 .....60 B1
Maybury Wk BUCK/MIL ST2 .....46 C4
Mayer Av NEWUL ST5 .....59 H2
Mayer Bank LEEK ST13 .....53 E1
Mayers Ct LEEK ST13 .....30 C4
Mayer St HAN ST1 .....5 G2
Mayfair Dr END/WER ST9 .....39 G5
Mayfield Av NEWUL ST5 .....5 K1
    NEWUL ST5 .....2 A5
Mayfield Cl LEEK ST13 .....30 A4
Mayfield Crs HAN ST1 .....5 K2
Mayfield Dr BLYBR/FOR ST11 .....81 H2
Mayfield Pl NEWUL ST5 .....60 A1
Mayfield Pl East STOKE ST4 .....67 G2
Mayfield Pl West STOKE ST4 .....67 G2
Mayfield Rd BIDD ST8 .....27 H2
Maylea Crs HAN ST1 .....53 C2
Mayneford Pl STOKE ST4 .....77 H1
Mayne St HAN ST1 .....77 H1
May Pl NEWUL ST5 .....60 A1
    .....60 H5
May St BURS/TUN ST6 .....45 F5
    NEWUL ST5 .....58 C3
Maythorne Rd LNGTN ST3 .....79 G1
McGough St BURS/TUN ST6 .....44 B5
McKellin Cl ALS/KID ST7 .....22 A4
Mc Kinley St STOKE ST6 * 44 B2
Mead Av ALS/KID ST7 .....25 E1
Meadowbrook Ct STONE ST15 .....91 G5
Meadow Cl BLYBR/FOR ST11 .....82 A4
    BLYBR/FOR ST11 .....82 D2
Meadow Cl ALS/KID ST7 .....36 C1
    BARL ST12 .....86 C3
Meadow Cft ALS/KID ST7 .....35 G1
Meadowcroft Av LNGTN ST3 .....81 G1
Meadow Dr CDLE ST10 .....74 D4
    LNGTN ST3 .....79 G2
Meadow La NEWUL ST5 .....78 C5
    STOKE ST4 .....
Meadow Pl BURS/TUN ST6 .....81 F1
Meadow Rd BARL ST12 .....86 D4
    BURS/TUN ST6 .....37 G5
    NEWUL ST5 .....51 F3
Meadowside BIDD ST8 .....37 F2
    STOKE ST4 .....78 B3
Meadowside Av ALS/KID ST7 .....41 E5
Meadowside La ALS/KID ST7 .....25 H1
Meadows Rd ALS/KID ST7 .....22 C5
The Meadows END/WER ST9 .....39 H4
Meadow St BUCK/MIL ST2 .....46 D5
    NEWUL ST5 .....51 F3
Meadow Vw BURS/TUN ST6 .....46 A3
Meadow Wy ALS/KID ST7 .....24 A5
    NEWUL ST5 .....90 C5
Meads Rd STOKE ST4 .....23 F4
The Mead STOKE ST4 .....78 B3
Meaford Av STONE ST15 .....90 C1
Meaford Dr LNGTN ST3 .....69 G4
Meakin Av NEWUL ST5 .....59 E4
Meakin Cl CDLE ST10 .....84 C1
    CONG CW12 .....13 F1
    STONE ST15 .....91 F5
Media Wy HAN ST1 .....60 D1
Medina Wy ALS/KID ST7 .....22 C5
Medway Dr BIDD ST8 .....19 H4
Medway Pl NEWUL ST5 .....66 D3
Meerbrook Cl STOKE ST6 .....78 B5
Megacre ALS/KID ST7 .....42 A4
Meigh Rd END/WER ST9 .....64 A1
Meigh St HAN ST1 .....5 C3
Meiklejohn Pl BURS/TUN ST6 .....37 E5
Meirhay Rd LNGTN ST3 .....70 B5
Meir Dr LNGTN ST3 .....80 C1
Meir St BURS/TUN ST6 .....44 C2
Meir Vw LNGTN ST3 .....71 E5
Melbourne St LNGTN ST3 .....70 B2
Melchester Gv LNGTN ST3 .....80 C1
Melfont St BURS/TUN ST6 .....44 C3
Mellelden Wy STOKE ST4 .....41 F5
Mellard St ALS/KID ST7 .....41 F5
    NEWUL ST5 .....2 B1
Mellors Bank ALS/KID ST7 .....26 A2
Mellor St ALS/KID ST7 .....36 D2
Melrose Av HAN ST1 .....53 G1
    LNGTN ST3 .....89 E1
    NEWUL ST5 .....66 C2
Melrose Pl LEEK ST13 .....30 A4
Melstone Av BURS/TUN ST6 .....44 D3
Melton Cl CONG CW12 .....7 F4
Melton Dr CONG CW12 .....7 F4
Melville Cl NEWUL ST5 .....77 E1
Melville St HAN ST1 .....5 J5
Melvyn Crs NEWUL ST5 .....52 A2
Menai Dr BIDD ST8 .....27 H2
Mendip Cl NEWUL ST5 .....66 A3
Mendip Pl NEWUL ST5 .....59 E1
Mercer Av STONE ST15 .....91 F4
Mercer St LNGTN ST3 .....79 H1
Mercia Crs BURS/TUN ST6 .....53 E3
Merelake Rd ALS/KID ST7 .....34 A3
Meremore Dr NEWUL ST5 .....42 D4
Mereside Av CONG CW12 .....7 F5
Mere Side Cl HAN ST1 .....60 D2
Merevale Av BUCK/MIL ST2 .....62 C2
Meriden Rd NEWUL ST5 .....67 E5
Merino Cl LNGTN ST3 .....80 A2

Merlin Cl BURS/TUN ST6 .....37 E3
Merlin Wy ALS/KID ST7 .....26 B5
Merrial St NEWUL ST5 .....3 G3
Merrion Dr BURS/TUN ST6 .....45 F4
Mersey Rd HAN ST1 .....66 C4
Mersey St HAN ST1 .....4 D5
Merthyr Gv BIDD ST8 .....28 A2
Merton St LNGTN ST3 .....70 A3
MetcalFe Rd BURS/TUN ST6 .....44 D3
Mews Cl BUCK/MIL ST2 .....46 A1
The Mews NEWUL ST5 * 52 B5
Michael Cl LNGTN ST3 .....71 F4
Michaels Cl NEWUL ST5 .....52 A2
Michigan Gv STOKE ST4 .....78 B2
Mickleby Wy BLYBR/FOR ST11 .....81 G3
Middle Cross St LNGTN ST3 .....70 A3
Middlefield Rd BUCK/MIL ST2 .....63 F4
Middle La CONG CW12 .....8 B5
Middleton Cl BURS/TUN ST6 .....46 A5
Midfield Cl BIDD ST8 .....19 G5
Midhurst Cl ALS/KID ST7 .....36 D3
Midway Dr BLYBR/FOR ST11 .....82 A4
The Midway HAN ST1 .....2 D4
Milan Dr NEWUL ST5 .....66 A1
Milan Gv LNGTN ST3 .....70 C3
Milborne Dr NEWUL ST5 .....67 E2
Milburn Rd BURS/TUN ST6 .....53 F2
Mile Ct NEWUL ST5 .....67 F2
Milehouse La NEWUL ST5 .....51 H5
Miles Green Rd ALS/KID ST7 .....49 C1
Milford Rd NEWUL ST5 .....2 B5
Milford St STOKE ST4 .....69 F2
Milgreen Av HAN ST1 .....53 H2
Milk St CONG CW12 .....8 B4
    LEEK ST13 .....31 E2
Milland Gv STOKE ST4 .....78 B4
Millbank Pl NEWUL ST5 .....59 F5
Millbank St LNGTN ST3 .....70 A4
Millbridge Cl LNGTN ST3 .....81 F4
Millbrook Gv BUCK/MIL ST2 .....46 C5
Millbrook Wy CDLE ST10 .....75 E5
Mill Cl BLYBR/FOR ST11 .....71 G4
Millend La NEWUL ST5 .....41 E1
Millennium Wy NEWUL ST5 .....43 F4
Millers Ca STONE ST15 .....90 D3
Millers La BUCK/MIL ST2 .....46 C5
Miller St NEWUL ST5 .....3 F2
Millers Vw ALS/KID ST7 .....35 G5
    CDLE ST10 .....75 E5
Millers Whf ALS/KID ST7 .....23 G1
Millett Rd BUCK/MIL ST2 .....62 C1
Millfield Crs BUCK/MIL ST2 .....46 C5
Mill Gn CONG CW12 .....8 B4
Mill Gv ALS/KID ST7 .....34 D2
    CDLE ST10 .....75 E5
Mill Hayes Rd BIDD ST8 .....27 G5
    BURS/TUN ST6 .....44 C5
Mill Hill Crs BUCK/MIL ST2 .....45 E2
Millhouse Dr CDLE ST10 .....85 F1
Millicent St STOKE ST4 .....62 A5
Mill La ALS/KID ST7 .....25 C1
    AUD/MAD/W CW3 .....56 B5
    CONG CW12 .....13 C2
    SBCH CW11 .....14 B5
Milmead ALS/KID ST7 .....23 H1
Mill Ri ALS/KID ST7 .....35 F2
Millrise Rd BUCK/MIL ST2 .....46 C5
Mill Rd CDLE ST10 .....75 E5
Millstone Av ALS/KID ST7 .....35 F2
Millstream Cl CDLE ST10 .....75 E5
Mill St CONG CW12 .....8 B4
    LEEK ST13 .....30 C3
    NEWUL ST5 .....58 C3
    STONE ST15 .....90 D3
Milltown Wy LEEK ST13 .....31 F5
Mill Vw BURS/TUN ST6 .....45 H1
Millwalk Av STONE ST15 .....91 F4
Millward Rd BUCK/MIL ST2 .....63 E1
Mill Waters CDLE ST10 .....75 E5
Milner Ter LEEK ST13 .....31 F3
Milnes Cl LNGTN ST3 .....69 G5
Milton Crs ALS/KID ST7 .....34 C3
Milton Rd BUCK/MIL ST2 .....46 B5
    HAN ST1 .....54 A2
    HAN ST1 .....5 H1
Milvale St BURS/TUN ST6 .....52 C2
Milward Gv LNGTN ST3 .....80 D4
Minard Gv LNGTN ST3 .....71 E3
Minden Gv BURS/TUN ST6 .....53 H1
Mineal Rd BUCK/MIL ST2 .....63 F5
Minerva Cl BIDD ST8 .....27 G3
Minerva Rd STOKE ST4 .....69 F1
Minfield Cl ALS/KID ST7 .....35 G3
Minnie Cl ALS/KID ST7 .....49 C2
Minshall St STOKE ST4 .....68 C2
Minster St BURS/TUN ST6 .....44 C3
Minton Cl CDLE ST10 .....84 D1
    CONG CW12 .....13 F1
Minton St NEWUL ST5 .....52 B4
    STOKE ST4 .....3 K4
Miranda Gv BURS/TUN ST6 .....44 B5
Mitchell Av ALS/KID ST7 .....34 D2
Mitchell Dr ALS/KID ST7 .....34 D2
Mitchell St BURS/TUN ST6 .....44 D5
Moat La ALS/KID ST7 .....40 C4
The Moat LNGTN ST3 .....71 F5
Mobberley Rd BURS/TUN ST6 .....44 B4
Moddershall Oaks STONE ST15 .....88 D5
Moffat Gv BUCK/MIL ST2 .....63 G5
Moffatt Wy NEWUL ST5 .....57 H2
Mollison Rd LNGTN ST3 .....81 E2
Monaco Pl NEWUL ST5 .....59 E5
Monkhouse Cl NEWUL ST5 .....57 F4
Monkhouse CDLE ST10 .....74 D4
Monkleigh Cl STOKE ST4 * 78 B5
Monks Cl NEWUL ST5 .....67 E1
Monkton Cl ALS/KID ST7 .....79 C1
Monmouth Pl NEWUL ST5 .....57 F3
Monsal Gv HAN ST1 .....54 B4
Montfort Pl NEWUL ST5 .....66 D1
Montgomery Ct NEWUL ST5 .....2 B1
Montgomery Pl LNGTN ST3 .....71 F5
Montrose St STOKE ST4 .....69 F2
Monty Pl LNGTN ST3 .....69 H2
Monument La BARL ST12 .....86 A5
Monument Rd ALS/KID ST7 .....34 D5

Monument Vw ALS/KID ST7 .....41 H4
Monville Cl BLYBR/FOR ST11 .....81 G3
Monyash Dr LEEK ST13 .....31 F4
Moody St CONG CW12 .....8 B5
Moor Cl BIDD ST8 .....20 A4
Moorcroft Av NEWUL ST5 .....66 D4
Moorcroft Cl CDLE ST10 .....84 C1
Moore St BURS/TUN ST6 .....53 E2
Moorfield Av BIDD ST8 .....19 G5
Moorfields LEEK ST13 .....31 G3
Moorhead Dr END/WER ST9 .....47 H2
Moorhouse Av ALS/KID ST7 .....23 C4
Moorhouse St LEEK ST13 .....31 E4
Moorings CONG CW12 .....12 C1
Moorland Rd ALS/KID ST7 .....35 H5
    BIDD ST8 .....19 H5
    BURS/TUN ST6 .....45 F5
    LEEK ST13 .....31 G4
Moorland Vw BURS/TUN ST6 .....45 G5
Moorland Wk CDLE ST10 .....74 D4
Moor La CDLE ST10 .....75 F3
Moorson Av ALS/KID ST7 .....17 F5
Moorsyde Rd STONE ST15 .....92 A2
Moorthorne Crs NEWUL ST5 .....51 C3
Moorview Gdns ALS/KID ST7 .....26 C5
Moran Rd NEWUL ST5 .....59 F2
Moresby Cl BUCK/MIL ST2 .....46 D5
Moreton Av ALS/KID ST7 .....35 H3
Moreton Cl ALS/KID ST7 .....35 H3
    END/WER ST9 .....64 A2
Moreton Dr ALS/KID ST7 .....22 D5
Moreton Pde ALS/KID ST7 .....37 E5
Morgan Wy BURS/TUN ST6 .....53 E5
Morley Dr CONG CW12 .....13 E1
Morley St HAN ST1 .....4 D4
    LEEK ST13 .....30 C4
Mornington Rd HAN ST1 .....53 H1
Morpeth St LNGTN ST3 .....70 A4
Morston Dr NEWUL ST5 .....66 D5
Mortimer Pl LNGTN ST3 .....70 D3
Morton St BURS/TUN ST6 .....52 C2
Morville Cl ALS/KID ST7 .....62 A5
Mosedale Av LNGTN ST3 .....70 C3
Mossfield Crs ALS/KID ST7 .....35 H1
Mossfield Dr BIDD ST8 .....28 A1
Mossfield Rd LNGTN ST3 .....63 E5
Moss Flds ALS/KID ST7 .....22 C5
Moss Green Bd BUCK/MIL ST2 .....63 F5
Moss Gv NEWUL ST5 .....42 D5
Moss Hl END/WER ST9 .....47 F1
Mossland Rd LNGTN ST3 .....70 A2
Moss La ALS/KID ST7 .....25 E4
    CDLE ST10 .....75 E1
    CONG CW12 .....8 C1
Mossley Ct CONG CW12 .....12 D2
Mossley Garth Cl CONG CW12 .....13 E1
Moss Pl ALS/KID ST7 .....17 E1
Moss Ri NEWUL ST5 .....42 C5
Moss Rd CONG CW12 .....12 C4
Moss Side NEWUL ST5 .....46 A1
Moss Wy ALS/KID ST7 .....35 H4
Moston St BURS/TUN ST6 .....53 H1
Mott Pl BURS/TUN ST6 .....52 B1
Mounfield Pl STOKE ST4 .....80 D1
Mount Av NEWUL ST5 .....60 D5
    STONE ST15 .....90 C1
Mountbatten Wy CONG CW12 .....8 B4
Mount Cl STONE ST15 .....91 G5
Mount Crs STONE ST15 .....90 C1
Mountford St BURS/TUN ST6 .....44 D5
Mount Pl BLYBR/FOR ST11 .....81 G3
Mount Pleasant ALS/KID ST7 .....25 H1
    HAN ST1 .....4 C5
    LEEK ST13 .....30 D5
    NEWUL ST5 .....51 E5
    NEWUL ST5 .....51 E3
Mount Pleasant Rd
    ALS/KID ST7 .....25 H1
Mount Rd ALS/KID ST7 .....35 H2
    BLYBR/FOR ST11 .....81 G3
    LEEK ST13 .....31 G3
Mountside Gdns LEEK ST13 .....31 G5
Mountsorrel Cl STOKE ST4 .....78 B5
Mount St HAN ST1 .....5 H1
The Mount ALS/KID ST7 .....25 E1
    ALS/KID ST7 .....35 G2
    CONG CW12 .....7 H2
    NEWUL ST5 .....51 E5
Mousley St BURS/TUN ST6 .....52 B1
Mow Cop Rd ALS/KID ST7 .....26 A2
Mow La ALS/KID ST7 .....19 E3
    ALS/KID ST7 .....25 H1
    CONG CW12 .....12 C4
    CONG CW12 .....18 D1
Moxley Av HAN ST1 .....53 H2
Mulberry Gdns NEWUL ST5 .....67 E2
Mulberry Wy LEEK ST13 .....31 F5
Mulgrave St HAN ST1 .....53 F2
Mulliner Cl BUCK/MIL ST2 * 63 F1
Munro St STOKE ST4 .....68 A2
Munster Ter BURS/TUN ST6 .....67 H2
Murhall St BURS/TUN ST6 .....52 C2
Murray St BURS/TUN ST6 .....36 A4
Myatt St HAN ST1 .....53 H4
Mynors St HAN ST1 .....5 H2
Myott Av LNGTN ST3 .....2 C5
Myrtle Av LNGTN ST3 .....71 F4

N

Nabbs Cl ALS/KID ST7 .....35 H1
Nabbswood Rd ALS/KID ST7 .....35 H1
Nab Hill Av LEEK ST13 .....30 B3
Nab Hill Cl LEEK ST13 .....30 B3
Nanny Goat La STONE ST15 .....90 D2
Nantwich Rd ALS/KID ST7 .....33 H5
Napier St STOKE ST4 .....68 D1
Naples Cl LNGTN ST3 .....70 C3
Naples Dr NEWUL ST5 .....66 B1

Narvik Crs BURS/TUN ST6 .....45 F4
Naseby Rd CONG CW12 .....7 G4
Nashe Dr LNGTN ST3 .....69 G5
Nash Peake St BURS/TUN ST6 .....44 B3
Nash St NEWUL ST5 .....59 E2
Navigation Loop STONE ST15 .....90 B1
Navigation Rd BURS/TUN ST6 .....52 D2
Navigation St BURS/TUN ST6 .....52 C2
Naylor St BURS/TUN ST6 .....44 D1
Naylor Yd LEEK ST13 .....30 D3
Neale Dr BUCK/MIL ST2 .....54 D4
Neath Cl LNGTN ST3 .....70 B4
Nelian Crs BURS/TUN ST6 .....45 H5
Nelson Bank ALS/KID ST7 .....35 G4
Nelson Cl ALS/KID ST7 .....33 H1
Nelson Pl HAN ST1 .....5 H4
Nelson Rd STOKE ST4 .....3 K4
Nelson St CONG CW12 .....8 B4
    LEEK ST13 .....31 E2
    NEWUL ST5 * 52 A4
    STOKE ST4 .....68 D2
Nephew St BURS/TUN ST6 .....52 C2
Neptune Gv HAN ST1 .....54 B3
Ness Gv CDLE ST10 .....84 B1
Nethercote Pl BUCK/MIL ST2 .....47 E4
Netherton Gv BUCK/MIL ST2 .....47 E4
Netley Pl LNGTN ST3 .....79 E5
Nevada La BURS/TUN ST6 .....53 F1
Neville St STOKE ST4 .....67 H3
Nevin Av BIDD ST8 .....27 G3
Newark Gv BURS/TUN ST6 .....36 A4
New Av BLYBR/FOR ST11 .....83 E5
Newborough Cl HAN ST1 .....54 A4
Newburn Gv STOKE ST4 .....78 B2
Newburn Gv LNGTN ST3 .....79 E3
Newby Ct CONG CW12 .....11 G1
Newcastle La STOKE ST4 .....67 G1
Newcastle Rd ALS/KID ST7 .....43 E1
    AUD/MAD/W CW3 .....56 B5
    CONG CW12 .....7 H4
    LEEK ST13 .....30 C5
    SBCH CW11 .....14 B1
    SBCH CW11 .....15 G1
    STOKE ST4 .....67 G2
    STOKE ST4 .....77 E2
    STONE ST15 .....90 B2
Newcastle St BURS/TUN ST6 .....52 B1
    NEWUL ST5 .....58 C2
    STOKE ST4 .....90 C2
New Century St HAN ST1 .....4 C3
New Chapel La BURS/TUN ST6 .....44 D2
Newchapel Rd ALS/KID ST7 .....25 H5
New Close Av BLYBR/FOR ST11 .....82 C3
Newcomen Gv BURS/TUN ST6 .....63 F5
Newfield St BURS/TUN ST6 .....59 E2
Newfold Crs BURS/TUN ST6 .....38 C3
Newford Crs BUCK/MIL ST2 .....46 B5
New Haden Rd CDLE ST10 .....70 B5
New Hall Rd LNGTN ST3 .....70 B5
New Haven Gv STOKE ST4 .....78 B5
New Hayes Rd BURS/TUN ST6 .....44 B2
Newhouse Rd BUCK/MIL ST2 .....54 D4
Newington Gv STOKE ST4 .....78 B2
New Inn La SBCH CW11 .....14 C3
    STOKE ST4 .....77 H2
New King St ALS/KID ST7 .....35 G4
New Kingsway LNGTN ST3 .....71 E3
Newlands Cl NEWUL ST5 .....60 C5
Newlands Dr CONG CW12 .....7 F4
Newlands St ALS/KID ST7 .....35 F2
New La BURS/TUN ST6 .....38 D2
Newleigh St ALS/KID ST7 .....36 C5
Newlyn Av CONG CW12 .....12 D2
Newman Cl CONG CW12 .....7 F4
    STONE ST15 .....91 E5
Newmarket Wy CDLE ST10 .....75 E2
Newmill St BUCK/MIL ST2 .....46 C5
Newmount Rd STOKE ST4 .....69 H2
Newpool Rd BIDD ST8 .....27 E2
Newpool Ter BIDD ST8 .....27 F5
Newport Gv NEWUL ST5 .....43 E4
Newport La BURS/TUN ST6 .....52 C1
Newport La BURS/TUN ST6 .....52 C1
Newquay Ct CONG CW12 .....11 C2
Newquay CONG CW12 .....11 C2
Newram Wy CDLE ST10 .....41 C4
    AUD/MAD/W CW3 .....56 A5
    BUCK/MIL ST2 .....63 H1
    CDLE ST10 .....73 E4
    CONG CW12 .....11 G5
Newshaw Wk HAN ST1 .....5 H3
Newstead Rd BUCK/MIL ST2 .....54 D4
New St BIDD ST8 .....28 B2
    BIDD ST8 .....28 B2
    BURS/TUN ST6 .....44 D5
    CONG CW12 .....8 C5
    LEEK ST13 .....31 E3
Newton Rd NEWUL ST5 .....51 H3
Newton St STOKE ST4 .....3 J7
Newtown ALS/KID ST7 .....36 C1
Nicholas St LNGTN ST3 .....77 H1
Nicholas Gv ALS/KID ST7 .....30 A5
Nicholas St BURS/TUN ST6 .....52 C1
Nicholl's La STONE ST15 .....91 E1
Nicholls St STOKE ST4 .....68 B3
Nicholson Wy LEEK ST13 .....90 B3
Nidderdale Cl CONG CW12 .....9 E2
Nightingale Wy ALS/KID ST7 .....22 D5
Nile St BURS/TUN ST6 .....52 C1
Noblett Rd HAN ST1 .....54 A2
Norbury Av BUCK/MIL ST2 .....46 C5
Norbury Ct STONE ST15 .....90 D5
Norbury Dr CONG CW12 .....8 C3
Norfolk Cl NEWUL ST5 .....59 E1
Norfolk Gv BIDD ST8 .....19 G4
Norfolk Rd ALS/KID ST7 .....35 H2
    CONG CW12 .....8 C3
Norfolk St HAN ST1 .....4 D7
Normacot Grange Rd
    LNGTN ST3 .....80 D3
Normacot Rd LNGTN ST3 .....70 D4
Norman Av BURS/TUN ST6 .....44 D3
Normandy Gv BUCK/MIL ST2 .....46 C4
Norman Gv NEWUL ST5 .....60 B2
Normanton Gv LNGTN ST3 .....70 B1

Norris Rd BURS/TUN ST6 .....44 D3
Northam Rd HAN ST1 .....53 H5
North Av LEEK ST13 .....30 C4
Northcote Pl NEWUL ST5 .....3 F2
Northcote St STOKE ST4 .....61 F5
Northesk Pl NEWUL ST5 .....66 C2
Northesk St STONE ST15 .....90 C2
Northfield Dr BIDD ST8 .....20 A4
Northfleet St BUCK/MIL ST2 .....62 C1
Northgate Cl STOKE ST4 .....77 H1
North Rd HAN ST1 .....54 D3
North Pl BUCK/MIL ST2 .....53 F2
North St ALS/KID ST7 .....25 H2
    CONG CW12 .....8 B4
    LEEK ST13 .....30 D3
    NEWUL ST5 .....3 F5
    NEWUL ST5 .....58 B2
    STOKE ST4 .....61 E4
North Ter NEWUL ST5 .....51 H4
North Wk LNGTN ST3 .....81 F1
North West Ter BURS/TUN ST6 .....45 F5
Northwood Cl NEWUL ST5 .....67 F5
Northwood Gn NEWUL ST5 .....5 J3
Northwood La NEWUL ST5 .....5 J2
Northwood Park Rd HAN ST1 .....5 J2
Norton Av BURS/TUN ST6 .....45 H1
Norton Crs BURS/TUN ST6 .....53 H1
Norton Hall Cl BURS/TUN ST6 .....46 A3
Norton La BURS/TUN ST6 .....46 A3
Norton Rd BUCK/MIL ST2 .....46 D5
Norwich Pl NEWUL ST5 .....67 F2
Norwich Rd BUCK/MIL ST2 .....63 F2
Novi La LEEK ST13 .....31 F2
Nunn's Cl LNGTN ST3 .....71 F2
Nunn St LEEK ST13 .....30 C3
Nursery Av END/WER ST9 .....34 D2
Nursery Cl ALS/KID ST7 .....34 D2
    CDLE ST10 .....74 C4
Nursery Dr BIDD ST8 .....19 G3
Nursery La BUCK/MIL ST2 .....47 E3
    .....8 C5
Nursery Rd ALS/KID ST7 .....25 E5
Nursery St STOKE ST4 .....68 A2
Nutbrook Cl STOKE ST4 .....68 C5
Nyewood Av LNGTN ST3 .....70 B2

O

Oakamoor Rd CDLE ST10 .....75 F3
Oak Av ALS/KID ST7 .....33 G1
Oakdale NEWUL ST5 .....67 E4
Oakdene Av BLYBR/FOR ST11 .....82 C4
Oakdene Cl ALS/KID ST7 .....51 G5
    NEWUL ST5 .....51 G5
Oakdene Wy BIDD ST8 .....27 H1
Oakham Wy ALS/KID ST7 .....25 E2
Oakham Wy BUCK/MIL ST2 .....63 E2
Oakhill Av ALS/KID ST7 .....43 H5
Oakhurst Crs LNGTN ST3 .....81 E4
Oaklands Av NEWUL ST5 .....52 A3
Oak La CONG CW12 .....18 B2
Oak Lea LEEK ST13 .....30 A5
Oakleigh Ct CONG CW12 .....7 G4
    STONE ST15 .....91 G5
Oakley Pl BURS/TUN ST6 .....37 E5
Oakmoor Rd CDLE ST10 .....75 G3
Oak Pl LNGTN ST3 .....70 D5
Oak Rd NEWUL ST5 .....58 D2
    STONE ST15 .....91 E5
Oakshaw Gv STOKE ST4 .....78 B4
Oak St ALS/KID ST7 .....15 G5
    CDLE ST10 .....74 D4
    NEWUL ST5 .....60 B1
Oaktree La ALS/KID ST7 .....42 D1
Oaktree Rd STOKE ST4 .....78 B4
Oakville Av BURS/TUN ST6 .....45 F4
Oakwell Gv LNGTN ST3 .....80 A1
Oakwood Rd LNGTN ST3 .....80 B3
    LNGTN ST3 .....79 E1
Oban Cl NEWUL ST5 .....59 F4
Obelisk Wy CONG CW12 .....8 A3
Oberon Cl BURS/TUN ST6 .....45 H5
Occupation St NEWUL ST5 .....2 D5
Oddfellows STONE ST15 * 90 D3
Odell Gv BURS/TUN ST6 .....44 C5
Ogden Rd HAN ST1 .....5 F5
Ogmore Gv LNGTN ST3 .....81 E2
Old Brownhills LEEK ST13 .....53 F1
Oldares Rd STOKE ST4 .....78 B5
Old Butt La ALS/KID ST7 .....34 D1
Old Chapel Cl NEWUL ST5 .....57 G4
Oldcott Cl ALS/KID ST7 .....36 A3
Oldcott Dr ALS/KID ST7 .....36 A3
Oldcourt St BURS/TUN ST6 .....44 D5
Oldfield Av BURS/TUN ST6 .....45 H1
Oldfield Dr STONE ST15 .....91 F5
Oldfield St STOKE ST4 .....69 G2
Old Hall Dr NEWUL ST5 .....51 G1
Old Hall St HAN ST1 .....5 F4
Oldham St HAN ST1 .....5 H6
Oldhill Cl ALS/KID ST7 .....43 E1
Old Knutsford Rd ALS/KID ST7 .....23 H3
Old Liverpool Rd NEWUL ST5 .....58 C2
Oldmill St STOKE ST4 .....3 K3
Old Rectory Rd STONE ST15 .....91 E5
Old Rd ALS/KID ST7 .....41 G5
    BARL ST12 .....86 C5
    STOKE ST4 .....61 E5
Old Road St STONE ST15 * 90 D2
Old Town Rd HAN ST1 .....5 F1
Old Tramway STOKE ST4 .....69 F2
Oldway Pl STONE ST15 .....70 A2
Old Whart Pl HAN ST1 .....5 G4
Old Whieldon Rd STOKE ST4 .....68 C1
Oliver Rd STOKE ST4 .....3 J7
Olof Palme Gv LNGTN ST3 .....70 A1
Omega Wy STOKE ST4 .....78 A2

Onsetter Rd BUCK/MIL ST2 ....63 F5
Onslow Dr NEWUL ST5 ....51 H1
Ontario Cl STONE ST4 ....11 H5
Opal Rd STOKE ST4 ....69 E2
Orb St HAN ST1 ....4 E5
Orchard Cl STONE ST15 ....90 C4
Orchard Crs ALS/KID ST7 ....34 D2
Orchard Gdns LEEK ST13 ....30 B5
Orchard Pl BARL ST12 ....86 D4
Orchard Ri BLYBR/FOR ST11 ....82 A3
The Orchards LNGTN ST3 ....69 E5
Orchard St NEWUL ST5 ....52 A4
Orchid Gv STOKE ST4 ....3 K2
Orford Rd END/WER ST9 ....39 H4
Orford St BURS/TUN ST6 ....52 B2
Orford Wy LNGTN ST3 ....79 E2
Orgreaves Cl NEWUL ST5 ....51 C1
Orgreave St BURS/TUN ST6 ....53 F1
Oriel St STOKE ST4 ....61 E5
Orion Ct NEWUL ST5 ....59 F4
Orion St BURS/TUN ST6 ....45 G5
Orkney Av ALS/KID ST7 ....36 D3
Orlestone Pl BURS/TUN ST6 ....37 F4
Orme Rd BIDD ST8 ....15 F4
Orme St BURS/TUN ST6 ....52 C1
Ormonde St STOKE ST4 ....69 F2
Orpheus Gv HAN ST1 ....54 A3
Orwell Dr NEWUL ST5 ....59 G2
Orwell Pl NEWUL ST5 ....59 D2
Orwell Pl NEWUL ST5 ....66 D3
Osborne Rd STOKE ST4 ....3 K4
Osborne St LEEK ST13 ....31 F5
Osbourne Rd STOKE ST4 ....69 F2
Oslo Gv HAN ST1 ....54 A5
Osprey Av ALS/KID ST7 ....81 E3
Osprey Vw ALS/KID ST7 ....26 B5
Ostend Pl NEWUL ST5 ....66 B1
Oswald Av LNGTN ST3 ....71 F4
Oulton Dr CONG CW12 ....7 F4
Oulton Ms STONE ST15 ....90 D2
Oulton Rd BURS/TUN ST6 * 37 F4
CDLE ST10 ....75 F4
STONE ST15 ....90 D1
Outclough Rd BIDD ST8 ....7 H1
Ovaldene Wy STOKE ST4 ....78 D3
The Oval LNGTN ST3 ....69 G5
Overdale Pl LEEK ST13 ....30 A4
Overhouse St BURS/TUN ST6 ....44 A1
Overland Dr BURS/TUN ST6 ....38 C5
Oversley Rd BURS/TUN ST6 ....37 E4
Over The Hl BIDD ST8 ....20 C3
Overton Cl STOKE ST4 ....8 A4
Overwood Pl BURS/TUN ST6 ....53 H2
Oxford Av HAN ST1 ....53 H2
Oxford Crs STOKE ST4 ....61 E5
Oxford Rd BURS/TUN ST6 ....37 F4
NEWUL ST5 ....60 B3
Oxford St STOKE ST4 ....61 E5
Oxhay Vw NEWUL ST5 ....60 A1
Ox-Hey Crs BIDD ST8 ....19 H4
Ox-Hey Dr BIDD ST8 ....19 H5

P

Pacific Rd STOKE ST4 ....78 B5
Packett St STONE ST4 ....69 H5
Pack Horse La BURS/TUN ST6 ....52 C1
Paddock Rd STOKE ST4 ....78 A4
The Paddock CDLE ST10 ....74 D5
SBCH CW11 ....14 B4
Padgbury Cl CONG CW12 ....11 G1
Padgbury La CONG CW12 ....7 F2
Padston Dr ALS/KID ST7 ....22 C5
Padstow Wy STOKE ST4 ....78 B5
Padworth St LNGTN ST3 ....71 E4
Paladin Av NEWUL ST5 ....71 F3
Palatine Av NEWUL ST5 ....50 C5
Pall Mall HAN ST1 * 4 E4
Palmers Gn STOKE ST4 ....3 H4
Palmerston St HAN ST1 ....5 C7
NEWUL ST5 ....52 A4
Palmerston Wy BIDD ST8 ....19 H5
Palmer St LNGTN ST3 ....70 B5
Palmers Wy STOKE ST4 ....80 A2
Palomino Cl LNGTN ST3 ....54 B5
Pandora Gv HAN ST1 ....54 B5
Panturner Rd BUCK/MIL ST2 ....63 E5
Paradise St BURS/TUN ST6 ....44 B5
Paragon Av NEWUL ST5 ....66 D4
Paragon Cl CDLE ST10 ....74 C5
Paragon Rd BURS/TUN ST6 ....70 B4
Paris Av NEWUL ST5 ....50 B5
Parish Cl ALS/KID ST7 ....22 D4
Park Av ALS/KID ST7 ....35 E5
CDLE ST10 ....75 E5
LNGTN ST3 ....71 E2
NEWUL ST5 ....52 A4
STONE ST15 ....90 D2
Park Bank CONG CW12 ....8 D5
Park Cl AUD/MAD/WD ST4 ....56 A4
Park Ct NEWUL ST5 * 51 E2
Park Dr BARL ST12 ....86 C4
CDLE ST10 ....75 F3
STONE ST15 ....77 G5
Parkend BLYBR/FOR ST11 ....82 C2
Parker-Jervis Rd LNGTN ST3 ....70 D3
Parker St HAN ST1 ....4 D3
Park Farm Wy BURS/TUN ST6 ....86 B4
Parkfield Rd STOKE ST4 ....80 A1
Parkfields END/WER ST9 ....39 H4
Parkfields Cl BARL ST12 ....86 C4
NEWUL ST5 ....58 A2
Park Hall Av LNGTN ST3 ....71 G5
Park Hall Crs LNGTN ST3 ....71 E3
Park Hall Rd LNGTN ST3 ....70 C2
Park Hall St LNGTN ST3 ....70 A3
Parkhead Crs LNGTN ST3 ....71 E4
Parkhead Dr LNGTN ST3 ....71 E3
Parkhead Gv LNGTN ST3 ....71 E3
Park House Dr STONE ST15 ....91 F4

Parkhouse Rd East
NEWUL ST5 ....43 E5
Parkhouse Rd West
NEWUL ST5 ....43 E5
Park La HAN ST1 ....4 C6
Parklands ALS/KID ST7 ....35 H2
BIDD ST8 ....20 D4
The Parklands CONG CW12 ....9 E5
Park La ALS/KID ST7 ....40 C1
BIDD ST8 ....27 G2
CDLE ST10 ....74 C3
CONG CW12 ....8 D5
Park Lane Cl CDLE ST10 ....74 C4
Park Pl STOKE ST4 ....69 E1
Park Rd BURS/TUN ST6 ....45 E5
CONG CW12 ....8 C4
LEEK ST13 ....31 G2
NEWUL ST5 ....58 B5
STOKE ST4 ....76 B1
Parkside STOKE ST4 ....78 B5
Parkside Crs END/WER ST9 ....39 H3
Parkside Dr NEWUL ST5 ....60 B1
Parkside Gv NEWUL ST5 ....60 B1
The Parks STOKE ST4 ....78 D5
Park St STOKE ST4 ....69 F1
Park Vw BLYBR/FOR ST11 ....82 A4
CONG CW12 * 8 C2
Parkview Cl LNGTN ST3 ....69 E5
Park View Rd ALS/KID ST7 ....47 E4
Park View Rd ALS/KID ST7 ....25 G5
Park Wy BLYBR/FOR ST11 ....82 A4
Parkway STOKE ST4 ....77 G3
STONE ST15 ....91 F4
The Parkway HAN ST1 ....5 F7
Parkwood Av STOKE ST4 ....77 H5
Parliament Rw HAN ST1 ....5 F3
Parliament St HAN ST1 ....5 F3
Parsonage St BURS/TUN ST6 ....44 B2
Parson St CONG CW12 ....8 A5
Parton Gv STOKE ST4 ....71 E5
Partridge Cl CONG CW12 ....12 C1
LNGTN ST3 ....81 E3
Patch Meadow Rd CDLE ST10 ....74 B4
Patrick Pl BIDD ST8 ....37 F1
Patterdale St BURS/TUN ST6 ....45 E3
Pavilion Dr HAN ST1 ....4 A1
Pavilion Wy CONG CW12 ....7 H4
Paxton St HAN ST1 ....5 G6
Paynter St STOKE ST4 ....69 F2
Peacehaven St STOKE ST4 ....78 C5
Peacock Hay Rd ALS/KID ST7 ....43 E2
Peacock Cl STOKE ST4 ....76 D2
Peacock Rd NEWUL ST5 ....51 F4
Peacock Vw STOKE ST4 ....62 B3
Peak Dale Av BURS/TUN ST6 ....35 H4
Peake St NEWUL ST5 ....59 E1
Pear Lee LEEK ST13 ....31 F4
Pearl Gv LNGTN ST3 ....81 E2
Pear Pl BUCK/MIL ST2 ....63 F5
Pearson Dr STONE ST15 ....91 F4
Pear Tree La NEWUL ST5 ....50 D1
Pear Tree Rd ALS/KID ST7 ....41 H5
Peascroft Rd BURS/TUN ST6 ....45 H2
Pebble Mill St HAN ST1 ....60 D1
Peckforton Vw ALS/KID ST7 ....35 G4
Peck Mill La BIDD ST8 ....37 G2
Pedley Gv BURS/TUN ST6 ....45 E3
Peebles Rd NEWUL ST5 ....57 H2
Peel Dr CONG CW12 ....11 H3
Peel Hollow ALS/KID ST7 ....40 C5
Peel La CONG CW12 ....12 A3
Peel St LNGTN ST3 ....71 E4
NEWUL ST5 ....52 A4
Pegasus Gv BURS/TUN ST6 ....45 H5
Peggy's Bank ALS/KID ST7 ....49 H1
Pegroy Gv BURS/TUN ST6 ....45 H4
Pelham St HAN ST1 ....5 G6
Pemberton Dr LNGTN ST3 ....81 E5
Pembridge Rd LNGTN ST3 ....79 E3
Pembroke Dr NEWUL ST5 ....2 A6
STOKE ST4 ....91 F4
Pembroke Rd BUCK/MIL ST2 ....46 C5
Penarth Gv HAN ST1 ....4 A1
Penarth Pl NEWUL ST5 ....2 B6
Pendine Gv HAN ST1 ....69 H1
Penfleet Av LNGTN ST3 ....81 E1
Pengrove Cl BURS/TUN ST6 ....36 C3
Penkhull New Rd STOKE ST4 ....69 E2
Penkhull Ter STOKE ST4 ....61 E5
Penk Rd BLYBR/FOR ST11 ....82 C3
Penkville St STOKE ST4 ....68 A2
Penmark Gv LNGTN ST3 ....80 C2
Pennere Dr END/WER ST9 ....64 A1
NEWUL ST5 ....77 E1
Pennell St BUCK/MIL ST2 ....54 D5
Pennine Wy BIDD ST8 ....20 A3
NEWUL ST5 ....59 E1
Pennington Cl LNGTN ST3 ....71 G5
Pennyfields Rd ALS/KID ST7 ....36 B5
Pennymore St STOKE ST4 ....78 B2
Penport Gv LNGTN ST3 ....69 G5
Penrhyn Av BURS/TUN ST6 ....45 F5
Penrith Cl STOKE ST4 ....78 C4
Penrith Ct CONG CW12 ....7 G5
NEWUL ST5 ....60 D1
Pensford Gv HAN ST1 ....54 B4
Pentland Gv NEWUL ST5 ....59 E1
Penton Pl LNGTN ST3 ....79 E5
Pen-y-Bont Wk BIDD ST8 ....28 A2
Penylan Cl STOKE ST4 ....78 C4
Perceval St HAN ST1 ....5 K1
Percival Dr END/WER ST9 ....47 E5
Percy James Cl ALS/KID ST7 ....23 C4
Percy St HAN ST1 ....5 F4
Peregrine Gv LNGTN ST3 ....81 E4
Perivale Cl HAN ST1 ....54 C3
Perkins St HAN ST1 ....36 A4
Perry Cl HAN ST1 ....5 G4
Perth St STOKE ST4 ....69 G2
Perthy Gv STOKE ST4 ....77 H5
Perton Wood Vw LNGTN ST3 ....69 F5

Petersfield Rd BURS/TUN ST6 ....37 E4
Petrel Gv LNGTN ST3 ....81 F3
Pevensey Gv LNGTN ST3 ....70 A1
Philip St STOKE ST4 ....69 E1
Phillips Cl STONE ST15 ....91 G4
Phillipson Wy BURS/TUN ST6 ....53 H1
Phoenix Cl BURS/TUN ST6 ....36 A1
Phoenix St BURS/TUN ST6 ....44 B3
Picasso Ri LNGTN ST3 ....81 F4
Piccadilly HAN ST1 ....5 F3
Piccadilly Ar HAN ST1 * 4 E3
Piccadilly St BURS/TUN ST6 ....44 B3
Pickering Cl LNGTN ST3 ....79 C1
Pickfords Yd ALS/KID ST7 * 24 D5
Pickmere Cl BUCK/MIL ST2 ....46 D3
Pickwick Pl ALS/KID ST7 ....34 D1
Pickwood Av LEEK ST13 ....31 F4
Pickwood Cl LEEK ST13 ....31 F4
Picton St HAN ST1 ....5 H4
LEEK ST13 ....30 C3
Pidduck St BURS/TUN ST6 ....52 C2
Pierce St BURS/TUN ST6 ....44 B3
Piggott Gv BUCK/MIL ST2 ....46 D2
Pikemere Rd ALS/KID ST7 ....22 D3
Pilkington Av NEWUL ST5 ....66 C1
Pillar Cl BUCK/MIL ST2 ....63 F5
Pilsbury St NEWUL ST5 ....59 G1
Pilsden Pl BLYBR/FOR ST11 ....81 C3
Pine Cl ALS/KID ST7 ....54 C4
Pine Ct BLYBR/FOR ST11 ....81 H2
Pinehurst Cl NEWUL ST5 ....66 D4
Pine Rd STOKE ST4 ....68 C3
Pinetree Dr BLYBR/FOR ST11 ....81 H5
Pinewood Crs LNGTN ST3 ....81 E1
Pinewood Gv BLYBR/FOR ST11 ....82 C4
NEWUL ST5 ....43 E5
LEEK ST13 ....30 D2
Pinfold Av BURS/TUN ST6 ....45 H2
Pingle La STONE ST15 ....79 C4
Pinhoe Pl LNGTN ST3 ....70 C4
Pinnox St BURS/TUN ST6 ....44 C4
Pioneer Pl BURS/TUN ST6 * 45 C3
The Pippins NEWUL ST5 ....67 E4
Pireford Pl NEWUL ST5 ....45 H5
Pirehill Rd NEWUL ST5 ....70 B3
Pirie Cl CONG CW12 ....9 E5
Pirie Rd CONG CW12 ....9 E5
Pitcairn St BURS/TUN ST6 ....44 C3
Pitcher La LEEK ST13 ....31 F4
Pitfield Av NEWUL ST5 ....60 B1
Pitgreen La NEWUL ST5 ....52 A3
Pit La ALS/KID ST7 ....42 C1
Pitsford St LNGTN ST3 ....70 C5
Pitts Hill Bank BURS/TUN ST6 ....44 D1
Pitt St East BURS/TUN ST6 ....53 F1
Plainfield Gv BUCK/MIL ST2 ....63 F4
The Plaisaunce NEWUL ST5 ....66 D1
Plane Gv NEWUL ST5 ....43 E5
Plantation Rd STOKE ST4 ....78 D4
Plant St CDLE ST10 ....75 E4
STONE ST15 ....70 A3
Platts Av END/WER ST9 ....39 C5
Pleasant St BURS/TUN ST6 ....53 H1
Plex St BURS/TUN ST6 ....44 A3
The Plex ALS/KID ST7 ....23 F4
Pleydell St HAN ST1 ....54 B2
Plough Cft ALS/KID ST7 ....22 C5
Plough St HAN ST1 ....53 H4
Plover Cl LNGTN ST3 ....81 E3
Plover Dr BIDD ST8 ....20 A5
Plumtree Gv HAN ST1 ....54 B3
Plymouth Gv NEWUL ST5 ....51 F2
Pochard Cl BURS/TUN ST6 ....45 C4
Podmore Av ALS/KID ST7 ....49 H3
Podmore La ALS/KID ST7 ....49 G3
Podmore St BURS/TUN ST6 ....53 E2
Pointon Gv BURS/TUN ST6 ....46 C1
Polperro Wy LNGTN ST3 ....81 E3
Pomona Ri BURS/TUN ST6 ....53 H1
Pool Dam NEWUL ST5 ....2 C4
Poole Av BUCK/MIL ST2 ....48 D4
Pooles La SBCH CW11 ....10 A3
Pooles Rd BIDD ST8 ....20 D5
Poolfield Av NEWUL ST5 ....59 F4
Poolfield Av North NEWUL ST5 ....2 A4
Poolfields Av BURS/TUN ST6 ....59 F4
Poolfields Cl NEWUL ST5 ....59 F4
Poolhill Cl LNGTN ST3 ....69 G5
Pool Side ALS/KID ST7 ....16 B5
Poolside NEWUL ST5 ....2 B5
STOKE ST4 ....69 H1
Poplar Av NEWUL ST5 ....59 C1
Poplar Cl BLYBR/FOR ST11 ....82 C4
CONG CW12 ....7 G3
NEWUL ST5 ....59 C1
STONE ST15 ....90 C4
Poplar Ct NEWUL ST5 ....59 C1
Poplar Dr ALS/KID ST7 ....35 G1
NEWUL ST5 ....59 C1
Poplar Gv LNGTN ST3 ....69 E5
NEWUL ST5 ....3 C2
Poppyfields ALS/KID ST7 ....22 D5
Porlock Gv STOKE ST4 ....78 B4
Porthill Bank NEWUL ST5 ....52 B2
Porthill Rd NEWUL ST5 ....52 A2
Porthill Rd BURS/TUN ST6 ....52 B2
Portland Cl BLYBR/FOR ST11 ....81 H3
BIDD ST8 ....19 H5
BLYBR/FOR ST11 ....82 D2
Portland Gv NEWUL ST5 ....50 B5
Portland Ms NEWUL ST5 ....52 A2
Portland Pl BARL ST12 ....87 F1
Portland Rd LNGTN ST3 ....69 H3
Portland St HAN ST1 ....66 D4
LEEK ST13 ....31 E3
Portland St North LEEK ST13 * 31 E3
Portland St South LEEK ST13 * 31 E3
Port St BURS/TUN ST6 ....79 G1
Port Vale St BURS/TUN ST6 ....52 C2
Post La END/WER ST9 ....39 H5
Potteries Wy HAN ST1 ....4 E1
HAN ST1 ....4 E5

Potters End BIDD ST8 ....19 F4
Poulson St STOKE ST4 ....61 F5
Pound Gdns BURS/TUN ST6 ....45 H2
Poundsgate Gv STOKE ST4 ....78 B2
Povey Pl NEWUL ST5 ....36 C3
Powderham Cl LNGTN ST3 ....36 C3
Powell St HAN ST1 ....4 C1
Power Gv LNGTN ST3 ....35 G1
Powy Dr ALS/KID ST7 ....35 G1
Premier Gdns ALS/KID ST7 ....75 D1
Prestbury Av NEWUL ST5 ....76 D1
Preston St BURS/TUN ST6 ....53 G1
Pretoria Rd HAN ST1 ....4 A6
Primitive Cl NEWUL ST5 ....43 H5
Price St BURS/TUN ST6 ....44 C2
Priestley Dr LNGTN ST3 ....70 B5
Priesty Ct CONG CW12 ....8 B5
Priesty Flds CONG CW12 ....8 C5
Prime St HAN ST1 ....5 K1
Primitive St ALS/KID ST7 ....26 A1
Primrose Gv NEWUL ST5 ....60 A2
Primrose Hl STOKE ST4 ....68 A5
Prince Charles Av LEEK ST13 ....31 C2
Prince George St CDLE ST10 ....74 D4
Prince's Rd STOKE ST4 ....60 D4
Princess Av ALS/KID ST7 ....41 F5
LEEK ST13 ....31 G1
Princess Dr LNGTN ST3 ....71 F4
Princess Sq ALS/KID ST7 * 32 B5
Princess St ALS/KID ST7 ....42 D1
BIDD ST8 ....27 H1
CONG CW12 ....8 B4
NEWUL ST5 ....59 E1
Prince's St STONE ST15 ....90 D3
Prince St LEEK ST13 ....31 E3
Princetown Cl LNGTN ST3 ....81 E3
Priorfield Cl LNGTN ST3 ....69 H5
Priory Av LEEK ST13 ....31 F3
Priory Cl CONG CW12 ....11 H3
Priory Rd BUCK/MIL ST2 ....54 D5
NEWUL ST5 ....2 B7
STONE ST15 ....90 D3
Prospect Rd LEEK ST13 ....30 D2
Prospect St BURS/TUN ST6 ....53 C2
Prospect Ter NEWUL ST5 ....2 B2
Providence St NEWUL ST5 ....53 H4
Provost Pl LEEK ST13 ....31 F2
Puddle Bank La CONG CW12 ....12 D5
Pullman Cl CDLE ST10 ....74 C5
Pump Bank NEWUL ST5 ....57 H5
Pump St LEEK ST13 ....31 E5
STOKE ST4 ....61 E5
Purbeck St BURS/TUN ST6 ....53 G2
Purser Crs NEWUL ST5 ....51 H4
Pyenest St HAN ST1 ....4 C7

Q

Quabbs La BLYBR/FOR ST11 ....83 E2
The Quadrangle END/WER ST9 ....39 H4
Quadrant Rd HAN ST1 ....4 E2
The Quadrant HAN ST1 * 5 E2
Quail Gv LNGTN ST3 ....81 E3
Quarry Av STOKE ST4 ....80 D4
Quarry Bank Rd NEWUL ST5 ....57 H4
Quarry Cl BUCK/MIL ST2 ....47 E3
Quarry Gv NEWUL ST5 ....57 H4
Quarry Ter ALS/KID ST7 ....55 G2
Quayside CONG CW12 ....12 C1
Queen Anne St STOKE ST4 ....78 A1
Queen Mary Rd STOKE ST4 ....78 A1
Queen Mary's Dr BARL ST12 ....87 E1
Queen's Av BURS/TUN ST6 ....44 C5
Queensberry Rd LNGTN ST3 ....70 B5
Queens Ct NEWUL ST5 ....2 E2
Queen's Dr BIDD ST8 ....27 H2
LEEK ST13 ....31 E3
Queensmead Rd LNGTN ST3 ....80 D3
Queens Pde NEWUL ST5 * 2 D3
Queens Park Av LNGTN ST3 ....79 H1
Queen's Rd BUCK/MIL ST2 ....54 C5
Queens Sq STONE ST15 ....90 D5
Queens Ter HAN ST1 ....5 H3
Queen St ALS/KID ST7 ....55 G1
ALS/KID ST7 ....41 E5
BURS/TUN ST6 ....52 D1
CDLE ST10 ....75 E4
LEEK ST13 ....31 E3
NEWUL ST5 ....2 E2
NEWUL ST5 ....51 H3
Queensway ALS/KID ST7 ....22 D5
BURS/TUN ST6 ....52 B3
STONE ST15 ....90 A4
Quinta Rd CONG CW12 ....7 H4
Quinton Gv NEWUL ST5 ....51 H5
Quinton Wk BURS/TUN ST6 ....45 G4

R

Rabone St BURS/TUN ST6 ....44 C3
Race Course NEWUL ST5 ....58 C3
Racecourse Rd STOKE ST4 ....68 A3
Rachel Gv STOKE ST4 ....69 H1
Radford Cl STOKE ST4 ....68 B3
Radford Rd STOKE ST4 ....3 K2
Radford St STOKE ST4 ....78 A1
Radley Wy END/WER ST9 ....64 B1
Radnor Cl CONG CW12 ....7 H4
Radway Green Rd
CW/SW CW2 ....32 A3
Raglan St LNGTN ST3 ....79 G1
Railton Av LNGTN ST3 ....79 G1
Railway Cl LNGTN ST3 ....70 D5
Railway Pas LEEK ST13 ....31 E5
Railway Rd BURS/TUN ST6 ....70 D5
Railway St BURS/TUN ST6 ....44 C4

Railway Ter LNGTN ST3 ....70 A4
Rainford Cl ALS/KID ST7 ....36 D2
Rainham Gv BURS/TUN ST6 ....37 E5
Rakeway Rd CDLE ST10 ....85 E1
Ralph Dr HAN ST1 ....54 A2
Ramage Gv LNGTN ST3 ....80 B1
Ramsay Cl BARL ST12 ....79 E5
Ramsey Rd NEWUL ST5 ....59 G2
Ramsey St STOKE ST4 ....68 C2
Ramshaw Gv LNGTN ST3 ....54 B5
Ramshaw Vw LEEK ST13 ....31 F1
Randle's Vw CONG CW12 ....13 G2
Ranelagh St HAN ST1 ....4 E5
Rangeley Vw STONE ST15 ....90 B5
Rangemore Ter NEWUL ST5 ....60 B1
Ransome Pl LNGTN ST3 ....70 C3
Ranworth Cl NEWUL ST5 ....66 D5
Rathbone Av NEWUL ST5 ....60 B1
Rattigan Dr LNGTN ST3 ....80 C2
Ratton St HAN ST1 ....5 A1
Ravenna Wy LNGTN ST3 ....70 C5
Ravenscliffe Rd ALS/KID ST7 ....35 G3
Ravens Cl ALS/KID ST7 ....41 G3
Raven's La ALS/KID ST7 ....41 E3
Ravenswood Cl NEWUL ST5 ....66 C4
Rawle Cl CDLE ST10 ....74 C4
Rawlins St HAN ST1 ....5 J1
Rayleigh Wy BUCK/MIL ST2 ....63 F3
Raymond Av HAN ST1 ....53 H2
Raymond St HAN ST1 ....53 H1
Reades La CONG CW12 ....13 F2
Reading Wy BUCK/MIL ST2 ....63 F3
Reads Rd STOKE ST4 ....62 B4
Rebecca St STOKE ST4 ....69 F1
Recorder Gv BLYBR/FOR ST11 ....37 F5
Recreation Rd LNGTN ST3 ....70 C5
Rectory Gdns ALS/KID ST7 ....34 D5
Rectory Rd HAN ST1 ....4 C6
Rectory St HAN ST1 ....4 C6
Rectory Vw ALS/KID ST7 ....34 D5
Red Bank LNGTN ST3 ....80 A1
Redbridge Cl STOKE ST4 ....77 H1
Redcar Rd STOKE ST4 ....78 A3
Reddish Av CONG CW12 ....8 B5
Red Hall La ALS/KID ST7 ....42 D4
Redheath Cl NEWUL ST5 ....57 H2
Redhill Dr CDLE ST10 ....85 E5
Redhills STONE ST15 ....91 E2
Redhills Rd BUCK/MIL ST2 ....54 C2
Red House Crs LNGTN ST3 ....69 C4
Redland Dr BUCK/MIL ST2 ....54 C2
The Redlands STONE ST15 ....91 E1
Red La BUCK/MIL ST2 ....47 E4
Red Lion Cl ALS/KID ST7 ....34 D4
Red Lion Pas HAN ST1 ....4 C3
Redman Gv BURS/TUN ST6 ....53 G2
Redmine Cl NEWUL ST5 ....51 F5
Redrock Crs ALS/KID ST7 ....36 A2
Redwing Dr BIDD ST8 ....20 A5
Redwood Av STOKE ST15 ....91 E5
Redwood Pl LNGTN ST3 ....80 D1
Reedbed Cl BURS/TUN ST6 ....45 G3
Reedham Wy BUCK/MIL ST2 * 63 F3
Reeves Av BURS/TUN ST6 ....45 E3
STONE ST15 ....59 H1
Refinery St HAN ST1 ....2 E5
Regency Cl ALS/KID ST7 ....42 D1
Regency Dr END/WER ST9 ....47 E2
Regent Av LNGTN ST3 ....80 B1
Regent Rd HAN ST1 ....5 F6
Regent St LEEK ST13 ....31 F3
STOKE ST4 ....67 H2
STONE ST15 ....90 C2
Reginald Mitchell Wy
LNGTN ST3 ....44 A2
Reginald St BURS/TUN ST6 * 53 E1
Regina St BURS/TUN ST6 ....53 E1
Reid St BURS/TUN ST6 ....52 C1
Rembrandt Wy LNGTN ST3 ....81 F4
Remer St BURS/TUN ST6 * 53 F1
Renard Wy LNGTN ST3 ....81 F3
Rendel Gv STONE ST15 ....90 B1
Renfrew Wy NEWUL ST5 ....59 F4
Renknown Cl NEWUL ST5 ....78 A1
Renown Cl BUCK/MIL ST2 ....62 B3
Repington Rd HAN ST1 ....54 A1
Repton Dr NEWUL ST5 ....66 B2
Reservoir Rd LNGTN ST3 ....70 C5
Reynolds Av NEWUL ST5 ....51 E5
Reynolds Rd BURS/TUN ST6 ....45 E5
Rhodes St HAN ST1 ....53 H1
Rhondda Av BURS/TUN ST6 ....44 B3
Rialto Rd BURS/TUN ST6 ....44 B3
Ribble Dr BIDD ST8 ....66 D5
Ribble Dr BIDD ST8 ....20 A5
Ribblesdale Av CONG CW12 ....9 E2
Ricardo St LNGTN ST3 ....79 H1
Riceyman Rd NEWUL ST5 ....43 H5
Richards Av BURS/TUN ST6 ....44 C3
Richardson Pl BURS/TUN ST6 ....37 F5
Richmond Av HAN ST1 ....53 C2
Richmond Dr NEWUL ST5 ....59 G2
Richmond Rd STOKE ST4 ....77 H1
Riddings Bank STOKE ST4 ....76 D5
Ridge Cl BARL ST12 ....86 D5
Ridge Crs LNGTN ST3 ....80 D4
Ridge Cft BIDD ST8 ....20 D4
Ridgecliffe BIDD ST8 ....20 D4
Ridge Hill Dr
AUD/MAD/WD CW3 ....56 D5
Ridgehouse Dr HAN ST1 ....4 C1
Ridge Rd BURS/TUN ST6 ....36 B5
Ridgmont Rd NEWUL ST5 ....51 H5
Ridgway Dr BLYBR/FOR ST11 ....81 H5
Ridgway Pl NEWUL ST5 ....51 E5
Ridgway Rd STOKE ST4 ....61 G3
Ridley St STOKE ST4 ....68 C2
Rigby Rd ALS/KID ST7 ....55 F4
Riley Av BURS/TUN ST6 ....45 F4
Riley St North BURS/TUN ST6 ....52 C1
Riley St South BURS/TUN ST6 ....52 D1

Rileys Wy ALS/KID ST7 ....41 H4
Rill St LNGTN ST3 ....69 H3
Rimini Cl LNGTN ST3 ....70 C2
Ringland Cl HAN ST1 ....5 H3
Ripon Av NEWUL ST5 ....72 B3
Ripon Rd LNGTN ST3 ....79 F2
Riseley Rd STOKE ST4 ....3 H4
Riverdale Dr BURS/TUN ST6 ....36 C3
Riverdane Rd STOKE ST4 ....8 D4
River Lea Ms AUD/MAD/W CW3 ...56 A5
Riverside Dr STOKE ST4 ....67 G5
Riversmead NEWUL ST5 ....66 D5
River St CONG CW12 ....8 B4
River Wy STONE ST15 ....90 D4
Rivington Crs BURS/TUN ST6 ....37 E5
Robert Heath St
  BURS/TUN ST6 * 45 G4
Roberts Av CONG CW12 ....59 C2
Roberts Cl ALS/KID ST7 ....49 H3
Robertson Dr NEWUL ST5 ....59 F1
Robertson Sq STOKE ST4 ....67 G3
Robert St BURS/TUN ST6 ....91 F5
Robertville Rd BUCK/MIL ST2 ...62 D1
Robina Dr CDLE ST10 ....75 E4
Robin Hl BIDD ST8 ....28 C1
Robin Hill Gv STONE ST15 ....69 H2
Robinson Av BURS/TUN ST6 ....53 H1
Robinson Rd STOKE ST4 ....77 H2
Robson St HAN ST1 ....4 D5
Roche Av LEEK ST13 ....31 F1
Rochester Rd LNGTN ST3 ....69 H2
Rochford Cl LEEK ST13 ....30 B4
Rockfield Av BUCK/MIL ST2 ....47 F5
Rock House Dr BARL ST12 ....86 D4
Rockside La ALS/KID ST7 ....34 C3
Rockside ALS/KID ST7 ....26 A2
Rode House Cl ALS/KID ST7 ....27 J1
The Rode ALS/KID ST7 ....23 F4
Rodgers Ct BURS/TUN ST6 * 36 A4
Rodgers St BURS/TUN ST6 ....36 A3
Roebuck St STOKE ST4 ....61 G4
Roe La NEWUL ST5 ....66 C5
Roe Pk CONG CW12 ....18 C4
Rogate Cl STOKE ST4 ....69 H1
Rogers Av NEWUL ST5 ....59 F1
Rogerstone Av STOKE ST4 ....67 G1
Rolfe Cl STOKE ST4 ....68 A5
Roma Cl LNGTN ST5 ....80 B2
Roman Dr NEWUL ST5 ....50 D4
Romer Side BUCK/MIL ST2 ....63 G4
Romford Pl LNGTN ST3 ....81 F3
Romney Av NEWUL ST5 ....51 C3
Ronald St LNGTN ST3 ....70 A5
Ronaldsway Dr NEWUL ST5 ....59 C2
Ronson Dr STOKE ST4 ....67 G3
Rood Hl CONG CW12 ....8 B4
Rood La CONG CW12 ....8 B4
Rookery Av LNGTN ST3 ....79 G1
Rookery La STOKE ST4 ....67 H4
Rookery Rd ALS/KID ST7 ....26 A5
The Rookery NEWUL ST5 ....58 C3
Roseacre NEWUL ST5 ....59 F5
Roseacre Gv LNGTN ST3 ....80 D4
Roseacre La BLYBR/FOR ST11...82 B4
Rose Bank St LEEK ST13 ....31 E3
Roseberry Dr
  AUD/MAD/W CW3 ....56 A5
Rosebery Cl BIDD ST8 ....20 A5
Rosebery St BURS/TUN ST6 ....44 D1
Roseland Crs BUCK/MIL ST2 ...46 D5
Rosemary Pl HAN ST1 ....54 A2
Rosendale Av NEWUL ST5 ....73 E3
Roseneath Pl BUCK/MIL ST2 ...46 D5
Rose St HAN ST1 ....5 J1
Rose Tree Av STOKE ST4 ....67 G5
Rosevale Ct NEWUL ST5 ....51 E1
Rosevale Rd NEWUL ST5 ....51 E1
Rosevale St BUCK/MIL ST2 ....46 D5
Roseville Dr CONG CW12 ....13 F2
Rosewood Av END/WER ST9 ....47 E2
Rossall Av NEWUL ST5 ....66 B3
Rossett Gv ALS/KID ST7 ....50 B4
Rosslyn Rd LNGTN ST3 ....70 A5
Rosvean Cl HAN ST1 ....4 E1
Rosy Bank BUCK/MIL ST2 ....47 E3
Rother Wk BURS/TUN ST6 ....45 E2
Rothesay Av NEWUL ST5 ....59 F5
Rothesay Rd LNGTN ST3 ....70 B5
Rothley Gn LNGTN ST3 ....79 F2
Rothsay Av HAN ST1 ....53 H1
Rothwell St STOKE ST4 ....67 H1
Rotterdam Av NEWUL ST5 ....59 F3
Rotterdam Rd NEWUL ST5 ....59 F3
Roughcote La LNGTN ST3 ....71 G1
Roughwood La SBCH CW11......14 C4
Roundfields BUCK/MIL ST2 ....47 E3
Roundway LNGTN ST3 ....68 D5
Roundwell St BURS/TUN ST6 ...44 B3
Rowanburn Cl LNGTN ST3 ....70 B2
Rowan Cl ALS/KID ST7 ....23 E2
  ALS/KID ST7 ....23 F5
  ALS/KID ST7 ....35 C5
  BIDD ST8 ....20 D5
  STONE ST15 ....90 D5
Rowan Gv LNGTN ST3 ....68 D4
Rowhurst Pl BURS/TUN ST6 ...45 G1
Rowhurst Pl BURS/TUN ST6 ...45 G1
Rowland St LNGTN ST3 ....79 H1
Rowley Av NEWUL ST5 ....72 B3
Row Moor Wy BURS/TUN ST6 ...46 A4
Rownall Pl LNGTN ST3 ....71 E5
Rownall Rd LNGTN ST3 ....71 E5
Rownall Vw LEEK ST13 ....30 B5
Roxburghe Av STOKE ST4 ....70 B5
Royal St STOKE ST4 ....69 C2
Royce Av BIDD ST8 ....27 F3
Roycroft Cl NEWUL ST5 ....51 H1
Royden Av HAN ST1 ....54 B5
Roylance St BURS/TUN ST6 ....45 E2
Royle St CONG CW12 ....8 B4
Royston Wk LNGTN ST3 ....70 A4
Royville St BURS/TUN ST6 ....53 H1
Ruabon Cl BIDD ST8 ....28 A2
Rubens Wy LNGTN ST3 ....81 F3

Rubian St STOKE ST4 * 69 F1
Rudyard Cl STOKE ST15 ....90 B1
Rudyard Gv NEWUL ST5 ....52 A5
Rudyard Rd BIDD ST8 ....20 D4
Rudyard Wy CDLE ST10 ....75 F3
Ruffin Ct STOKE ST15 ....91 F4
Rugby Cl NEWUL ST5 ....66 B2
Rugby Dr LNGTN ST3 ....79 H1
Runnymede STONE ST15 ....90 D5
Runnymede Cl BUCK/MIL ST2 ...62 D1
Rupert St BIDD ST8 ....19 C5
Rushcliffe Dr LNGTN ST3 ....81 F5
Rushmoor Gv
  BLYBR/FOR ST11 ....81 F3
Rushton Gv BURS/TUN ST6 ....53 E2
Rushton Rd BURS/TUN ST6 ....53 E5
Rushton Wy
  BLYBR/FOR ST11 ....82 C2
Ruskin Cl LNGTN ST3 ....70 B2
Ruskin Rd CONG CW12 ....8 A5
Rusper Cl HAN ST1 ....54 B3
Russell Av ALS/KID ST7 ....23 E5
Russell Cl CONG CW12 ....12 D2
Russell Pl BURS/TUN ST6 ....36 C5
Russell Rd BURS/TUN ST6 ....36 B5
Russell St LEEK ST13 ....30 D4
  LNGTN ST3 ....79 H1
  NEWUL ST5 ....52 A4
Russet Cl LNGTN ST3 ....81 E2
Rustington Av LNGTN ST3 ....70 C4
Ruston Av BURS/TUN ST6 ....37 F5
Rutherford Av NEWUL ST5 ....66 D4
Rutherford Pl STOKE ST4 ....3 J7
Ruthin Gv BIDD ST8 ....28 A2
Ruthin Rd BUCK/MIL ST2 ....63 F2
Rutland Cl CONG CW12 ....8 C5
Rutland Pl NEWUL ST5 ....67 E5
Rutland Rd ALS/KID ST7 ....35 G1
  LNGTN ST3 ....69 H5
Rutland St HAN ST1 ....4 C1
Ruxley Rd BUCK/MIL ST2 ....62 C1
Rydal Cl CONG CW12 ....7 G5
Rydal Wy ALS/KID ST7 ....23 E5
  NEWUL ST5 ....66 D3
Ryder Rd LNGTN ST3 ....81 E2
Rye Bank NEWUL ST5 ....2 D3
Rye Bank Crs NEWUL ST5 ....2 D3
Ryebrook Gv BURS/TUN ST6 ...36 D4
Rye Cl ALS/KID ST7 ....22 D5
Ryecroft NEWUL ST5 ....2 D2
Ryecroft Rd BURS/TUN ST6 ...46 A5
Ryedale Wy CONG CW12 ....1 F2
Ryehills ALS/KID ST7 ....41 C5
Ryeland Cl LNGTN ST3 ....80 A2

S

Sackville St STOKE ST4 ....3 H1
Saddler Av STONE ST15 ....91 F4
Saffron Cl STOKE ST4 ....81 E4
Sage Cl HAN ST1 ....5 F6
St Aidan's St BURS/TUN ST6 ...44 B2
St Andrews Crs HAN ST1 ....53 H2
St Andrews Dr ALS/KID ST7 ...46 C5
  NEWUL ST5 ....59 F4
St Andrews Gdns ALS/KID ST7 ...33 G1
St Andrew's Sq STOKE ST4 ....61 E4
St Anne's V BURS/TUN ST6 ....38 D3
St Ann St HAN ST1 ....5 H3
St Ann Wk HAN ST1 ....5 H3
St Anthony's Dr NEWUL ST5 ...59 F5
St Bartholomews Cl
  BURS/TUN ST6 ....46 A2
St Bernard Pl BUCK/MIL ST2 ...54 C4
St Bernards Pl BUCK/MIL ST2 ...54 C4
St Bernard's Rd NEWUL ST5 ...59 F2
St Chad's Cl STONE ST15 ....91 F4
St Chads Rd BURS/TUN ST6 ...44 C3
St Christopher Av STOKE ST4 ...3 K7
St Clair St LNGTN ST3 ....70 A5
St Davids Wy BIDD ST8 ....28 A2
St Edmund's Av NEWUL ST5 ...52 B2
St Edward St LEEK ST13 ....30 D3
St Gabriels Ct ALS/KID ST7 ....23 E5
St Georges Av
  BURS/TUN ST6 ....45 E2
  END/WER ST9 ....39 G5
St George's Av North
  NEWUL ST5 ....51 H4
St George's Av South
  NEWUL ST5 ....51 H4
St George's Av West
  NEWUL ST5 ....51 H4
St George's Crs STOKE ST4 ....78 A1
St George's Rd NEWUL ST5 ....2 B2
  STONE ST15 ....91 E5
St Gile's Rd NEWUL ST5 ....59 F2
St Gregory's Rd LNGTN ST3 ....69 G4
St Helier Cl NEWUL ST5 ....66 B4
St James Av CONG CW12 ....8 A5
St James Ct BIDD ST8 ....20 A2
St James Pl STOKE ST4 ....78 A1
St James St HAN ST1 ....4 D5
St John's Av NEWUL ST5 ....52 A5
  STONE ST15 ....67 G3
St Johns Pl BIDD ST8 ....27 H1
  NEWUL ST5 ....59 F2
St John's Rd BIDD ST8 ....27 H1
  CONG CW12 ....8 D2
St John's Sq BURS/TUN ST6 ...52 D1
St John's St HAN ST1 ....5 C1
St John's Wd ALS/KID ST7 ....35 F2
St Joseph St
  BURS/TUN ST6 * 36 A4
St Lucy's Dr NEWUL ST5 ....52 A2
St Luke's St NEWUL ST5 ....58 B2
St Margarets Ct
  BLYBR/FOR ST11 * 83 C5
St Margaret's Dr HAN ST1 ....54 A1
St Margarets Gv LNGTN ST3 ...69 E4
St Mark's Cl HAN ST1 ....4 D6
St Marks St HAN ST1 ....4 D6

St Martin's La LNGTN ST3 ....70 A3
St Martin's Rd ALS/KID ST7 ....43 E1
  NEWUL ST5 ....59 F4
St Marys Cl ALS/KID ST7 ....23 E5
St Mary's Dr NEWUL ST5 ....2 A4
St Mary's Rd LNGTN ST3 ....70 B2
  NEWUL ST5 ....52 B3
St Matthew St STOKE ST4 ....69 F1
St Michaels Cl STONE ST15 * ...91 E5
St Michaels Mt STONE ST15 ....91 F5
St Michael's Rd
  BURS/TUN ST6 ....44 D1
  NEWUL ST5 ....59 H1
St Nicholas Av BURS/TUN ST6 ...46 A2
St Patrick's Dr NEWUL ST5 ....59 F4
St Paul's Ct LNGTN ST3 ....69 F5
St Paul's Rd NEWUL ST5 ....2 A3
St Paul St BURS/TUN ST6 ....52 C1
St Peters Rd CONG CW12 ....12 C1
St Saviour's St ALS/KID ST7 ....34 D2
St Thomas Pl STOKE ST4 ....67 H1
St Thomas St ALS/KID ST7 ....26 B1
St Vincent Pl NEWUL ST5 * 59 E2
St Vincent Rd STONE ST15 ....93 H5
Salcombe Pl HAN ST1 ....50 D1
Salem St HAN ST1 ....4 C4
Salisbury Av HAN ST1 ....61 Q3
Salisbury Cl
  AUD/MAD/W CW3 ....56 B5
Salisbury St BURS/TUN ST6 ....44 C5
  STONE ST15 ....30 D5
Salkeld Pl BURS/TUN ST6 ....45 F1
Salop Gv NEWUL ST5 ....67 E3
Salop Pl ALS/KID ST7 ....25 G5
Salters Cl END/WER ST9 ....64 B3
Salters La END/WER ST9 ....64 B1
Sampson St HAN ST1 ....4 D2
Samuel St ALS/KID ST7 ....26 A5
Sandbach Rd North
  ALS/KID ST7 ....23 E5
Sandbach Rd South
  ALS/KID ST7 ....23 F5
Sandcrest Pl LNGTN ST3 ....80 C1
Sandford St LNGTN ST3 * 70 A2
  NEWUL ST5 ....59 F4
Sandgate St LNGTN ST3 ....70 B4
Sandhurst Av LNGTN ST3 ....80 D1
Sandhurst Cl NEWUL ST5 ....51 H4
Sandhurst Pl NEWUL ST5 ....80 D2
Sandiway Pl HAN ST1 * 54 A3
Sandon Av NEWUL ST5 ....66 C2
Sandon Old Rd LNGTN ST3 ....80 D3
Sandon Rd LNGTN ST3 ....80 D5
Sandon St HAN ST1 ....4 B4
  LEEK ST13 ....30 D5
Sandown Pl ALS/KID ST7 ....23 E5
Sandown Rd BURS/TUN ST6 ...47 E4
Sandra Cl BURS/TUN ST6 ....45 E4
Sandringham Crs STOKE ST4 ...78 A1
Sandringham Rd CONG CW12......8 D5
Sandsdown Cl BIDD ST8 ....19 G4
Sandside Rd ALS/KID ST7 ....22 C5
Sands La BURS/TUN ST6 ....28 C5
Sands Rd ALS/KID ST7 ....26 C2
Sandwell Pl LNGTN ST3 ....80 C2
Sandwick Crs HAN ST1 ....54 B4
Sandwood Crs LNGTN ST3 ....70 A2
Sandyfield Ct BIDD ST8 ....19 C4
Sandyfield Rd HAN ST1 ....5 K1
Sandylands Crs ALS/KID ST7 ...23 H5
Sandy La BUCK/MIL ST2 ....47 E4
  BURS/TUN ST6 ....38 D5
  CONG CW12 ....6 D4
  CONG CW12 ....12 C2
  CONG CW12 ....11 E5
  NEWUL ST5 ....60 A2
Sandy Rd BIDD ST8 ....19 G5
  BURS/TUN ST6 ....36 B4
Sangster La BURS/TUN ST6 ...45 H4
Sant St BURS/TUN ST6 ....52 C1
The Saplings NEWUL ST5 ....67 E4
Saracen Wy LNGTN ST3 ....81 E1
Sargeant Av BURS/TUN ST6 ...52 B2
Sark Cl NEWUL ST5 ....66 A3
Sark Pl LNGTN ST3 ....70 B1
Sarver La CDLE ST10 ....73 E5
Saturn Rd BURS/TUN ST6 ....38 D5
Saunders Rd NEWUL ST5 ....53 H5
Sawyer Dr BIDD ST8 ....19 G4
Saxifrage Dr STONE ST15 ....91 F5
Scarlett St NEWUL ST5 ....52 A1
Scarratt Cl BLYBR/FOR ST11 ...82 D2
Scarratt Dr BLYBR/FOR ST11 ...82 D2
Sceptre St HAN ST1 ....4 E5
School Cl ALS/KID ST7 ....42 A5
  LEEK ST13 ....30 B5
School La BIDD ST8 ....20 D3
  BLYBR/FOR ST11 ....71 H5
  CDLE ST10 ....73 F3
  CONG CW12 ....11 H2
  LNGTN ST3 ....79 G2
School Rd BUCK/MIL ST2 ....54 C4
School St LNGTN ST3 ....30 D5
  NEWUL ST5 ....51 F5
  NEWUL ST5 ....57 H1
  STONE ST15 ....67 G4
Scot Hay Rd ALS/KID ST7 ....49 G5
Scotia Rd BURS/TUN ST6 ....44 D4
Scott Cl ALS/KID ST7 ....15 G5
Scott Lidgett Rd
  BURS/TUN ST6 ....52 B2
Scott Rd BURS/TUN ST6 ....44 D1
Scott St NEWUL ST5 ....2 E5
Scragg St ALS/KID ST7 ....25 H1
Scrimshaw Dr
  BURS/TUN ST6 ....45 F5
Scrivener Rd STOKE ST4 ....60 D3
Seabridge La NEWUL ST5 ....66 A5
Seabridge Rd NEWUL ST5 ....2 B6

Seaford St STOKE ST4 ....61 F3
Seagrave Av CDLE ST10 ....66 C1
Seagrave Pl NEWUL ST5 ....66 C5
Seaton Cl LNGTN ST3 ....80 C2
Sebring Av LNGTN ST3 ....80 C2
Second Av ALS/KID ST7 ....55 F5
  BUCK/MIL ST2 ....55 F5
  NEWUL ST5 ....52 A2
Sedbergh Cl NEWUL ST5 ....66 A3
Seddon Rd LNGTN ST3 ....80 C2
Seedfields Rd LNGTN ST3 ....69 E4
Sefton Av CONG CW12 ....13 E1
  HAN ST1 ....54 A2
Sefton Rd LNGTN ST3 ....70 C5
Selborne St HAN ST1 ....4 B4
Selborne Rd LNGTN ST3 ....30 D5
Selbourne Dr BURS/TUN ST6 ...36 C4
Selby Cl NEWUL ST5 ....66 C5
Selby St LNGTN ST3 ....71 F2
Selby Wy LNGTN ST3 ....79 E3
Selworthy Rd BURS/TUN ST6 ...46 C1
Selwyn St STOKE ST4 ....68 B1
Semper Cl CONG CW12 ....12 C5
Settle Gv LNGTN ST3 ....66 C5
Seven Arches Wy STOKE ST4 ...61 G5
Sevenoaks Cv LNGTN ST3 ....81 F4
Severn Cl BIDD ST8 ....20 C4
  CONG CW12 ....12 D1
Severn Dr NEWUL ST5 ....66 C5
Severn St HAN ST1 ....53 F4
Seymour St HAN ST1 ....5 J4
Shackleton Dr BURS/TUN ST6 ...44 A2
Shackson Cl HAN ST1 ....4 D7
Shady Gv ALS/KID ST7 ....23 F4
Shaftesbury Av
  NEWUL ST5 ....45 E4
Shakerley Av CONG CW12 ....8 D4
Shakespeare Cl LNGTN ST3 ...35 F3
  BUCK/MIL ST2 ....46 C4
Shakespeare Ct BIDD ST8 ....27 G1
Sheldon Av END/WER ST9 ....47 E2
Shallowford Ct HAN ST1 ....4 B3
Shannon Ct BURS/TUN ST6 * ...36 A4
Shannon Dr BURS/TUN ST6 ....35 H4
Shardlow Cl STOKE ST4 ....69 H5
  STONE ST15 ....91 F5
Sharman Cl STOKE ST4 ....60 D5
Sharron Dr LEEK ST13 ....31 F3
Shaw Pl LNGTN ST3 ....31 F5
Shawport Av NEWUL ST5 ....57 G1
Shaw St BIDD ST8 ....27 C1
  HAN ST1 ....4 B1
  NEWUL ST5 ....2 C2
Sheaf Pas LNGTN ST3 ....70 A4
Sheaf St HAN ST1 ....4 C6
Shearer St HAN ST1 ....4 C7
Sherford Rd NEWUL ST5 ....66 E3
Shelburne St STOKE ST4 ....68 A2
Sheldon Av CONG CW12 ....13 E1
Sheldon Gv NEWUL ST5 ....51 F3
Sheldrake Gv STOKE ST4 ....69 H1
Shelford Rd BURS/TUN ST6 ....36 D5
Shelley Cl ALS/KID ST7 ....15 G5
  ALS/KID ST7 ....35 F3
Shelley Dr CDLE ST10 ....74 C5
Shelley Rd LNGTN ST3 ....71 F2
Shelley Wd CDLE ST10 ....75 E5
Shelton Farm Rd HAN ST1 ....4 D7
Shelton New Rd HAN ST1 ....4 C7
  STOKE ST4 ....3 H5
Shelton Old Rd STOKE ST4 ....61 F4
Shemilt Crs BURS/TUN ST6 ....45 G5
Shenton St LNGTN ST3 ....70 B2
Shepherd St BIDD ST8 ....27 G1
Shepley Cl STONE ST15 ....91 F4
Shepley Gv LNGTN ST3 ....79 E3
Sheppard St STOKE ST4 ....68 A1
Sherborne Ct STOKE ST4 ....79 E5
Sherborne Dr NEWUL ST5 ....69 F5
Sheridan Gdns LNGTN ST3 ....69 F5
Sheridan Wy STONE ST15 ....91 H4
Sheriden Wy NEWUL ST5 ....59 E2
Sheringham Pl NEWUL ST5 ....52 B5
Sherratt Cl CONG CW12 ....8 C5
Sherratt St BURS/TUN ST6 ....45 G3
Sherwin Rd BURS/TUN ST6 ....44 D5
Sherwood Rd LNGTN ST3 ....80 D5
Shetland Rd HAN ST1 ....69 F4
Shillingford Dr STOKE ST4 ....78 B2
Shilton Cl STOKE ST4 ....67 H2
Shinwell Gv LNGTN ST3 ....81 E2
Shipley Pl BURS/TUN ST6 ....45 F5
Shirburn Rd LEEK ST13 ....31 F5
Shirley Rd HAN ST1 ....4 E6
Shirley St BURS/TUN ST6 ....52 B1
  LEEK ST13 ....30 D5
Shoobridge St LEEK ST13 ....31 E4
Shop La CONG CW12 ....2 C4
Short Bambury St LNGTN ST3 ...70 B1
Short St NEWUL ST5 ....70 B4
Shorwell Gv BURS/TUN ST6 ....44 D5
Shotsfield Pl BUCK/MIL ST2 ...46 C5
Shotsfield St BUCK/MIL ST2 ...46 C5
Showan Av NEWUL ST5 ....60 B1
Shrawley Rd ALS/KID ST7 ....48 C2
Shrewsbury Dr NEWUL ST5 ....43 E4
Shughborough Cl
  END/WER ST9 ....64 A2
Sidcot Pl HAN ST1 ....53 H2
Sideway Rd STOKE ST4 ....68 B3
Sidings Pl LNGTN ST3 ....80 H3
Sidings Rd STONE ST15 ....90 C2
The Sidings CDLE ST10 ....75 E4
  STONE ST15 ....91 E3
Sidmouth Av NEWUL ST5 ....51 E5
Silk St CONG CW12 ....8 C4
  LEEK ST13 ....30 D5
Sillitoe Pl STOKE ST4 ....68 A1
Silverbank Av BURS/TUN ST6 ...37 G5
Silver Cl BIDD ST8 ....19 G5
Silverdale Rd NEWUL ST5 ....2 A4
Silvergate Ct CONG CW12 ....12 C2
Silvermine Cl ALS/KID ST7 ....35 H1

Silver Rdg BARL ST12 ....86 C5
Silverstone Av CDLE ST10 ....75 E4
Silverstone Crs BURS/TUN ST6 ...36 C4
Silver St BURS/TUN ST6 ....46 A2
  CDLE ST10 ....75 F1
Silverton Cl NEWUL ST5 ....51 C1
Silverwood ALS/KID ST7 ....35 H2
Simeon St LNGTN ST3 ....91 F5
Simon Av STOKE ST4 ....3 K7
Simonburn Av STONE ST15 ....1 A3
Simon Pl STOKE ST4 ....61 F3
Simpson St HAN ST1 ....5 H7
  NEWUL ST5 ....51 H4
Sinclair Av ALS/KID ST7 ....22 D5
Siskin Pl LNGTN ST3 ....81 F3
Sitwell Gv LNGTN ST3 ....70 B5
Skellern Av BURS/TUN ST6 ....45 G5
Skellern St ALS/KID ST7 ....34 D1
Skipacre Av BURS/TUN ST6 ....45 G5
Skye Cl LNGTN ST3 ....70 C4
Slacken La ALS/KID ST7 ....34 B1
Slaidburn Gv HAN ST1 ....54 B4
Slaney St NEWUL ST5 ....3 F6
Slapton Cl BUCK/MIL ST2 ....62 B3
Slater St BIDD ST8 ....27 G1
  BURS/TUN ST6 ....46 A2
The Sleeve LEEK ST13 ....30 B5
Slindon Cl NEWUL ST5 ....42 D5
Slippery La HAN ST1 ....4 D4
Sloane Wy STOKE ST4 ....69 H1
Smallwood Cl NEWUL ST5 ....42 D5
Smallwood Gv HAN ST1 ....54 B3
Smith Child St BURS/TUN ST6 ...44 B2
Smith Cl ALS/KID ST7 ....22 D4
Smithfield Ct HAN ST1 ....4 E6
Smithpool Rd STOKE ST4 ....68 D2
Smiths Buildings
  LNGTN ST3 ....81 E1
Smiths Pas STOKE ST15 ....69 G2
Smith St LNGTN ST3 ....70 A3
Smithyfield Rd
  BURS/TUN ST6 ....45 H2
Smithy La BIDD ST8 ....19 H3
  CDLE ST10 ....84 D2
Smokies Wy BIDD ST8 ....19 C4
Sneyd Av LEEK ST13 ....30 D4
  NEWUL ST5 ....59 F5
Sneyd Crs NEWUL ST5 ....59 F5
Sneyd Hl BURS/TUN ST6 ....53 F1
Sneyd Pl BURS/TUN ST6 ....36 A5
Sneyd St NEWUL ST5 ....53 F5
  LEEK ST13 ....30 D4
Sneyd Ter NEWUL ST5 ....58 B2
Sneyd Wood Vw
  BURS/TUN ST6 ....53 C2
Sneyd Wy LNGTN ST3 ....71 F5
Snow Hl HAN ST1 ....4 C6
Soames Crs LNGTN ST3 ....69 H1
Solly Crs CONG CW12 ....7 G5
Solway Gv STOKE ST4 ....70 C3
Somerby Rd HAN ST1 ....54 B5
Somerset Av ALS/KID ST7 ....35 F1
Somerset Cl CONG CW12 ....13 E1
Somerset Rd HAN ST1 ....5 J5
Somerton Rd END/WER ST9 ....64 A1
Somerton Wy LNGTN ST3 ....70 B2
Somerville Av NEWUL ST5 ....60 B1
Sophia Wy NEWUL ST5 ....51 H1
Sorrel Cl BUCK/MIL ST2 ....62 C1
Sorrento Gv LNGTN ST3 ....70 C5
Soudern Wy LNGTN ST3 ....70 B5
Southall Wy BUCK/MIL ST2 ....62 C3
Southampton St HAN ST1 ....5 F1
South Bank Gv CONG CW12 ....8 D5
Southbank St LEEK ST13 ....31 E4
Southborough Crs
  BURS/TUN ST6 ....45 F2
South Cheshire Wy
  ALS/KID ST7 ....15 G4
Southdown Cl LNGTN ST3 ....80 A2
Southern Wy BURS/TUN ST6 ...45 H5
Southgate Av STOKE ST4 ....78 C4
Southlands Av LNGTN ST3 ....79 H1
  NEWUL ST5 ....60 A1
Southlands Cl LEEK ST13 ....30 B3
Southlands Rd CONG CW12 ....13 E1
South Pl BURS/TUN ST6 ....37 H5
South St ALS/KID ST7 ....54 D4
  BURS/TUN ST6 ....37 H5
South Ter NEWUL ST5 ....52 A4
  STOKE ST4 ....68 A3
South Vw BIDD ST8 ....19 C5
South Wk LNGTN ST3 ....81 F1
South Wolfe St BURS/TUN ST6 ...61 F5
Spalding Pl BUCK/MIL ST2 ....63 G4
Sparch Av NEWUL ST5 ....52 A5
Sparch St NEWUL ST5 ....52 A5
Sparch Hollow NEWUL ST5 ....52 A5
Spark St STOKE ST4 ....61 E5
Spark Ter STOKE ST4 ....61 E5
Sparrowbutts Gv ALS/KID ST7 ...36 A1
Sparrow St BURS/TUN ST6 ....53 H4
Sparrow Ter NEWUL ST5 ....51 H5
Spa St BURS/TUN ST6 ....53 C2
Speakman St LNGTN ST3 ....70 B5
Spedding Rd STOKE ST4 ....62 A4
Spedding Wy BIDD ST8 ....20 A5
Speedwall St LNGTN ST3 ....70 A2
Speedwell Rd NEWUL ST5 ....43 F5
Spencer Av END/WER ST9 ....30 D5
  LEEK ST13 ....30 D5
Spencer Cl ALS/KID ST7 ....22 B4
Spencer Pl NEWUL ST5 ....51 E5
Spencer Rd STOKE ST4 ....61 C4
Spencroft Rd NEWUL ST5 ....52 D1
Sperry Cl BLYBR/FOR ST11 ....81 F3
Spey Av ALS/KID ST7 ....36 A1
Spinney Cl END/WER ST9 ....39 G3
The Spinney ALS/KID ST7 ....49 C4
  AUD/MAD/W CW3 ....56 C4
Spire Cl BURS/TUN ST6 ....46 A3
Spitfire Wy BURS/TUN ST6 ....44 A2
Spode Cl CDLE ST10 ....74 C5

Spode Gv NEWUL ST5 ....66 D4
Spode St STOKE ST4 ....68 B2
Spoutfield Rd STOKE ST4 ....60 D3
Spout La BURS/TUN ST6 ....47 E5
Spragg House La
 BURS/TUN ST6 ....45 H4
Spragg St CONG CW12 ....8 C4
Spratslade Dr LNGTN ST3 ....69 H5
Spring Bank ALS/KID ST7 ....25 G1
Springbank Av END/WER ST9 ......39 G5
Spring Cl ALS/KID ST7 ....15 C5
Spring Crs BURS/TUN ST6 ....39 E4
Springcroft BLYBR/FOR ST11 ......82 B4
Springfield Cl LEEK ST13 ....31 F4
 NEWUL ST5 ....51 F3
Springfield Ct LEEK ST13 ....31 F3
Springfield Crs LNGTN ST3 ....69 H5
Springfield Dr ALS/KID ST7 ....34 D3
 BLYBR/FOR ST11 ....31 F3
Springfield Rd BIDD ST8 ....27 H1
 LEEK ST13 ....31 F4
Springfields Dr CONG CW12 ....8 B4
Springfields Rd NEWUL ST5 ....67 G1
Spring Garden Rd LNGTN ST3 .....69 H5
Spring Gdns BLYBR/FOR ST11 .....82 D2
Springhead Cl ALS/KID ST7 ....30 C4
Spring Rd NEWUL ST5 ....70 C5
Springside Pl LNGTN ST3 ....79 E3
Spring St CONG CW12 ....8 C5
 STOKE ST4 ....7 G4
Springwood Dr STONE ST15 ....91 G4
Springwood Rd NEWUL ST5 ....50 C1
Sprink Bank Rd BURS/TUN ST6 ...45 E1
Sprink La CONG CW12 ....8 C4
Sprinkwood Gv LNGTN ST3 ....71 E4
Sproston Rd BURS/TUN ST6 ....44 D1
Spruce Gv ALS/KID ST7 ....23 H1
Spur St HAN ST1 ....5 H7
The Square BLYBR/FOR ST11 ......72 A5
 NEWUL ST5 ....66 C5
Squires Vw STOKE ST4 ....51 E5
Squirrel Hayes Av BIDD ST8 ....28 A2
The Squirrels NEWUL ST5 ....67 E4
Stadium Ct BURS/TUN ST6 ....53 E3
Stadmorslow La ALS/KID ST7 .....26 D4
Stafford Av NEWUL ST5 ....5 C7
Stafford Cl STONE ST15 ....90 D4
Stafford Crs NEWUL ST5 ....67 E3
Stafford La HAN ST1 ....5 G5
Stafford St STOKE ST4 ....90 D4
Staffordshire Moorlands Wks
 BURS/TUN ST6 ....38 B5
 CDLE ST10 ....74 B2
 CONG CW12 ....7 G4
Staffordshire Wy ALS/KID ST7 ....18 C5
Stafford St HAN ST1 ....2 E4
 NEWUL ST5 * 2 E4
 STONE ST15 ....90 D3
Staines Ct STONE ST15 ....7 G4
Stallington Cl BLYBR/FOR ST11 ...89 H1
Stallington Gdns
 BLYBR/FOR ST11 ....82 B4
Stallington Rd LNGTN ST3 ....89 F3
Stamer St STOKE ST4 ....68 B1
Standard St STOKE ST4 ....68 D1
Standerstoft Pl
 BURS/TUN ST6 ....37 F5
Stanfield Crs CDLE ST10 ....84 D1
Stanfield Rd BURS/TUN ST6 ....45 E5
Stanfield St LNGTN ST3 ....70 B1
Stanhope St HAN ST1 ....4 E6
Stanier St NEWUL ST5 ....2 B3
 STOKE ST4 ....69 E1
Stanley Bank END/WER ST9 ....47 H1
Stanley Ct ALS/KID ST7 ....23 E4
Stanley Dr NEWUL ST5 * 42 C5
Stanley Gv BUCK/MIL ST2 ....46 D4
 NEWUL ST5 * 60 B2
Stanley Matthews Wy
 STOKE ST4 ....68 C4
Stanley Moss La END/WER ST9 ...47 G1
Stanley Moss Rd
 END/WER ST9 ....47 G1
Stanley Rd BIDD ST8 ....19 G3
 END/WER ST9 ....47 F2
 NEWUL ST5 ....60 B2
 STOKE ST4 ....52 B5
Stanley St BIDD ST8 ....19 G5
 BURS/TUN ST6 ....44 C2
 LEEK ST13 ....30 D4
Stannerhouse La SBCH CW11 .....14 A2
Stangate Pl HAN ST1 ....5 H7
Stanmore Rd LNGTN ST3 ....71 F5
Stanton Cl NEWUL ST5 ....59 F2
Stanton Rd LNGTN ST3 ....81 E1
Stanway Av BURS/TUN ST6 ....53 G2
Stanways La BIDD ST8 ....20 D3
Stapleton Crs LNGTN ST3 ....79 E5
Star & Carter Rd LNGTN ST3 ......80 C2
Starling Cl ALS/KID ST7 ....26 C5
Starwood Rd LNGTN ST3 ....80 C2
Statham St HAN ST1 ....4 D5
Station Ap STONE ST15 ....90 C1
Station Bridge Rd
 STOKE ST4 ....69 E2
Station Crs BURS/TUN ST6 ....45 H4
Station Dr NEWUL ST5 ....57 F4
Station Gv BUCK/MIL ST2 ....46 C5
Station Rd ALS/KID ST7 ....36 D2
 ALS/KID ST7 ....23 E5
 ALS/KID ST7 ....25 E1
 ALS/KID ST7 ....35 F2
 ALS/KID ST7 ....46 D2
 BARL ST12 ....86 D4
 BIDD ST8 ....19 G4
 CDLE ST10 ....74 D5
 END/WER ST9 ....39 H4
 NEWUL ST5 ....57 G4
 NEWUL ST5 ....57 G4

NEWUL ST5 ....58 B2
STOKE ST4 ....61 F4
STONE ST15 ....90 C2
Station St BURS/TUN ST6 ....52 D2
 LEEK ST13 ....30 C4
Station Vw LNGTN ST3 ....81 E1
Station Wks ALS/KID ST7 ....49 F2
Staveley Av STOKE ST4 ....62 C1
Staveley Pl NEWUL ST5 ....58 B2
Stedman St HAN ST1 ....53 H4
Steele Av BURS/TUN ST6 ....45 F4
Steel St STOKE ST4 ....3 K5
Stellar St BURS/TUN ST6 ....44 C2
Stephens Wy ALS/KID ST7 ....41 H4
Sterling Cl CONG CW12 ....12 A1
Sterndale Dr NEWUL ST5 ....66 D4
 STOKE ST4 ....69 H1
Stevenson Rd BUCK/MIL ST2 .....54 C5
Steventon Pl BURS/TUN ST6 ......52 D1
Stewart St STOKE ST4 ....69 H1
Stile Cl BIDD ST8 ....27 F3
Stirling Cl BUCK/MIL ST2 ....63 G5
Stockfield Rd LNGTN ST3 ....80 D3
Stockholm Gv HAN ST1 ....54 A2
Stockwell Gv LNGTN ST3 ....70 B1
Stockwell St LEEK ST13 ....30 D3
Stockwood Rd NEWUL ST5 ....66 B3
Stoke Old Rd STOKE ST4 ....3 H3
Stoke Rd STOKE ST4 ....61 F5
Stokesay Gv BURS/TUN ST6 * 53 E2
Stone Bank Rd ALS/KID ST7 ......35 G3
Stone Chair La ALS/KID ST7 ......17 E5
Stonefield Sq STONE ST15 ....90 D2
Stonehaven Gv HAN ST1 ....5 G7
Stonehouse Crs END/WER ST9 ...64 B1
Stonehouse Gn CONG CW12 ....8 B4
Stonehouse Rd END/WER ST9 ....64 B1
Stoneleigh Rd BURS/TUN ST6 .....45 E1
 STONE ST15 ....67 H5
 STOKE ST4 ....67 H5
Stone St STOKE ST4 ....61 E5
Stonewall Rd BUCK/MIL ST2 ......58 D3
Stonewood Cl STOKE ST4 ....67 G4
Stoneycroft BUCK/MIL ST2 ....46 D4
Stoneyfields BIDD ST8 ....20 D4
Stoneyfields Av
 BUCK/MIL ST2 ....46 D4
Stoneyfields Ct NEWUL ST5 ....3 C1
Stoney La END/WER ST9 ....39 G4
Stoney Lea BURS/TUN ST6 ....53 E3
Stony La CONG CW12 ....12 A1
Stopsley Cl CONG CW12 ....54 D4
Stormont Cl BURS/TUN ST6 ....45 G4
Stowford Gv STOKE ST4 ....78 B2
Stradbroke Dr LNGTN ST3 ....79 C1
Strand Cl BUCK/MIL ST2 ....62 C2
The Strand HAN ST1 ....69 H4
Strangman St LEEK ST13 ....30 D4
Stranraer Cl LNGTN ST3 ....71 F5
Stratford Av NEWUL ST5 ....60 B1
Stratford Cl BLYBR/FOR ST11 .....82 C2
 STOKE ST4 ....46 B4
Stratheden Rd BURS/TUN ST6 ....45 F4
Street La SBCH CW11 ....15 C3
Stretton Rd NEWUL ST5 ....54 B2
Stringer Ct BURS/TUN ST6 ....54 A2
Stringer's St BIDD ST8 ....19 C5
Stroma Cl BURS/TUN ST6 ....52 D2
Stross Av BURS/TUN ST6 ....44 D1
Stroud Cl HAN ST1 ....81 F5
Stuart Cl STONE ST15 ....90 C5
Stuart Cl North STONE ST15 ......90 C5
Stuart Gv NEWUL ST5 ....52 A5
Stuart Rd HAN ST1 ....5 C7
Stubbs Dr STONE ST15 ....91 C4
Stubbsfield Rd NEWUL ST5 ....3 F6
Stubbs La HAN ST1 ....5 C5
Stubbs St BURS/TUN ST6 ....52 C1
 NEWUL ST5 ....2 B2
Sturgess St STOKE ST4 ....68 A1
Sudbourne Cl ALS/KID ST7 ....36 C3
Sudbury Pl NEWUL ST5 ....66 D5
Sudgrove Pl LNGTN ST3 ....81 F3
Sudlow St BURS/TUN ST6 ....52 C1
Suffolk Cl CONG CW12 ....8 B3
 CONG CW12 ....67 F3
Suffolk Rd LNGTN ST3 ....80 A2
Summerbank Rd
 BURS/TUN ST6 ....44 B2
Summerfield ALS/KID ST7 ....35 H2
Summerhill Dr NEWUL ST5 ....42 D5
Summer Rw LNGTN ST3 ....69 H5
Summer St STOKE ST4 ....68 A2
Summerville Rd STOKE ST4 ....67 C4
Sunbury Cl STOKE ST4 ....78 C4
Sundorne Pl BUCK/MIL ST2 ....62 D2
Sunningdale Cl STONE ST15 ......90 D4
Sunningdale Cl
 BURS/TUN ST6 ....45 E3
Sunningdale Gv NEWUL ST5 ......50 D1
Sunny Bank BURS/TUN ST6 ....52 C3
Sunnycroft Av LNGTN ST3 ....79 G1
Sunnyfield Gv BUCK/MIL ST2 .....47 E5
Sunny Hollow NEWUL ST5 ....60 A1
Sunnyside ALS/KID ST7 ....35 H2
Sunnyside Av BURS/TUN ST6 .....44 D3
Sunridge Cl BUCK/MIL ST2 ....46 D4
Sun St CDLE ST10 ....75 E4
 HAN ST1 ....4 C6
Surrey Cl CONG CW12 ....75 E4
Surrey Dr CDLE ST10 ....35 G1
Surrey Rd ALS/KID ST7 ....35 C1
Surtees Gv STOKE ST4 ....69 H2
Sussex Dr ALS/KID ST7 ....35 F1
Sussex Pl STOKE ST4 ....46 E2
 LNGTN ST3 ....36 A1
Sutherland Av LNGTN ST3 ....79 H1
Sutherland Crs
 BLYBR/FOR ST11 ....82 A4
Sutherland Rd BUCK/MIL ST2 ....66 B2
Sutherland Pl LNGTN ST3 ....70 B5
Sutherland Rd BARL ST12 ....86 A3

LNGTN ST3 ....70 A4
STONE ST15 ....91 E5
Sutherland St STOKE ST4 ....68 C1
Sutton Dr STOKE ST4 ....67 H5
Sutton Pl BURS/TUN ST6 ....45 F1
Sutton St NEWUL ST5 ....51 F3
Swaffham Wy
 BUCK/MIL ST2 ....63 F2
Swainsley Cl BURS/TUN ST6 ......53 E2
Swaledale Av CONG CW12 ....9 F2
Swallow Cl ALS/KID ST7 ....35 G1
 LNGTN ST3 ....81 E5
Swallow Cft LNGTN ST3 ....30 B5
Swallow Dr ALS/KID ST7 ....34 A3
Swallowmore Vw
 ALS/KID ST7 * 34 C3
Swallow Rd ALS/KID ST7 ....36 C2
Swallow Wk BIDD ST8 ....27 H1
Swanage Cl LNGTN ST3 ....81 F5
Swan Bank ALS/KID ST7 ....34 C4
Swan Cl ALS/KID ST7 ....34 C3
Swan Gv BURS/TUN ST6 ....44 B5
Swanland Gv LNGTN ST3 ....70 B3
Swan La STOKE ST4 ....67 G4
Swan Pas BLYBR/FOR ST11 ....22 A2
Swan Sq BURS/TUN ST6 ....52 D1
Swan St CONG CW12 ....8 C5
 STOKE ST4 ....61 E4
Swanton Pl STOKE ST4 ....77 H4
Swaythling Gv ALS/KID ST7 ....34 A3
Sweettenham Cl ALS/KID ST7 ....23 E5
Swettenham Cl ALS/KID ST7 .....23 E5
Swift Cl ALS/KID ST7 ....35 H1
Swift Dr BIDD ST8 ....20 A5
Swift Pl LNGTN ST3 ....70 D2
Swinburne Cl LNGTN ST3 ....69 F4
Swingle Hill Rd LNGTN ST3 ....69 F4
Swithin Dr STOKE ST4 ....69 H1
Sycamore Av ALS/KID ST7 ....23 H1
 BIDD ST8 ....20 A3
 LNGTN ST3 ....81 E5
Sycamore Gdns
 BURS/TUN ST6 ....52 B1
Sycamore Gv BUCK/MIL ST2 ......58 D4
 NEWUL ST5 ....60 B1
Sycamore Rd STONE ST15 ....91 E5
Sydenham Pl BUCK/MIL ST2 ......46 B5
Sylvan Cv STOKE ST4 ....67 G4
Sylvester St BURS/TUN ST6 ......53 E1
Sytch Rd BURS/TUN ST6 ....38 C3

T

Talbot St HAN ST1 ....5 C6
 LEEK ST13 ....31 E4
Talke Rd ALS/KID ST7 ....35 F2
 NEWUL ST5 ....42 D3
 NEWUL ST5 ....43 F5
Tall Ash Av CONG CW12 ....9 E3
Tallis Gv HAN ST1 ....53 G2
Tally Cl BUCK/MIL ST2 ....63 F5
Talsarn Gv STOKE ST4 ....78 C4
Tamar Cl CONG CW12 ....12 D1
Tamar Gv CDLE ST10 ....35 H1
Tamar St STOKE ST4 ....69 F1
Tame Cl BIDD ST8 ....19 H4
Tanners Rd BUCK/MIL ST2 ....54 D2
Tansey Cl BUCK/MIL ST2 ....62 C1
Tape St CDLE ST10 ....74 D4
Tara Gv BUCK/MIL ST2 ....62 C1
Target Cl ALS/KID ST7 ....35 E5
Tarleton Rd HAN ST1 ....5 J5
Tarporley Gv STOKE ST4 ....67 G2
Tarragon Dr LNGTN ST3 ....81 E4
Tarvin Gv BURS/TUN ST6 ....36 D5
Tasman Sq HAN ST1 ....5 J7
Tatton Cl ALS/KID ST7 * 23 E5
 LEEK ST13 ....30 A5
Tatton St LNGTN ST3 ....70 A5
Taunton Pl NEWUL ST5 ....51 F2
Taunton Wy BUCK/MIL ST2 ....46 D2
Taurus Gv BURS/TUN ST6 ....36 D5
Tavistock Crs NEWUL ST5 ....66 C2
Tavistock Pl STOKE ST4 ....3 J2
Tawney Cl ALS/KID ST7 ....35 H1
Tawney Crs LNGTN ST3 ....71 F4
Tay Cl BIDD ST8 ....19 H4
 CDLE ST10 ....75 E2
 LNGTN ST3 ....70 A2
Taylor Av NEWUL ST5 ....52 A5
Taylor Cl ALS/KID ST7 ....54 D5
Taylor St BURS/TUN ST6 ....52 A5
 NEWUL ST5 ....52 A5
Taynton Cl BURS/TUN ST6 ....37 E5
Teal Vw BURS/TUN ST6 ....45 H4
Tean Rd CDLE ST10 ....84 D2
Telford Cl ALS/KID ST7 ....35 E2
 CONG CW12 ....9 F5
Telford Wy BURS/TUN ST6 ....45 E3
Tellwright Gv NEWUL ST5 ....51 G3
Tellwright St BURS/TUN ST6 .....52 A5
Templar Crs NEWUL ST5 ....51 H1
Templar Ter NEWUL ST5 ....60 A5
Temple St STOKE ST4 ....68 D1
Templeton Av BUCK/MIL ST2 .....62 D2
Tenby St NEWUL ST5 ....51 E2
Tenford La CDLE ST10 ....84 D5
Tennant Pl NEWUL ST5 ....51 H2
Tennyson Av ALS/KID ST7 ....35 C3
Tennyson Cl ALS/KID ST7 ....15 C5
 CDLE ST10 ....74 B5
Tennyson Gdns LNGTN ST3 ......81 E5
Tercel Gv LNGTN ST3 ....81 E5
Tern Av ALS/KID ST7 ....36 A1
Tern Cl BIDD ST8 ....20 A5
The Terrace CDLE ST10 ....74 C4
Terrington Dr NEWUL ST5 ....66 D5
Terry Cl LNGTN ST3 ....71 F4
Terson Wy LNGTN ST3 ....70 D3

Tewkesbury Gv
 BUCK/MIL ST2 ....54 C1
Thackeray Dr LNGTN ST3 ....69 G5
Thames Cl CONG CW12 ....12 D1
Thames Dr BIDD ST8 ....19 H4
 CDLE ST10 ....85 E1
Thames Rd NEWUL ST5 ....66 C4
Thanet St NEWUL ST5 ....69 G4
Thatcher Cl STOKE ST4 ....79 E5
Thatcher Gv BIDD ST8 ....19 F5
Thelma Av BURS/TUN ST6 ....38 D4
Theodore Rd BUCK/MIL ST2 ......62 D1
Theresa Cl STOKE ST4 ....68 A5
Third Av ALS/KID ST7 ....22 D5
 BUCK/MIL ST2 ....55 F5
Thirlmere Ct CONG CW12 ....7 C5
Thirlmere Gv NEWUL ST5 ....66 D2
Thirlmere Pl NEWUL ST5 ....66 D2
Thirsk Pl NEWUL ST5 ....66 D2
Thistleberry Av NEWUL ST5 ....59 F5
The Thistles NEWUL ST5 ....59 F5
Thistley Hough STOKE ST4 ....67 H1
Thomas Av NEWUL ST5 ....51 G1
 STONE ST15 ....90 C5
Thomas Cl ALS/KID ST7 ....23 G4
Thomas St ALS/KID ST7 ....34 C3
 ALS/KID ST7 ....42 A4
 BIDD ST8 ....19 G4
 LEEK ST13 ....30 C5
Thompstone Av NEWUL ST5 ......59 F5
Thomson Gdns CONG CW12 ......7 G4
Thorley Dr CDLE ST10 ....75 F5
Thornburrow Dr STOKE ST4 ....3 K6
Thorncliff Gv HAN ST1 ....54 A4
Thorncliff Sq BUCK/MIL ST2 ......62 C1
Thorncliff Vw LEEK ST13 ....31 G1
Thorndyke St HAN ST1 ....4 C6
Thorneycroft Av
 BURS/TUN ST6 ....45 F4
Thornfield Av LEEK ST13 ....31 G4
Thornham Cl NEWUL ST5 ....66 D5
Thornhill Dr
 AUD/MAD/W CW3 ....56 A5
Thornhill Rd BUCK/MIL ST2 ....63 G4
Thornley Rd BURS/TUN ST6 ......44 D3
Thornton Rd STOKE ST4 ....54 C4
Thorpe Gn LNGTN ST3 ....79 F3
Thorpe Ri CDLE ST10 ....75 E1
Three Fields Cl CONG CW12 ......7 G4
Thurlwood Dr
 BURS/TUN ST6 * 26 B5
Thursfield Av ALS/KID ST7 * 26 A5
Thursfield Pl BURS/TUN ST6 .....45 H2
Thurston Wy BUCK/MIL ST2 ......66 D5
Thyme Gv ALS/KID ST7 ....81 H4
Tibb St ALS/KID ST7 ....54 D5
Tiber Dr NEWUL ST5 ....50 D4
Tickhill La BLYBR/FOR ST11 ......72 C1
Tidebrook Pl BURS/TUN ST6 ......36 C4
Tideswell Rd LNGTN ST3 ....70 A2
Tidnock Av CONG CW12 ....8 B2
Tierney St HAN ST1 ....5 H1
Tilbrook Cl BUCK/MIL ST2 ....63 E4
Tilehurst Pl LNGTN ST3 ....79 E1
Tilley La LNGTN ST3 ....75 B1
Tilewright Cl ALS/KID ST7 ....35 H1
Tilling Dr STONE ST15 ....90 D5
Tilson Av STOKE ST4 ....60 D5
Tilstone Cl ALS/KID ST7 ....63 E4
Timble Av BUCK/MIL ST2 ....53 E4
Timmis St HAN ST1 ....54 A5
Timor Gv STOKE ST4 ....78 B2
Timothy Cl LNGTN ST3 ....70 A1
Tintagel Pl BUCK/MIL ST2 ....63 F4
Tintern St HAN ST1 ....5 J4
Tintern St HAN ST1 ....5 J4
Tipping Av LNGTN ST3 ....81 F1
Tirley St STOKE ST4 ....52 B5
Tissington Pl
 BLYBR/FOR ST11 ....81 G3
Tittensor Rd BARL ST12 ....86 B5
 NEWUL ST5 ....67 E2
Titterton St STOKE ST4 ....58 C1
Tittesworth Av LEEK ST13 ....31 F2
Tiverton Rd BUCK/MIL ST2 ....63 E3
Toft End Rd NEWUL ST5 ....45 F4
Tolkien Wy STOKE ST4 ....5 H5
Tollgate Cl ALS/KID ST7 ....34 C3
Tomfields ALS/KID ST7 ....49 H1
Tomlinson Dr
 BURS/TUN ST6 * 52 B1
Tommy's La CONG CW12 ....8 D5
Tonbridge Av BURS/TUN ST6 .....45 H2
Toney Pl BUCK/MIL ST2 ....62 B1
Tongue La BURS/TUN ST6 ....38 A3
Tontine Sq HAN ST1 ....5 F3
Tontine St HAN ST1 ....5 F3
Tony Waddington Pl
 STOKE ST4 ....68 C3
Top Chapel La
 BURS/TUN ST6 ....38 D2
Topham Pl BUCK/MIL ST2 ....62 B1
Top Rd BIDD ST8 ....21 E3
Top Station Rd ALS/KID ST7 ......26 A1
Torres Wk HAN ST1 ....5 K1
Torridon Cl STOKE ST4 ....78 C4
Tor St HAN ST1 ....5 J3
Torvale Dr BIDD ST8 ....20 A5
Tower Cl BIDD ST8 ....27 F2
Tower Hill Rd ALS/KID ST7 ....38 C2
 BIDD ST8 ....26 D2
Tower Sq BURS/TUN ST6 ....36 B5
Town End CDLE ST10 ....74 C4
Townfield Cl ALS/KID ST7 ....34 D1
Town Rd HAN ST1 ....53 H4
 HAN ST1 ....5 H2
Townsend La ALS/KID ST7 ....46 A4
Townsend Pl BUCK/MIL ST2 ......62 D1
Townsend Rd CONG CW12 ....8 C5
Trade St STOKE ST4 ....61 F5
Trafalgar Rd STOKE ST4 ....3 J4
Trafalgar St HAN ST1 ....5 G2
Trafford Cl LEEK ST13 ....31 F4
Transport La LNGTN ST3 ....69 H4

Tranter Rd BUCK/MIL ST2 ....54 D3
Travers St HAN ST1 ....5 G2
Trecastle Gv LNGTN ST3 ....80 C1
Tregaron Rd LNGTN ST3 ....64 A1
Tregemma Gv LNGTN ST3 ....63 H1
Tregew Pl NEWUL ST5 ....58 D2
Tregowan Cl BURS/TUN ST6 ......85 E1
Trent Cl CDLE ST10 ....85 E1
Trent Gv BIDD ST8 ....90 C5
 NEWUL ST5 ....77 H3
Trentfields Rd BUCK/MIL ST2 .....46 C4
Trent Gv BIDD ST8 ....62 H1
 NEWUL ST5 ....77 H3
Trentham Ct STOKE ST4 * 77 H3
Trentham Gardens Cl
 STOKE ST4 ....77 H5
Trentham Ms NEWUL ST5 ....52 A5
Trentham Ms STOKE ST4 * 54 B3
Trentham Rd NEWUL ST5 ....76 C2
 STOKE ST4 ....78 D3
Trentley Dr BIDD ST8 ....20 D5
Trentley Rd STOKE ST4 ....78 A3
Trentmill Rd HAN ST1 ....5 J6
Trent Rd BLYBR/FOR ST11 ....82 C2
Trentside Rd BURS/TUN ST6 ......46 C1
Trent Vale Rd STOKE ST4 ....62 B1
Trent Wk HAN ST1 ....67 H2
Trentway Cl BUCK/MIL ST2 ....62 C2
Trevithick Cl BUCK/MIL ST2 ....63 F5
Trevor Dr BLYBR/FOR ST11 ....71 H4
Trimley Wy BUCK/MIL ST2 ....62 C2
Trimpos CDLE ST10 ....74 A3
Triner Pl BURS/TUN ST6 ....46 A2
Trinity Cl BUCK/MIL ST2 ....63 E4
Trinity Dr STOKE ST4 ....90 C2
Trinity Pde HAN ST1 * 5 G3
Trinity St HAN ST1 ....4 E5
Troutbeck Av CONG CW12 ....7 C5
Troutdale Cl STOKE ST4 ....62 C1
Trowbridge Crs
 STOKE ST4 ....63 E2
Trubshaw Br BURS/TUN ST6 ......52 B1
Trubshaw Pl ALS/KID ST7 ....35 H5
Truro Cl CONG CW12 ....12 C2
Truro Pl BUCK/MIL ST2 ....63 E4
Tudor Cv NEWUL ST5 ....59 C3
 STONE ST15 ....90 C5
Tudor Cl BIDD ST8 ....68 A1
Tudor Rose Wy
 BURS/TUN ST6 ....45 H4
Tudor Wy CONG CW12 ....44 D2
Tudor Wy CONG CW12 ....12 B1
Tulip Gv NEWUL ST5 ....60 A2
Tulley Pl BUCK/MIL ST2 ....57 H2
Tulsa Cl BUCK/MIL ST2 ....62 C1
Tunbridge NEWUL ST5 ....57 H2
Tunley Gv STONE ST15 ....90 C2
Tunnicliffe Cl LNGTN ST3 ....70 C4
Tunstall Rd BIDD ST8 ....27 C1
Turin Cl LNGTN ST3 ....70 A3
Turin Dr NEWUL ST5 ....70 A3
Turnberry Dr STOKE ST4 ....77 H2
Turner Av ALS/KID ST7 ....42 A5
Turner Crs NEWUL ST5 ....51 F3
Turner St HAN ST1 ....54 A4
Turnhill Gv NEWUL ST5 ....70 A3
Turnhurst Rd BURS/TUN ST6 .....36 D4
Turnlake Cl BIDD ST8 ....27 F2
Turnock St BUCK/MIL ST2 ....54 A5
Tuscan Cl CDLE ST10 ....84 C1
Tuscan St LNGTN ST3 ....70 A3
Tuscan Wy NEWUL ST5 ....50 D3
Tutbury Gv LNGTN ST3 ....70 B5
Tweed Gv NEWUL ST5 ....66 C5
Tweed St STOKE ST4 ....66 C5
Twemlow St HAN ST1 ....4 B4
Twigg St BUCK/MIL ST2 ....62 D2
Twyning Gv ALS/KID ST7 ....79 F5
Tyler Gv BUCK/MIL ST2 ....52 C1
 STONE ST15 ....90 D4
Tyndall Pl STOKE ST4 ....3 J6
Tyneham Gv BUCK/MIL ST2 ......46 C4
Tyne Wy NEWUL ST5 ....54 B1
Tynwald Gra NEWUL ST5 ....59 C2
Tyrell Gv HAN ST1 ....54 B1

U

Ubberley Rd BUCK/MIL ST2 ....62 D2
Uffington Pde BUCK/MIL ST2 .....63 E4
Ullswater Av BURS/TUN ST6 ......79 F4
Ullswater Dr CDLE ST10 ....75 E5
 STONE ST15 ....91 G4
Ullswater Rd CONG CW12 ....7 C5
Ulster Ter STOKE ST4 ....68 A2
Ulverston Rd LNGTN ST3 ....73 F5
Umberleigh Rd LNGTN ST3 ....79 E3
Under The HI BIDD ST8 ....20 C4
Underwood Rd NEWUL ST5 ....55 H3
Unicorn Pl BURS/TUN ST6 ....44 D1
Union St CONG CW12 ....8 A5
 HAN ST1 ....4 E1
 LEEK ST13 ....31 E3
Unity Av HAN ST1 ....53 H2
Unity Wy ALS/KID ST7 ....34 D3
Uplands Av BURS/TUN ST6 ....36 D5
Uplands Dr END/WER ST9 ....64 A1
Uplands Rd BUCK/MIL ST2 ....54 D2
Uplands BIDD ST8 ....20 A3
Upper Belgrave Rd
 LNGTN ST3 ....80 B1
Upper Crs STOKE ST4 ....3 J5
Upper Cross St LNGTN ST3 ....70 A3
Upper Furlong St STOKE ST4 .....68 D1
Upper Hilchurch St HAN ST1 ......5 G2
Upper Huntbach St HAN ST1 .....5 G2

Upper Market Sq HAN ST1 .....5 F3
Upper Marsh NEWUL ST5 .....60 B1
Upper Normacot Rd
  LNGTN ST3 .....70 B5
Urmston Pl LNGTN ST3 .....79 F1
Utterly Side BUCK/MIL ST2 .....63 E4
Uttoxeter Rd
  BLYBR/FOR ST11 .....82 A3
  LNGTN ST3 .....70 A4
  STONE ST15 .....91 H5

V

Vale Gdns ALS/KID ST7 .....23 G4
Valentine Rd ALS/KID ST7 .....35 G2
Vale Pl HAN ST1 .....4 D1
Vale Pleasant NEWUL ST5 .....58 C2
Valerian Wy LNGTN ST3 .....81 E4
Vale St NEWUL ST5 .....5 H1
  NEWUL ST5 .....58 B2
  STOKE ST4 .....61 F5
Vale Vw NEWUL ST5 .....52 B2
Valley Cl ALS/KID ST7 .....22 B5
Valley Dr LEEK ST13 .....30 A4
Valley Park Wy LNGTN ST3 .....69 F4
Valley Rd STOKE ST4 .....71 F4
  STONE ST15 .....90 D4
Valley Vw CONG CW12 .....8 A4
Vancrey Crs CONG CW12 .....8 D4
Vaudrey Dr CONG CW12 .....8 D4
Venn Pl HAN ST1 .....5 H7
Ventnor Gv LNGTN ST3 .....79 F4
Venton Cl BURS/TUN ST6 .....46 A2
Verney Wy LNGTN ST3 .....79 F3
Vernon Av ALS/KID ST7 .....41 F4
  CONG CW12 .....12 D2
Vernon Cl ALS/KID ST7 .....41 F4
Vernon Rd STOKE ST4 .....61 F4
Verona Gv LNGTN ST3 .....70 C5
Vessey Ter NEWUL ST5 .....2 E5
Valley Vw CONG CW12 .....8 A4
Vicarage Crs BARL ST12 .....86 A4
  BLYBR/FOR ST11 .....71 H4
  NEWUL ST5 .....3 F6
Vicarage La BARL ST12 .....87 G5
  STOKE ST4 .....67 G5
Vicarage Rd LEEK ST13 .....31 E3
  STOKE ST4 .....60 D4
Vichy Cl NEWUL ST5 .....59 E5
Vickers Rd BURS/TUN ST6 .....45 E1
Victoria Av ALS/KID ST7
  ALS/KID ST7 .....49 G2
  HAN ST1 .....4 E7
Victoria Park Rd
  BURS/TUN ST6 .....44 C2
Victoria Pl NEWUL ST5 * 51 E2
  STOKE ST4 .....69 E1
Victoria Rd NEWUL ST5 .....3 F4
  STOKE ST4 .....61 H4
Victoria Av BIDD ST8 .....27 G4
Victoria Sq HAN ST1 .....5 F5
Victoria St CDLE ST10 .....74 D4
  LEEK ST13 .....31 F3
  NEWUL ST5 .....2 E5
  NEWUL ST5 .....58 C2
  NEWUL ST5 .....3 H1
  STOKE ST4 .....90 D1
Victory Crs CONG CW12 .....90 C2
Victory Crs CDLE ST10 .....75 E3
Vienna Pl NEWUL ST5 .....66 A1
Vienna Wy LNGTN ST3 .....79 F3
Viggars Pl NEWUL ST5 .....59 F2
Villa Cl BIDD ST8 .....27 G2
The Village CONG CW12 .....11 G2
The Villas STOKE ST4 .....68 A2
Villa St STOKE ST4 .....68 A2
Villiers St LNGTN ST3 .....79 H1
Vincent St HAN ST1 .....5 J1
Vine Bank Rd ALS/KID ST7 .....35 C1
Vinebank St STOKE ST4 .....68 A1
Vine Rw STOKE ST4 .....68 A1
Viscount Wk LNGTN ST3 .....80 D3
Vivian Rd STOKE ST4 .....69 F1
Vowchurch Wy BUCK/MIL ST2 .....63 E3

W

Wade Av NEWUL ST5 .....52 B3
Wadebridge Rd
  BUCK/MIL ST2 .....62 D3
Wade Cl CDLE ST10 .....84 D1
Wade St BURS/TUN ST6 .....45 F5
Wadham St STOKE ST4 .....61 F5
Waggs Rd CONG CW12 .....11 G5
Wagg St CONG CW12 .....8 B5
Wain Av BURS/TUN ST6 .....46 A1
Wainfleet Rd STOKE ST4 .....59 F4
Wain Dr STOKE ST4 .....67 G1
Wain St BURS/TUN ST6 .....44 D5
Wainwright Wk HAN ST1 .....5 J3
Wakefield St STOKE ST4 .....67 H3
Walcot Gv BUCK/MIL ST2 .....62 C3
Walfield Av CONG CW12 .....8 B2
Walgrave Cl CONG CW12 .....7 C5
Walker Rd BURS/TUN ST6 .....44 D2
Walkersgreen Rd
  NEWUL ST5 .....42 D4
Walkers La ALS/KID ST7 .....16 B3
Walker St NEWUL ST5 .....44 B4
Waklate Av NEWUL ST5 .....5 H5
The Walks LEEK ST13 .....30 C4
Wallbridge Cl LEEK ST13 .....30 B5
Wallbridge Dr LEEK ST13 .....30 B4
Walley Dr BURS/TUN ST6 .....44 B5
Walley Pl BURS/TUN ST6 .....53 E2
Walley's Dr NEWUL ST5 .....60 B2
Walley St BIDD ST8 .....19 G5
  BURS/TUN ST6 .....53 E2
Wallhill La CONG CW12 .....10 D1

Wallis Pl BUCK/MIL ST2 .....54 D4
Wallis St STOKE ST4 .....69 F1
Wallis Wy BUCK/MIL ST2 .....46 C4
Wallworth's Bank CONG CW12 .....8 C5
Walmer Pl LNGTN ST3 .....69 H2
Walmer St LNGTN ST3 .....5 G4
Walnut Cv NEWUL ST5 .....50 D1
Walnut Ri CONG CW12 .....7 H5
Walpole St LNGTN ST3 .....70 B2
Walsingham Gdns
  NEWUL ST5 .....66 D5
Walton Crs STOKE ST4 .....68 C2
Walton Gv ALS/KID ST7 .....34 C3
Walton Rd NEWUL ST5 .....51 F5
Walton Rd STOKE ST4 .....67 H4
Walton Wy ALS/KID ST7 .....34 C5
  STONE ST15 .....90 C4
Warburton St BURS/TUN ST6 .....53 E2
Wardle Crs LEEK ST13 .....30 C5
Wardle La BUCK/MIL ST2 .....47 E5
Wardle St BURS/TUN ST6 .....44 C3
Ward Pl BURS/TUN ST6 .....45 F1
Wards La CONG CW12 .....13 C2
Warm Cft STONE ST15 .....91 F4
Warmson Cl LNGTN ST3 .....70 A1
Warner St HAN ST1 .....4 E5
Warren Rd BURS/TUN ST6 .....57 F5
Warren St LNGTN ST3 .....5 J4
Warrilowheath Rd
  NEWUL ST5 .....42 C5
Warrington Dr LEEK ST13 .....30 A3
Warrington Rd STOKE ST4 .....61 H3
Warrington St STOKE ST4 .....69 E1
Warsill Cv LNGTN ST3 .....70 B3
Warwick Av CDLE ST10 .....74 C5
  LNGTN ST3 .....80 D1
  NEWUL ST5 .....67 E3
Warwick Cl ALS/KID ST7 .....35 C1
Warwick Gv NEWUL ST5 .....60 C1
Warwick Gv BIDD ST8 .....27 C1
  HAN ST1 .....5 H5
  NEWUL ST5 .....51 E3
Washerwall St BUCK/MIL ST2 .....63 F4
Washington Cl BIDD ST8 .....19 G3
Washington St
  BURS/TUN ST6 .....44 C4
Watchfield Cl LNGTN ST3 .....80 D1
Waterbeck Gv STOKE ST4 .....78 C5
Waterdale Gv LNGTN ST3 .....70 C4
Watergate St BURS/TUN ST6 .....44 B4
Water Glades Cl HAN ST1 .....60 D2
Waterhead Rd LNGTN ST3 .....80 D1
Watering Trough Bank
  AUD/MAD/W CW3 .....56 D4
Waterloo Rd BURS/TUN ST6 .....35 C1
Waterloo Rd BURS/TUN ST6 .....53 E5
Waterloo St HAN ST1 .....5 H4
  LEEK ST13 .....31 E3
Watermeet St HAN ST1 .....60 D1
Watersedge Gv HAN ST1 .....60 D2
Waterside Dr LNGTN ST3 .....79 E3
Watersmeet Ct STONE ST15 .....91 F5
Water St NEWUL ST5 .....3 F5
  NEWUL ST5 .....42 D4
  STOKE ST4 .....68 A2
Watery La CONG CW12 .....11 G3
  LNGTN ST3 .....80 B1
Watford St STOKE ST4 .....5 H3
Watkin St STOKE ST4 .....68 D2
Watlands Av NEWUL ST5 .....52 A4
Watlands Rd ALS/KID ST7 .....41 C4
Watlands Vw NEWUL ST5 .....51 H5
Watson Rd STOKE ST4 .....67 H5
Watson St STOKE ST4 .....60 D4
Watt Pl CDLE ST10 .....74 D4
Waveney Gv NEWUL ST5 .....66 D5
Waverley Pl NEWUL ST5 .....63 C2
Waverton Rd BUCK/MIL ST2 .....63 C2
Wavertree Av ALS/KID ST7 .....25 E1
Wayfield Gv STOKE ST4 .....3 H1
Wayside Av NEWUL ST5 .....52 A5
Wayside Linley ALS/KID ST7 .....33 H1
Wayte St HAN ST1 .....5 J4
Weaver Cl ALS/KID ST7 .....22 C5
  BIDD ST8 .....19 H4
  CDLE ST10 .....75 E2
Weaver Pl NEWUL ST5 .....66 D3
Weavers La STONE ST15 .....91 F5
Weaver St HAN ST1 .....4 D6
Webberley La LNGTN ST3 .....70 A4
Webb St LNGTN ST3 .....71 F4
Webster Av LNGTN ST3 .....70 C2
Webster St NEWUL ST5 .....2 E5
Wedgewood Av ALS/KID ST7 .....41 H5
  STOKE ST4 .....90 B5
Wedgwood Av NEWUL ST5 .....66 B1
Wedgwood Dr BARL ST12 .....86 D1
Wedgwood La BARL ST12 .....87 E1
  BIDD ST8 .....19 H5
Wedgwood Pl BURS/TUN ST6 .....44 D5
Wedgwood Rd ALS/KID ST7 .....34 D5
  CDLE ST10 .....84 C1
  STOKE ST4 .....69 F1
Wedgwood St NEWUL ST5 .....52 B2
Weighton Gv BUCK/MIL ST2 .....63 C3
Weir Gv ALS/KID ST7 .....35 G1
Welbeck Pl BUCK/MIL ST2 .....55 E4
Welby St STOKE ST4 .....68 C1
Weldon Av LNGTN ST3 .....71 F3
Welland Gv NEWUL ST5 .....66 C4
Wellbank Ct CONG CW12 * 8 C5
Wellbury Cl STOKE ST4 .....78 C5
Weller St STOKE ST4 .....3 K5
Welles St HAN ST1 .....4 D7
Wellfield Rd BUCK/MIL ST2 .....63 E3
Wellington Cl CONG CW12 .....8 A5
Wellington Rd ALS/KID ST7 .....35 G2
  HAN ST1 .....5 H3
Wellington St HAN ST1 .....5 H5
  LEEK ST13 .....30 D3
  NEWUL ST5 .....52 A4
Wellington Ter HAN ST1 .....5 H4
Well La ALS/KID ST7 .....23 E5
  BIDD ST8 .....19 G3

Wells Cl BIDD ST8 .....19 H5
Well St ALS/KID ST7 .....25 G1
  BIDD ST8 .....27 G1
  BLYBR/FOR ST11 .....82 C2
  CDLE ST10 .....75 G4
  HAN ST1 .....5 G4
  LEEK ST13 .....31 E4
  NEWUL ST5 .....2 E4
Wem Gv NEWUL ST5 .....43 E4
Wendover Gv BUCK/MIL ST2 .....62 D5
Wenfor Cl BUCK/MIL ST2 .....62 D3
Wenger Crs STOKE ST4 .....77 H5
Wenham Dr LNGTN ST3 .....81 F3
Wenlock Cl BURS/TUN ST6 .....37 F1
  NEWUL ST5 .....43 E4
Wensleydale Av CONG CW12 .....9 E2
Wensleydale Cl HAN ST1 .....53 H2
Wentlows Av CDLE ST10 .....84 D5
Wentlows Rd CDLE ST10 .....84 D5
Wentworth Dr NEWUL ST5 .....26 A5
Wentworth Gv HAN ST1 .....54 B2
Werburgh Dr STOKE ST4 .....77 H3
Wereton Rd ALS/KID ST7 .....41 F5
Werrington Rd BUCK/MIL ST2 .....62 C1
Wesker Pl LNGTN ST3 .....70 D5
Wesley Av ALS/KID ST7 .....33 H1
Wesley Dr STOKE ST4 .....91 F5
Wesley Pl ALS/KID ST7 .....49 F2
  NEWUL ST5 .....51 E1
Wesley St ALS/KID ST7 .....50 A1
  BIDD ST8 .....27 G1
  BURS/TUN ST6 .....44 B5
Wessex Dr STOKE ST4 .....78 A2
Westacre HAN ST1 .....66 D2
West Av ALS/KID ST7 .....34 C2
  HAN ST1 .....3 H1
  STOKE ST4 .....60 D4
West Bank STOKE ST4 .....68 A1
Westbourne Cl LEEK ST13 .....30 A3
Westbourne Dr
  BURS/TUN ST6 .....44 C1
Westbourne Ms CONG CW12 * 7 H5
West Brampton NEWUL ST5 .....2 D2
Westbury Cl HAN ST1 .....54 B4
Westbury Rd NEWUL ST5 .....66 D4
Westcliffe Av NEWUL ST5 .....51 G4
West Crs HAN ST1 .....54 A1
West End Av LEEK ST13 .....30 C4
West End Cottages
  CONG CW12 .....8 A5
Westerby Dr END/WER ST9 .....64 A1
Westerham Cl STOKE ST4 .....77 H5
Westfield Av ALS/KID ST7 .....41 E5
Westfield Rd ALS/KID ST7 .....26 A1
  BUCK/MIL ST2 .....62 D1
Westfields LEEK ST13 .....31 E4
Westfield Wk HAN ST1 .....54 A5
Westhead Wk HAN ST1 .....4 C5
Westholme Cl CONG CW12 .....7 H4
Westlands ALS/KID ST7 .....41 H4
Westlands Av NEWUL ST5 .....59 F5
The Westlands CONG CW12 .....8 A5
Westland St STOKE ST4 .....61 E5
Westmarsh Gv BURS/TUN ST6 .....45 E2
Westmill St HAN ST1 .....5 G7
Westminster Pl STOKE ST4 .....78 A1
Westminster Rd LEEK ST13 .....31 F2
Westmorland Av ALS/KID ST7 .....35 H1
Westmorland Cl
  BURS/TUN ST6 .....37 E3
Weston Cl BUCK/MIL ST2 .....64 A1
  NEWUL ST5 .....59 F1
Weston Coyney Rd
  LNGTN ST3 .....70 C4
Weston Dr LNGTN ST3 .....71 E3
Westonfields Dr LNGTN ST3 .....70 C4
Weston Rd LNGTN ST3 .....71 E3
Weston St LEEK ST13 .....31 F3
  LNGTN ST3 .....70 B2
Westonview Av LNGTN ST3 .....70 B2
West Pde NEWUL ST5 .....66 D2
Westport Lake Rd
  BURS/TUN ST6 .....44 B5
Westport Rd BURS/TUN ST6 .....44 C5
West Prec HAN ST1 * 5 F4
West Rd CONG CW12 .....7 H4
Westsprink Crs LNGTN ST3 .....70 C4
West St ALS/KID ST7 .....25 H2
  BIDD ST8 .....27 G1
  CONG CW12 .....8 A4
  LEEK ST13 .....31 F2
  LNGTN ST3 .....71 F2
  NEWUL ST5 .....2 E5
  NEWUL ST5 .....52 B2
  NEWUL ST5 .....58 B3
West Ter BURS/TUN ST6 .....53 E1
West Vw NEWUL ST5 .....88 D1
Westview Cl LEEK ST13 .....30 B3
Westville Dr CONG CW12 .....7 G5
Westwood Gv LEEK ST13 .....30 C3
Westwood Heath Rd
  LEEK ST13 .....30 B4
Westwood Park Av LEEK ST13 .....30 A5
Westwood Park Dr LEEK ST13 .....30 A5
Westwood Rd LEEK ST13 .....71 F5
  LNGTN ST3 .....52 B5
Wetherby Cl CDLE ST10 .....51 E2
  NEWUL ST5 .....51 E2
Wetherby Rd STOKE ST4 .....78 B3
Wettenhall Dr LEEK ST13 .....30 A4
Weybourne Av BUCK/MIL ST2 .....46 D5
Whalley Av STOKE ST4 .....3 K7
Wharfe Cl CONG CW12 .....8 A4
Wharfedale Rd CONG CW12 .....9 E2
Wharf La CONG CW12 .....17 H1
Wharf Pl STOKE ST4 .....68 D1
Wharf Rd BIDD ST8 .....19 G5
  HAN ST1 .....5 H5
Wharf Ter AUD/MAD/W CW3 .....56 D4
Whatmore St BURS/TUN ST6 .....45 G5
Wheatfields BURS/TUN ST6 .....45 H4
Wheatly Av STOKE ST4 .....67 G1
Wheelock Cl ALS/KID ST7 .....22 C5

Wheelock Wy ALS/KID ST7 * 35 H1
Whetstone Rd BIDD ST8 .....19 G3
Whieldon Crs STOKE ST4 * 68 C2
Whieldon Rd STOKE ST4 .....68 C1
Whisper La NEWUL ST5 .....76 A3
Whitaker Rd LNGTN ST3 .....69 E4
Whitbread Dr BIDD ST8 .....20 A5
Whitchurch St LNGTN ST3 .....43 E4
Whitcliffe Pl LNGTN ST3 .....69 F4
Whitcombe Rd LNGTN ST3 .....71 E5
Whitebridge La STONE ST15 .....90 B1
Whitehall Av ALS/KID ST7 .....35 F1
White Hall Rd ALS/KID ST7 .....35 F1
Whitehaven Dr HAN ST1 .....53 H2
Whitehead Rd BURS/TUN ST6 .....45 F1
Whitehill Rd ALS/KID ST7 .....35 H1
Whitehouse Rd
  BUCK/MIL ST2 .....54 C4
  NEWUL ST5 .....59 H1
Whitehouse Rd North
  NEWUL ST5 .....51 H5
Whitemill La STONE ST15 .....90 C4
Whiteridge Rd ALS/KID ST7 .....63 F4
Whitesands Gv LNGTN ST3 .....81 F4
Whitestone Cl ALS/KID ST7 .....81 F4
Whitethorn Av BARL ST12 .....86 D4
Whitethorn Wy NEWUL ST5 .....43 E5
Whitfield Av NEWUL ST5 .....2 A5
Whitfield Rd ALS/KID ST7 .....35 H1
Whitfield St LEEK ST13 .....31 F3
Whitley Rd BURS/TUN ST6 .....37 H5
Whitmore Rd NEWUL ST5 .....66 A3
  NEWUL ST5 .....77 F2
Whitmore St HAN ST1 .....4 B6
Whitridge Gv BUCK/MIL ST2 .....63 F4
Whittle Rd LNGTN ST3 .....81 F2
Whygate Gv HAN ST1 .....54 B3
Wickenstones Ct BIDD ST8 * 27 H1
Widecombe Ct HAN ST1 .....54 B4
Wigmore Pl LNGTN ST3 .....70 A1
Wilbraham Rd BURS/TUN ST6 .....36 B5
Wilbraham's Wk ALS/KID ST7 .....41 F4
Wilbrahams Wy ALS/KID ST7 .....23 F4
Wild Goose Av ALS/KID ST7 .....26 B5
Wilding Rd BURS/TUN ST6 .....37 H5
Wileman Pl STOKE ST4 .....69 E1
Wileman St STOKE ST4 .....69 E1
Wilfred Pl STOKE ST4 .....3 K5
Wilkinson St BURS/TUN ST6 .....44 B4
Willbury St ALS/KID ST7 .....44 C2
Willatt Pl BUCK/MIL ST2 .....46 C5
Willdale Gv HAN ST1 .....54 B4
Willeton St BUCK/MIL ST2 .....62 C1
Willfield La ALS/KID ST7 .....26 B5
William Av BIDD ST8 .....27 H1
  LNGTN ST3 .....81 G2
William Birch Rd
  BUCK/MIL ST2 .....62 C3
William Cl BLYBR/FOR ST11 .....81 G3
William Clowes St
  BURS/TUN ST6 .....52 D1
William Coltman Wy
  BURS/TUN ST6 .....44 A1
William Fiske Ct STOKE ST4 .....67 H3
William Rd ALS/KID ST7 .....35 C1
William Ruston Rd
  BURS/TUN ST6 .....45 H5
Williamson Av BURS/TUN ST6 .....37 H5
Williamson St BURS/TUN ST6 .....44 C4
William St CONG CW12 .....9 E3
  STOKE ST4 .....69 E1
William Ter BURS/TUN ST6 .....44 D5
Willmer Crs ALS/KID ST7 .....25 H2
Willotts Hill Rd NEWUL ST5 .....58 B4
Willoughby St
  BURS/TUN ST6 .....36 B4
Willow Cl ALS/KID ST7 * 36 B4
  CDLE ST10 .....84 D5
Willowcroft Ri
  BLYBR/FOR ST11 .....81 G3
Willowcroft Wy ALS/KID ST7 .....68 C2
Willowdale Av STOKE ST4 .....68 C2
Willowfield Dr STOKE ST4 .....78 C3
Willow Gv LNGTN ST3 .....81 F4
Willow La LNGTN ST3 .....89 E2
Willow Pl BIDD ST8 .....20 D4
Willow Rd STOKE ST15 .....91 E4
Willow Rw LNGTN ST3 .....70 A1
Willows Dr LNGTN ST3 .....89 E1
The Willows LEEK ST13 .....30 B4
  STONE ST15 .....91 E5
Willow St CONG CW12 .....8 C4
Willow Tree Gv ALS/KID ST7 * 23 H1
  STOKE ST4 .....25 H5
Willow Wy BLYBR/FOR ST11 .....82 C2
Wilmot Cl NEWUL ST5 .....59 F1
Wilmot Dr NEWUL ST5 .....59 F1
Wilson Gv LNGTN ST3 .....80 C5
Wilson Rd STOKE ST4 .....77 H1
Wilson St BURS/TUN ST6 .....45 F4
  NEWUL ST5 .....2 D2
Wilson Wy BURS/TUN ST6 .....36 B5
Wilton St NEWUL ST5 .....59 G2
Wiltshire Dr CONG CW12 .....8 C3
Wiltshire Gv NEWUL ST5 .....67 E3
Wimberry Dr NEWUL ST5 .....42 D5
Wimborne Av LNGTN ST3 .....79 E3
Winchester Av BUCK/MIL ST2 .....62 D3
Winchester Dr NEWUL ST5 .....66 B3
Windermere CDLE ST10 .....75 F3
Windermere Rd NEWUL ST5 .....66 D3
Windermere St HAN ST1 .....53 F4
Windmill Av ALS/KID ST7 .....34 C5
Windmill Cl LNGTN ST3 .....88 D1
Windmill Hl LNGTN ST3 .....88 D1
Windmill St CDLE ST10 .....75 F3
  STOKE ST4 .....78 C5
Windsmoor St STOKE ST4 .....61 G2
Windsor Av LNGTN ST3 .....69 G3
Windsor Dr ALS/KID ST7 .....22 B4
  LEEK ST13 .....31 G2

Windsor Pl CONG CW12 .....8 D5
Windsor Rd STOKE ST4 .....78 A1
Windsor St NEWUL ST5 .....2 E3
Windy Arbour CDLE ST10 .....74 D5
Windycote La END/WER ST9 .....65 G2
Winghay Cl BURS/TUN ST6 .....52 A1
Winghay Pl BURS/TUN ST6 .....45 F2
Winghay Rd ALS/KID ST7 .....35 H1
Wingrove Av NEWUL ST5 .....80 B1
Winifred St HAN ST1 .....4 D1
Winnipeg Cl STOKE ST4 .....78 B2
Winpenny Rd NEWUL ST5 .....51 F1
Winsford Av LNGTN ST3 .....70 C5
Winston Av ALS/KID ST7 .....23 E4
Winston Pl BUCK/MIL ST2 .....62 C1
Winston Ter NEWUL ST5 .....52 A3
Winterbourne Gv LNGTN ST3 .....70 C4
Winterfield La LNGTN ST3 .....64 B5
Winterside Cl NEWUL ST5 .....42 D5
Wintonfield St STOKE ST4 .....61 C5
Winton Sq STOKE ST4 .....61 F4
Wise St LNGTN ST3 .....80 A1
Witchford Crs LNGTN ST3 .....79 F3
Witham Wy BIDD ST8 .....20 A4
Withies Rd STOKE ST4 .....58 B3
Withington Rd BURS/TUN ST6 .....37 F5
Woburn Cl STOKE ST4 * 71 F5
Woburn Dr CONG CW12 .....13 F2
Wolfe St STOKE ST4 .....68 B1
Wolseley Rd NEWUL ST5 .....51 H4
  STOKE ST4 .....67 H5
Wolstanholme Cl CONG CW12 .....12 D1
Wolstanton Rd NEWUL ST5 .....51 F3
Wolstern Rd LNGTN ST3 .....70 B2
Woodall St HAN ST1 .....53 F4
Woodbank St BURS/TUN ST6 .....52 D1
Woodberry Av STOKE ST4 .....67 H2
Woodbridge Rd NEWUL ST5 .....26 A2
Woodcock La ALS/KID ST7 .....42 A5
Woodcroft Av LNGTN ST3 .....30 C5
Woodcroft Rd LEEK ST13 .....30 C5
Wood Dr ALS/KID ST7 .....22 C5
Woodend St STOKE ST4 .....69 F1
Woodfield Ct LEEK ST13 .....31 F3
Woodford Gv ALS/KID ST7 .....23 H5
Woodgate St LNGTN ST3 .....81 E1
Woodhall Pl NEWUL ST5 .....57 H2
Woodhall Rd ALS/KID ST7 .....26 A5
Woodhead Rd BUCK/MIL ST2 .....55 F1
  BURS/TUN ST6 .....53 F4
Woodhouse St STOKE ST4 .....68 B1
Woodingdean Ct LNGTN ST3 .....70 B2
Woodkirk Cl BURS/TUN ST6 .....37 E3
Woodland Av BURS/TUN ST6 .....46 B2
  STOKE ST4 .....52 A4
Woodland Ct ALS/KID ST7 .....23 F4
Woodland Gv BURS/TUN ST6 .....45 H4
Woodland Hills
  AUD/MAD/W CW3 .....56 A3
Woodland Rd ALS/KID ST7 .....15 C5
Woodlands HAN ST1 * 52 D4
  CONG CW12 .....90 B3
  STONE ST15 .....90 B3
Woodlands Cl STONE ST15 .....90 B3
Woodlands Gv LNGTN ST3 .....89 E1
Woodlands La
  BLYBR/FOR ST11 .....82 D5
Woodlands Rd STOKE ST4 .....67 G3
Woodland St BIDD ST8 .....27 H1
  BURS/TUN ST6 .....44 C3
Woodman St BUCK/MIL ST2 .....46 B5
Woodpark La STOKE ST4 .....80 B3
Woodpecker Dr ALS/KID ST7 .....36 D2
Wood Pl LNGTN ST3 .....71 F5
Woodrow Wy NEWUL ST5 .....43 E5
Woodruff Cl ALS/KID ST7 .....34 D2
Woodshutt's St ALS/KID ST7 .....34 D2
Woodside ALS/KID ST7 .....25 E4
Woodside Av ALS/KID ST7 .....23 C4
  ALS/KID ST7 .....35 F2
  BURS/TUN ST6 .....38 D5
Woodside Dr NEWUL ST5 .....89 E1
Woodside Rd BUCK/MIL ST2 .....46 D5
Woodstock Cl NEWUL ST5 .....60 A1
Woodstock Rd
  BURS/TUN ST6 .....35 C4
Woodstock St BURS/TUN ST6 .....35 H3
Woodstone Av END/WER ST9 .....35 G5
Wood St ALS/KID ST7 .....41 C3
  CONG CW12 .....8 C4
  LEEK ST13 .....31 E4
  STOKE ST4 .....70 A3
Wood Ter HAN ST1 .....4 D6
The Wood LNGTN ST3 .....71 F5
Woodvale Crs END/WER ST9 .....39 G3
Wood Vw ALS/KID ST7 .....42 A5
Woodville Pl HAN ST1 .....71 E5
Woodville Rd LNGTN ST3 .....71 E5
Woodward St HAN ST1 .....5 H2
Woolaston Dr ALS/KID ST7 .....23 H5
Woolliscroft Av NEWUL ST5 .....60 B1
Woolliscroft Rd
  BUCK/MIL ST2 .....62 D1
Woolrich St BURS/TUN ST6 .....52 C2
Woolston Av CONG CW12 .....8 D4
Worcester Cl ALS/KID ST7 .....34 D4
Worcester Pl BUCK/MIL ST2 .....62 D3
Wordsworth Cl CDLE ST10 .....74 C5
Wordsworth Wy ALS/KID ST7 .....23 F4
Worrall St CONG CW12 .....12 A1
Worsley Dr CONG CW12 .....13 F1
Worth Cl LNGTN ST3 .....70 B3
Wraggs La BIDD ST8 .....20 D4
Wrenbury Cl NEWUL ST5 .....42 D5
Wren Cl STOKE ST4 .....20 A5
Wren Vw LNGTN ST3 .....70 B5
Wrexham Cl BIDD ST8 .....19 H4
Wright Av NEWUL ST5 .....51 E2
Wrighton Cl BUCK/MIL ST2 .....62 B2

Wright St *ALS/KID* ST7....................34 D2
Wroxham Wy *NEWUL* ST5...............66 D5
Wulfad Ct *STONE* ST4...................91 F4
Wulstan Dr *NEWUL* ST5.................60 A1
Wulstan Rd *BURS/TUN* ST6..........53 E3
Wyatt St *BURS/TUN* ST6...............36 A4
Wycliffe Rd *BURS/TUN* ST6...........52 D1
Wye Cl *CDLE* ST10.......................85 E1
Wye Rd *NEWUL* ST5.....................66 C4
Wymondley Gv *STOKE* ST4............78 B4
Wynbank Cl *ALS/KID* ST7..............49 C1
Wyndham Rd *LNGTN* ST3...............79 F3
Wynford Rd *BUCK/MIL* ST2............62 D3

Wynstay Ct *NEWUL* ST5................77 E1

Y

Yale St *BURS/TUN* ST6.................52 C2
Yardley Pl *LNGTN* ST3.................79 F4
Yardley St *BURS/TUN* ST6............46 B1
Yarlet Wk *LNGTN* ST3.................79 F4
Yarnbrook Gv *BURS/TUN* ST6........45 H5
Yarnfield Cl *LNGTN* ST3...............71 E5

Yateley Cl *BUCK/MIL* ST2............62 D2
Yates St *HAN* ST1............................4 D5
Yaxley Ct *NEWUL* ST5.................66 D5
Yaxley Pl *LNGTN* ST3.................79 F4
Yeaman St *STOKE* ST4................68 B1
Yeldham Pl *LNGTN* ST3...............79 F4
Yeovil Pl *LNGTN* ST3.................79 F4
Yew Tree Av *LNGTN* ST3.............69 E5
Yew Tree Cl *BUCK/MIL* ST2..........47 F5
Yew Tree Ct *ALS/KID* ST7............33 G1
Yew Tree La *CONG* CW12...............18 A3
Yew Tree Ter *ALS/KID* ST7............35 G5
York Ct *ALS/KID* ST7..................34 D4

BIDD ST8...................................19 H3
BLYBR/FOR ST11.........................82 D2
York Rd *LNGTN* ST3..................71 F4
York St *HAN* ST1...........................4 D2
LEEK ST13....................................31 E3
NEWUL ST5.....................................3 G5
STONE ST15................................90 D1
Youlgreave Av *BUCK/MIL* ST2.....62 B3
Youlton Pl *BUCK/MIL* ST2............62 D3
Younger St *STOKE* ST4...............68 D1
Young St *BURS/TUN* ST6.............36 D5
CDLE ST10...................................75 E4
Yoxall Av *STOKE* ST4..................60 D4

Z

Zamenhof Gv *BURS/TUN* ST6........45 G5
Zennor Gv *BUCK/MIL* ST2............62 D2
Zetland Pl *LNGTN* ST3................79 F4
Zion St *BURS/TUN* ST6.................3 G4
Zodiac Dr *BURS/TUN* ST6.............36 D5

Index - featured places

Abbey Hill Special School
  BUCK/MIL ST2........................55 E4
Abbey Hulton Primary School
  BUCK/MIL ST2........................54 C4
Abbey Vue Tennis Club
  LEEK ST13.............................30 D2
Ackers Crossing
  CONG CW12............................17 H5
Alexander Trading Estate
  HAN ST1....................................4 B6
Alexandra Infant School
  LNGTN ST3............................70 C5
Alexandra Junior School
  LNGTN ST3............................80 C1
Allerynes High School
  STONE ST15...........................91 E1
All Saints CE First School
  LEEK ST13.............................31 E5
Alsager CC
  ALS/KID ST7..........................23 F4
Alsager Golf & Country Club
  ALS/KID ST7..........................33 G2
Alsager Highfields
  Primary School
  ALS/KID ST7..........................23 F4
Alsager Leisure Centre
  ALS/KID ST7..........................22 D4
Alsager School
  ALS/KID ST7..........................22 D4
Apedale Business Park
  NEWUL ST5............................50 C2
Ash Green Primary School
  STOKE ST4.............................78 B3
Ashlands Medical Centre
  NEWUL ST5..............................4 A5
Astbury Golf Club
  CONG CW12............................12 C3
Astbury Mere Country Park
  CONG CW12..............................7 H5
Astbury St Marys CE
  Primary School
  CONG CW12............................11 H2
Audley CC
  ALS/KID ST7..........................41 E4
Aynsley Special School
  BLYBR/FOR ST11.....................81 H3
Ball Green Primary School
  BURS/TUN ST6........................45 H1
Banbury Nursery School
  ALS/KID ST7..........................34 D2
Barlaston CE (VC) First School
  BARL ST12.............................87 E3
Barlaston CC
  BARL ST12.............................87 F3
Barnfield Road Industrial Estate
  LEEK ST13.............................30 C5
Barnes Hall (Keele University)
  NEWUL ST5............................58 B5
Beeches Junior School
  BLYBR/FOR ST11.....................82 C3
Belgrave CE Primary School
  LNGTN ST3............................80 A1
Belgrave Medical Centre
  LNGTN ST3............................80 A1
Bentilee CP School
  BUCK/MIL ST2........................63 G4
Bentilee Nursery School
  BUCK/MIL ST2........................63 F3
Beresford Memorial CE
  First School
  LEEK ST13.............................31 F2
Beresford Trading Estate
  BURS/TUN ST6........................44 B1
Berry Hill High School
  BUCK/MIL ST2........................62 C2
Biddulph Community
  Health Centre
  BIDD ST8...............................27 H1
Biddulph Grange
  Country Park *BIDD* ST8.............20 B2
Biddulph Grange
  Gardens (NT) *BIDD* ST8............20 A2
Biddulph High School
  BIDD ST8...............................27 H3
Biddulph Valley Leisure Centre
  BIDD ST8...............................19 H4
Birches Head High School
  HAN ST1................................54 B2
Birches Head Medical Centre
  HAN ST1................................54 B3
Birchwood Nursery School
  ALS/KID ST7..........................35 G1
Bishop Rawle CE
  Primary School *CDLE* ST10........74 D5
Bishop Stamer Primary School
  STOKE ST4.............................68 B1
Blackfirs Primary School
  CONG CW12..............................7 F3
Blackfriars Special School
  NEWUL ST5............................59 E5
Blurton High School
  LNGTN ST3............................78 D1
Blurton & Newstead
  Health Centre *LNGTN* ST3.........79 F2
Blurton Primary School
  LNGTN ST3............................69 E5

Blythe Bridge High School
  BLYBR/FOR ST11.....................82 B3
Bradwell CP School
  NEWUL ST5............................51 G2
Bradwell Crematorium
  NEWUL ST5............................51 H1
Bradwell Hospital
  NEWUL ST5............................51 G2
Brampton House
  Business Centre *NEWUL* ST5........2 E2
Brampton Sidings
  Industrial Estate
  NEWUL ST5...............................2 D1
Bridestone Shopping Centre
  CONG CW12..............................8 B4
Bridge Industrial Estate
  BURS/TUN ST6........................53 F2
Brindley Mill
  LEEK ST13.............................30 C2
Britannia Park Industrial Estate
  BURS/TUN ST6........................53 F2
Brookhouses Industrial Estate
  CDLE ST10.............................74 B5
Brook Medical Centre
  BURS/TUN ST6........................45 G3
Brookside Industrial Estate
  BURS/TUN ST6........................52 A1
Brough Park Leisure Centre
  LEEK ST13.............................30 D3
Brownhills Business Park
  BURS/TUN ST6........................44 B4
Brownhills High School
  BURS/TUN ST6........................44 A4
Brown Lees Road
  Industrial Estate *BIDD* ST8.......27 F4
Brunswick Industrial Estate
  NEWUL ST5............................44 B5
Buglawton Hall School
  CONG CW12..............................9 G2
Buglawton Industrial Estate
  CONG CW12..............................8 D2
Buglawton Primary School
  CONG CW12..............................9 E3
Burnwood Primary School
  BURS/TUN ST6........................45 F2
Burslem CC
  BURS/TUN ST6........................53 E3
Burslem Golf Club
  BURS/TUN ST6........................45 E2
Burslem Health Centre
  BURS/TUN ST6........................53 E1
Bursley Primary School
  NEWUL ST5............................51 H1
The Business Centre
  BURS/TUN ST6........................53 F2
Business & Technology
  Centre
  CW/SHV CW2..........................32 C2
Cadmans Leisure Centre
  BURS/TUN ST6........................45 G4
California Business Park
  STOKE ST4.............................68 C3
Carmountside Cemetery
  BUCK/MIL ST2........................54 D1
Carmountside Crematorium
  BUCK/MIL ST2........................54 D1
Carmountside Primary
  School *BUCK/MIL* ST2...............55 E2
The Cartwright Industrial
  Estate *LNGTN* ST3...................69 G4
Castle Primary School
  ALS/KID ST7..........................26 B2
Caverswall CC
  LNGTN ST3............................71 G3
Cedars Medical Centre
  ALS/KID ST7..........................23 F5
Cedars (Newcastle Base)
  NEWUL ST5............................52 A4
Central Forest Park
  HAN ST1................................53 G3
Century Retail Park
  HAN ST1..................................4 C2
Ceramica
  BURS/TUN ST6........................52 D1
Chapel Museum
  ALS/KID ST7..........................26 B2
Cheadle CC
  CDLE ST10.............................75 E5
Cheadle High School
  CDLE ST10.............................74 D5
Cheadle Primary School
  CDLE ST10.............................74 D5
Cheadle Shopping Centre
  CDLE ST10.............................74 D4
Cheadle Swimming Pool
  CDLE ST10.............................75 E5
Chesterton Clinic
  NEWUL ST5............................51 E3
Chesterton High School
  NEWUL ST5............................51 E3
Chesterton Primary School
  NEWUL ST5............................51 F2
Childrens Clinic
  HAN ST1..................................4 C7
Christ Church CE First School
  STONE ST15...........................90 D2

Christ Church CE Middle School
  STONE ST15...........................90 D1
Christchurch CE Primary School
  STOKE ST4.............................69 E1
Church Lawton Primary School
  ALS/KID ST7..........................24 A3
Churnet View Middle School
  LEEK ST13.............................31 F1
Cinderhill Industrial Estate
  LNGTN ST3............................70 C5
  LNGTN ST3............................70 D5
City of Stoke-on-Trent
  Sixth Form College
  STOKE ST4.............................61 H5
Civic Centre & Kings Hall
  STOKE ST4.............................61 F5
Clayton Hall Business & Language
  College *NEWUL* ST5..................67 E4
Cleveland Trading Estate
  HAN ST1..................................4 D6
Clough Hall School
  ALS/KID ST7..........................35 F2
Cobridge Industrial Estate
  BURS/TUN ST6........................53 F5
Cockshute Industrial Estate
  STOKE ST4.............................60 D3
Congleton Business Centre
  CONG CW12..............................8 C4
Congleton Business Park
  CONG CW12..............................8 A3
Congleton Golf Club
  CONG CW12.............................13 F2
Congleton High School
  CONG CW12..............................7 E4
Congleton Leisure Centre
  CONG CW12..............................8 C4
Coppice Special School
  NEWUL ST5...............................2 D7
Cottage Delight at Number 64
  LEEK ST13.............................30 D4
Crackley Bank Primary School
  NEWUL ST5............................51 E1
Cranberry J & I School
  ALS/KID ST7..........................22 C5
Crescent Primary School
  LNGTN ST3............................71 G5
Croft Road Industrial Estate
  NEWUL ST5............................59 H2
Crown Hotel
  STONE ST15...........................90 D3
Dane Mill Business Centre
  CONG CW12..............................8 A4
Daneside Business Park
  CONG CW12..............................8 C3
Daneside Theatre
  CONG CW12..............................8 B4
Daven Primary School
  CONG CW12..............................8 C5
Dilhorne Endowed
  Primary School *CDLE* ST10.........75 F2
Dilhorne Recreation Centre
  CDLE ST10.............................73 E4
Dimensions Leisure Complex
  BURS/TUN ST6........................44 D4
Dove Bank Primary School
  ALS/KID ST7..........................35 G1
Draycott Manor Primary
  School *BLYBR/FOR* ST11............83 F5
Dudson Museum
  HAN ST1..................................4 E2
Dunrobin Street Medical Centre
  STOKE ST4.............................70 A5
Eaton Bank Industrial Estate
  CONG CW12..............................8 D3
Eaton Bank School
  CONG CW12..............................8 D2
Eaton Park Health Centre
  BUCK/MIL ST2........................62 C3
Eaton Park Primary School
  BUCK/MIL ST2........................62 C2
Edenhurst Preparatory
  School
  NEWUL ST5............................59 F5
Edensor CE Primary School
  LNGTN ST3............................69 G5
Edensor Technology College
  LNGTN ST3............................69 G4
Ellison Primary School
  NEWUL ST5............................52 B4
Endon Hall Primary School
  END/WER ST9.........................39 H3
Endon High School
  END/WER ST9.........................39 G5
English Martyrs RC Primary
  School *BIDD* ST8.....................27 H1
Etruria Trading Estate
  NEWUL ST5...............................3 H4
Etruscan Primary School
  HAN ST1..................................4 A4
  STOKE ST4.............................61 G3
Etruscan Trading Estate
  HAN ST1..................................4 C3
Excalibur Industrial Estate
  ALS/KID ST7..........................23 G5
Excalibur Primary School
  ALS/KID ST7..........................33 G1

Faculty of Contemporary Arts
  (Manchester Metropolitan
  University)
  ALS/KID ST7..........................22 C4
Far Green Industrial Estate
  HAN ST1................................53 G3
Fegg Hayes Health Centre
  BURS/TUN ST6........................37 F5
Fenpark Industrial Estate
  STOKE ST4.............................69 F2
Fenton Industrial Estate
  STOKE ST4.............................62 B1
Fenton Manor Swimming Pool
  STOKE ST4.............................61 H5
Festival Heights Retail Park
  HAN ST1................................53 E4
Festival Park
  HAN ST1...................................4 A1
Finney Gardens Sports Ground
  HAN ST1................................62 B1
Forest Park Primary School
  BUCK/MIL ST2........................47 E4
Forsbrook CE Primary School
  BLYBR/FOR ST11.....................82 B3
Forum Theatre
  HAN ST1..................................4 E4
Foxfield Steam Railway
  BLYBR/FOR ST11.....................82 C1
  CDLE ST10.............................72 D2
Freeport Talke Outlet Mall
  ALS/KID ST7..........................34 C5
Friarswood Primary School
  NEWUL ST5...............................2 C7
Fulford CP School
  BLYBR/FOR ST11.....................89 H5
Furlong Industrial Estate
  NEWUL ST5............................52 C2
Furlong Medical Centre
  BURS/TUN ST6........................44 B2
Gas Works Industrial Estate
  ALS/KID ST7..........................35 E1
Gladstone Primary School
  LNGTN ST3............................70 A2
Gladstone Working Pottery
  Museum *LNGTN* ST3..................70 A4
Glebe Primary School
  NEWUL ST5............................69 F1
Goldenhill Golf Club
  BURS/TUN ST6........................36 B4
Goldenhill Primary School
  BURS/TUN ST6........................35 H4
Goldenhill St Josephs Catholic
  Primary School
  BURS/TUN ST6........................36 B4
Grafton Infant School
  LNGTN ST3............................70 A3
Grange Primary School
  LNGTN ST3............................81 E3
Great Fenton Business Park
  STOKE ST4.............................68 D3
Greenbirches Industrial
  Estate *BURS/TUN* ST6...............44 B2
Greenfield Farm Industrial
  Estate *CONG* CW12...................7 H3
Greenway Bank Country Park
  BIDD ST8...............................28 A4
Greenway Hall Golf Club
  END/WER ST9.........................47 F2
Greenways Primary School
  END/WER ST9.........................47 E2
Grove House Clinic
  NEWUL ST5...............................2 E2
Grove Junior School
  HAN ST1................................53 H4
Grove Road Industrial Estate
  STOKE ST4.............................68 D3
Hales Hall Caravan & Camping
  Park *CDLE* ST10......................75 F3
Hamilton Infant School
  HAN ST1................................53 H4
Hanford Clinic
  NEWUL ST5............................77 H2
Hanley Business Park
  HAN ST1..................................4 E6
Hanley Cemetery
  STOKE ST4.............................61 E5
Hanley Park
  HAN ST1..................................5 G3
Hanley St Lukes CE Primary
  School *HAN* ST1........................5 H5
Hanley Shopping Centre
  HAN ST1..................................4 D4
Hanley Town FC
  BUCK/MIL ST2........................54 C5
Harley Street Medical Centre
  HAN ST1..................................5 G5
Harpfield Primary School
  HAN ST1..................................3 H4
Hartshill Business Park
  NEWUL ST5...............................2 E4
Hartshill & Newcastle CC
  HAN ST1................................67 F2
Hassell Primary School
  NEWUL ST5...............................2 E4
Havannah Business Centre
  CONG CW12..............................8 D1

Havannah Primary School
  CONG CW12..............................8 D1
Haydon House Hotel
  STOKE ST4...............................3 J2
Haywood High School
  BURS/TUN ST6........................45 E4
The Haywood Hospital
  BURS/TUN ST6........................45 E3
Heathfield Special School
  BURS/TUN ST6........................45 F1
Hempstalls Primary School
  NEWUL ST5............................59 H1
Heron Cross Primary School
  STOKE ST4.............................68 D3
High Carr Business Park
  NEWUL ST5............................43 F4
Highfield Hall
  STOKE ST4.............................30 B1
Hillside Primary School
  BUCK/MIL ST2........................47 E4
Hill Top CP School
  STOKE ST4.............................52 D1
Hill Top Primary School
  ALS/KID ST7..........................34 D4
HM Young Offenders Institution
  Werrington House
  END/WER ST9.........................64 C1
Holden Lane High School
  Sports College *NEWUL* ST5........54 A1
Holden Lane Primary School
  HAN ST1................................54 B2
Holditch Industrial Estate
  NEWUL ST5............................51 F4
Hollywall Primary School
  BURS/TUN ST6........................36 A5
Hot Lane Industrial Estate
  BURS/TUN ST6........................53 F1
Hyde Park Trading Estate
  STOKE ST4.............................68 C1
Imex Business Park
  STOKE ST4.............................69 F2
Innkeeper's Lodge
  STOKE ST4.............................78 B4
Innovation Centres
  NEWUL ST5............................58 C5
Jackfield County Infants School
  ALS/KID ST7..........................34 C5
Jamage Industrial Estate
  ALS/KID ST7..........................34 C5
James Brindley High School
  BURS/TUN ST6........................36 D5
John Baskeyfield VC CE (C)
  Primary School
  BURS/TUN ST6........................44 D5
Joiner's Square
  Industrial Estate *HAN* ST1..........5 G6
Joiner's Square Primary School
  HAN ST1..................................5 H6
Jubilee Pool
  NEWUL ST5...............................2 E3
Keele Golf Club
  NEWUL ST5............................58 B4
Keele Leisure Centre
  NEWUL ST5............................58 B5
Keele University
  NEWUL ST5............................58 B5
Keele University
  (Hartshill Campus)
  STOKE ST4...............................3 K5
Keele University
  (Hospital Campus)
  STOKE ST4...............................3 G6
Kemball Special School
  STOKE ST4.............................69 F2
Kidsgrove Medical Centre
  ALS/KID ST7..........................36 A1
Kidsgrove Ski Centre
  ALS/KID ST7..........................35 F4
Kidsgrove Sports Centre
  ALS/KID ST7..........................35 F2
Kingsfield First School
  BIDD ST8...............................19 H5
Kingsland CE Primary School
  BUCK/MIL ST2........................54 C5
Knutton Infant Welfare
  Centre & Clinic *NEWUL* ST5........59 F2
Knutton Recreation Centre
  NEWUL ST5............................59 E2
Knutton St Marys CE Primary
  School *NEWUL* ST5...................59 E2
Knypersley First School
  BIDD ST8...............................27 F2
Knypersley Sports Club
  BIDD ST8...............................27 G3
Lambs House School
  CONG CW12..............................8 D3
Langdale Infant School
  NEWUL ST5............................66 D2
Leek College of FE & School
  of Art *LEEK* ST13....................30 D3
Leek County First School
  LEEK ST13.............................31 F4
Leek County High School
  LEEK ST13.............................31 F3
Leek Health Centre
  LEEK ST13.............................31 F4

Leek Moorlands Hospital
LEEK ST13 ....**31** F4
Leek Town FC
LEEK ST13 ....**30** B3
The Limes Industrial Estate
LEEK ST13 ....**31** F2
Linley Trading Estate
ALS/KID ST7 ....**34** C2
Little Moreton Hall (NT)
CONG CW12 ....**17** E3
Little Stoke CC **91** H5
Longbridge Hayes Industrial
Estate *BURS/TUN* ST6 ....**52** A1
Longton CC
LNGTN ST3 ....**79** F2
Longton High School
LNGTN ST3 ....**70** D5
Longton Leisure Centre
LNGTN ST3 ....**69** H4
Longton Neighbourhood
College *LNGTN* ST3 ....**70** A4
Longton Town Hall Cinema
LNGTN ST3 ....**69** H3
Longus Industrial Estate
BURS/TUN ST6 ....**44** B1
Lonpark Industrial Estate
LNGTN ST3 ....**70** A4
Loomer Road Industrial Estate
NEWUL ST5 ....**50** D4
Lord Nelson Industrial Estate
NEWUL ST5 ....**5** H5
Lucy Wedgwood Health Centre
NEWUL ST5 ....**53** E1
Lyme Brook Mental Health
Centre *NEWUL* ST5 ....**51** G2
Manor Hill First School
STONE ST15 ....**90** B4
Manor House Hotel
ALS ST7 ....**33** G1
Maple Court Primary School
BUCK/MIL ST2 ....**63** F4
Marcus Industrial Estate
HAN ST1 ....**62** B1
Marifield Primary School
CONG CW12 ....**8** A5
The Marsh Primary School
BLYBR/FOR ST11 ....**82** B4
Maryhill High School
ALS/KID ST7 ....**25** G5
Maryhill Primary School
ALS/KID ST7 ....**25** H5
May Bank Business Centre
NEWUL ST5 ....**52** B5
May Bank Infant School
NEWUL ST5 ....**60** B1
Meadows Community School
NEWUL ST5 ....**59** E2
Meadows Primary School
AUD/MAD/W CW3 ....**56** C4
Meir Health Centre
LNGTN ST3 ....**80** D1
Meir Heath CP School
LNGTN ST3 ....**89** E1
Meir Heath CC
LNGTN ST3 ....**89** E2
Members Business Centre
NEWUL ST5 ....**2** E1
Merryfield Special School
NEWUL ST5 ....**51** H5
Metro Business Park
HAN ST1 ....**4** C4
Michelin Sports Centre
STOKE ST4 ....**67** G5
Middlehurst Special School
ALS/KID ST7 ....**36** D4
Mill Hill Primary School
BURS/TUN ST6 ....**44** D2
Milton Primary School
BUCK/MIL ST2 ....**46** D5
The Mitchell High School
BUCK/MIL ST2 ....**63** E1
Mitchell Memorial Youth Centre
& Theatre *HAN* ST1 ....**4** D4
Moody Street Medical Centre ...**8** B5
Moorcroft Medical Centre
HAN ST1 ....**5** H5
Moor First School
BIDD ST8 ....**20** D4
Moorland Medical Centre
LEEK ST13 ....**31** E3
Moorlands Sixth Form Centre
CDLE ST10 ....**74** D5
Moorpark County Junior
School *BURS/TUN* ST6 ....**45** E5
Mossley CE Primary School
CONG CW12 ....**13** F2
Mount Industrial Estate
STONE ST15 ....**90** D1
Mount Pleasant CP School
STONE ST15 ....**68** D2
Mow Cop Castle (NT)
ALS/KID ST7 ....**26** B1
Nelson Industrial Estate
ALS/KID ST7 ....**34** C2
Newcastle Business Centre
NEWUL ST5 ....**51** G1
Newcastle Community
High School *NEWUL* ST5 ......**59** F5
Newcastle Museum & Art
Gallery *NEWUL* ST5 ....**3** F1
Newcastle Town FC
NEWUL ST5 ....**67** F1
Newcastle-under-Lyme College
NEWUL ST5 ....**2** B1
NEWUL ST5 ....**2** D3
Newcastle-under-Lyme College
(Trinity Site)
NEWUL ST5 ....**2** A2

Newcastle-under-Lyme Golf
Club *NEWUL* ST5 ....**66** B1
Newcastle-under-Lyme IT
Learning Centre *NEWUL* ST5 ..**2** E3
Newcastle-under-Lyme School
NEWUL ST5 ....**3** F4
New Cheadle Hospital
CDLE ST10 ....**74** D5
Newfields Industrial Estate
BURS/TUN ST6 ....**44** B1
New Ford Primary School
BURS/TUN ST6 ....**45** H5
New Forest Industrial Estate
HAN ST1 ....**53** G4
Newhouse Special School
BUCK/MIL ST2 ....**54** D4
New Parkhall Industrial Estate
LNGTN ST3 ....**70** B1
Newstead Industrial Trading
Estate *STOKE* ST4 ....**78** D3
Newstead Primary School
LNGTN ST3 ....**79** F4
New Victoria Theatre
NEWUL ST5 ....**3** G1
North Primary School
BURS/TUN ST6 ....**53** F2
North Staffordshire City General
Hospital *STOKE* ST4 ....**3** G7
North Staffordshire Hospital
(Hartshill Site) *STOKE* ST4 ....**3** K5
North Staffordshire Maternity
Hospital *STOKE* ST4 ....**3** H6
The North Staffordshire Nuffield
Hospital *NEWUL* ST5 ....**67** E4
North Staffordshire Regional
Film Theatre *STOKE* ST4 ....**61** F4
North Staffordshire Royal
Infirmary *STOKE* ST4 ....**60** D5
Northwood Infant School
HAN ST1 ....**5** J2
Northwood Stadium
HAN ST1 ....**5** K3
Norton Industrial Estate
BURS/TUN ST6 ....**46** A3
Norton Primary School
BURS/TUN ST6 ....**46** B3
Oakhill Primary School
STOKE ST4 ....**67** H4
The Octagon Shopping Centre
HAN ST1 ....**4** B5
Odeon Cinema & Hot Shots
Snooker *HAN* ST1 ....**4** A3
Oldfields Business Park
BURS/TUN ST6 ....**69** F3
Old Man of Mow
ALS/KID ST7 ....**18** B5
Our Lady & St Benedict
Primary School
BUCK/MIL ST2 ....**54** C4
Our Lady & St Werburghs RC (A)
Primary School *NEWUL* ST5 ...**66** D3
Our Ladys RC Primary School
STOKE ST4 ....**68** D1
Oxhey First School
BIDD ST8 ....**20** A4
Packmoor Primary School
HAN ST1 ....**36** D2
Painsley Catholic High School
CDLE ST10 ....**74** D5
Paramount Business Park
BURS/TUN ST6 ....**53** E1
Park Hall Country Park
LNGTN ST3 ....**71** E1
Parkhall Industrial Estate
LNGTN ST3 ....**70** C1
Park Hall Primary School
LNGTN ST3 ....**71** E3
Parkhouse Industrial Estate
NEWUL ST5 ....**51** F1
Park Middle School
BIDD ST8 ....**27** G2
The Picture House
BURS/TUN ST6 ....**45** H4
Pikemere Primary School
ALS/KID ST7 ....**22** D3
Pirehill First School
STONE ST15 ....**90** C5
Porthill Clinic
NEWUL ST5 ....**52** A3
Porthill Park CC
NEWUL ST5 ....**52** A5
Port Vale FC (Vale Park)
BURS/TUN ST6 ....**45** E5
The Potteries Business Centre
HAN ST1 ....**4** A2
The Potteries Museum & Art
Gallery *HAN* ST1 ....**4** E4
Potteries Shopping Centre
HAN ST1 ....**5** F2
Power Wash Trading Estate
BIDD ST8 ....**27** F4
Premier Travel Inn
NEWUL ST5 ....**43** F5
The Priory CE Primary School
STOKE ST4 ....**77** H2
Quality Hotel
HAN ST1 ....**4** D3
Queens Primary School
NEWUL ST5 ....**69** G2
Queensway Industrial
Estate
BURS/TUN ST6 ....**52** A1
The Quinta Primary School
CONG CW12 ....**16** A3
Radnor Park Trading Estate
CONG CW12 ....**7** F2
Ravenside Retail Park
ALS/KID ST7 ....**61** H4
Ravensmead Primary School
ALS/KID ST7 ....**41** G3

Red House FC
BLYBR/FOR ST11 ....**71** H4
Regent College
HAN ST1 ....**4** B7
Regent Theatre
HAN ST1 ....**4** E4
Reginald Mitchell Primary School
ALS/KID ST7 ....**34** D2
Ribble Industrial Estate
NEWUL ST5 ....**52** D2
Richard Heathcote
Community Primary School
ALS/KID ST7 ....**49** G3
The Roaches School (Upper)
BIDD ST8 ....**27** F2
Rode Heath Primary School
ALS/KID ST7 ....**23** H1
Roebuck Shopping Centre
NEWUL ST5 ....**6** C4
Rosevale Business Park
NEWUL ST5 ....**51** F1
Roundwell Place Day Hospital
BURS/TUN ST6 ....**44** B3
Rowhurst Industrial Estate
NEWUL ST5 ....**50** C2
Royal Doulton Visitor Centre
BURS/TUN ST6 ....**53** E1
Ryandra Business Park
STONE ST15 ....**74** B5
St Annes CE Primary School
BURS/TUN ST6 ....**38** D2
St Augustines RC Primary
School *LNGTN* ST3 ....**80** D2
St Chads CE Primary School
NEWUL ST5 ....**42** D4
St Dominics Catholic
Primary School
STONE ST15 ....**90** D3
St Dominics Independent Junior
School *STONE* ST15 ....**61** E4
St Dominics Priory School
STONE ST15 ....**90** C2
St Edwards CE Middle School
LEEK ST13 ....**30** B4
St Filumenas RC Primary School
BLYBR/FOR ST11 ....**72** A5
St Gabriel's RC Primary School
ALS/KID ST7 ....**23** E5
St George & St Martins RC Primary
School *HAN* ST1 ....**53** H3
St Giles RC (A) Primary School
CDLE ST10 ....**74** D4
St Giles & St Georges CE Primary
School *NEWUL* ST5 ....**2** D3
St Gregorys RC Primary School
LNGTN ST3 ....**69** H5
St John Fisher Catholic High
School *NEWUL* ST5 ....**2** B1
St Johns CE Primary School
NEWUL ST5 ....**57** H5
St John the Evangelist RC
Primary School
ALS/KID ST7 ....**35** F1
St Josephs College
STOKE ST4 ....**67** H4
St Lukes CE Primary School
NEWUL ST5 ....**57** H2
St Lukes CE (VC) Primary School
END/WER ST9 ....**39** G4
St Margarets CE Junior School
NEWUL ST5 ....**52** A5
St Margaret Ward Catholic
School *BURS/TUN* ST6 ....**44** D1
St Maria Goretti
Catholic Primary School
BUCK/MIL ST2 ....**63** E2
St Mark's CE Primary School
HAN ST1 ....**4** D6
St Marys Catholic Primary
School *CONG* CW12 ....**8** B4
St Marys CE Primary School
BURS/TUN ST6 ....**44** B3
St Marys RC Primary School
BURS/TUN ST6 ....**45** H5
NEWUL ST5 ....**2** B3
St Matthews CE (A) Primary
School *LNGTN* ST3 ....**80** C5
St Michaels CE First School
STONE ST15 ....**91** F5
St Pauls Junior School
BURS/TUN ST6 ....**52** C1
St Peters CE (A) Primary School
BLYBR/FOR ST11 ....**71** H4
St Peters High School &
International Language
College *STOKE* ST4 ....**3** K7
St Peters Nursery School
CONG CW12 ....**8** B7
St Peters RC CP School
NEWUL ST5 ....**53** E3
St Saviours CE Primary School
ALS/KID ST7 ....**34** C2
St Teresas RC Primary School
STOKE ST4 ....**67** G5
St Thomas Aquinas RC
Primary School
STOKE ST4 ....**60** D3
St Thomas CE (A) Primary
School *ALS/KID* ST7 ....**35** G2
St Thomas More Catholic
College *LNGTN* ST3 ....**69** G4
St Wilfrids RC Primary School
BURS/TUN ST6 ....**44** D3
St Wulstans Catholic Primary
School *NEWUL* ST5 ....**52** B4
Saltway School
END/WER ST9 ....**64** B2
Sandford Hill Primary School
LNGTN ST3 ....**70** A1

Sandon High School
LNGTN ST3 ....**80** D2
Sarraine Industrial Estate
CDLE ST10 ....**74** B5
Scholar Green Primary School
ALS/KID ST7 ....**25** E2
Scotia Business Park
BURS/TUN ST6 ....**44** C4
Scott Lidgett Industrial Estate
BURS/TUN ST6 ....**53** F2
Seabridge Junior School
NEWUL ST5 ....**66** B3
Shelton Swimming Pool
STOKE ST4 ....**61** F3
Silverdale Business Park
NEWUL ST5 ....**58** D3
Silverdale CC
NEWUL ST5 ....**58** A3
Silverdale Health Centre
NEWUL ST5 ....**58** A5
Silverdale Primary School
NEWUL ST5 ....**58** C3
Sir Thomas Boughey High
School *ALS/KID* ST7 ....**49** F2
Smallthorne Cemetery
BURS/TUN ST6 ....**45** G5
Smallthorne Primary School
BURS/TUN ST6 ....**45** H4
Smithfield Shopping Centre
LEEK ST13 ....**31** H1
Sneyd CC
BURS/TUN ST6 ....**53** F2
Sneyd Green Primary School
BURS/TUN ST6 ....**53** G2
Sneyd Hill Trading Estate
BURS/TUN ST6 ....**45** F5
Sneyd Industrial Estate
BURS/TUN ST6 ....**53** F1
Sneyd Trading Estate
BURS/TUN ST6 ....**53** F1
Spode Museum
STOKE ST4 ....**61** F5
Springcroft Primary School
BLYBR/FOR ST11 ....**81** H3
Springfield Primary School
STOKE ST4 ....**67** F1
Springfield Special School
STOKE ST4 ....**31** F4
Springhead Primary School
ALS/KID ST7 ....**34** D5
Squirrel Hayes County First
School *BIDD* ST8 ....**27** H1
Staffordshire Magistrates Court
NEWUL ST5 ....**2** C2
Staffordshire University
HAN ST1 ....**4** C7
HAN ST1 ....**5** F4
STOKE ST4 ....**61** F4
Stallington Hospital
BLYBR/FOR ST11 ....**89** H2
Stanfield Hospital
BURS/TUN ST6 ....**45** E3
Station Industrial Estate
HAN ST1 ....**62** B1
Stoke Business Park
STOKE ST4 ....**61** F5
Stoke Cemetery
STOKE ST4 ....**3** K6
Stoke City FC
(Britannia Stadium)
STOKE ST4 ....**68** C3
Stoke Health Centre
STOKE ST4 ....**61** E5
Stoke-on-Trent RFC
STONE ST15 ....**88** A3
Stoke-on-Trent College
HAN ST1 ....**4** C7
Stoke-on-Trent College
(Burslem Campus)
BURS/TUN ST6 ....**45** F5
Stoke-on-Trent College
(Cauldon Campus)
STOKE ST4 ....**61** F3
Stoke-on-Trent College
of Art
STOKE ST4 ....**61** F4
Stoke-on-Trent Magistrates
Court *STOKE* ST4 ....**68** D1
Stoke Superbowl
HAN ST1 ....**4** A3
Stone CC
STONE ST15 ....**91** E4
Stone Golf Club
STONE ST15 ....**90** B3
Stone Tennis Club
STONE ST15 ....**90** C2
Stonewall Industrial Estate
NEWUL ST5 ....**58** D2
Stop Inn
NEWUL ST5 ....**51** G4
Studio 1 Health Centre
NEWUL ST5 ....**69** H3
Summerbank Primary School
BURS/TUN ST6 ....**44** A2
Sutherland Primary School
LNGTN ST3 ....**79** F1
Talke Clinic
ALS/KID ST7 ....**34** D5
Thistley Hough High School
STOKE ST4 ....**67** G1
Thursfield Primary School
BIDD ST8 ....**26** B5
Titanic Brewery
BURS/TUN ST6 ....**53** E3
Tittensor CE First School
BARL ST12 ....**86** A4
Town Road Business Quarter
HAN ST1 ....**53** H4
Townsend Primary School
BUCK/MIL ST2 ....**54** D5

Town Yard Industrial Estate
....**30** C4
Travelodge
ALS/KID ST7 ....**42** D2
CW/SHV CW2 ....**32** A5
Trentham RFC
STOKE ST4 ....**78** B4
Trentham Business Centre
STOKE ST4 ....**78** D3
Trentham Gdns
STOKE ST4 ....**77** H4
Trentham Golf Club
STOKE ST4 ....**78** B4
Trentham High School
STOKE ST4 ....**78** A2
Trentham Park Golf Club
STOKE ST4 ....**77** G3
Trent Hospital
STONE ST15 ....**90** C3
Trentside Business Park
STOKE ST4 ....**68** A3
Trentside Clinic
STOKE ST4 ....**90** D3
Trent Vale CE Primary School
STOKE ST4 ....**67** G4
Trent Vale Health Centre
STOKE ST4 ....**67** H3
Tunstall Cemetery
BURS/TUN ST6 ....**44** D2
Tunstall
Neighbourhood College
BURS/TUN ST6 ....**44** C4
Tunstall Road
Industrial Estate
BIDD ST8 ....**27** G4
Ubberley Health Centre
BUCK/MIL ST2 ....**63** E5
Unicorn Industrial Estate
BURS/TUN ST6 ....**52** B1
Vale FC
CONG CW12 ....**8** C3
Victoria Hall
HAN ST1 ....**5** F4
VUE Cinema
NEWUL ST5 ....**2** D4
Walton Priory Middle School
STONE ST15 ....**90** C5
War Memorial Hospital
CONG CW12 ....**12** D1
Wedgwood Memorial College
BARL ST12 ....**86** D3
Wedgwood's Monument
ALS/KID ST7 ....**42** B5
Wedgwood Visitor Centre
BARL ST12 ....**86** D1
Well Street Medical Centre
BIDD ST8 ....**27** H1
STOKE CT10 ....**75** E4
Werrington Primary School
END/WER ST9 ....**64** B1
Westcliffe Hospital
BURS/TUN ST6 ....**36** D4
West Heath Shopping Centre
CONG CW12 ....**7** G4
Westlake Trading Estate
BURS/TUN ST6 ....**44** B4
Westlands Primary School
NEWUL ST5 ....**66** B4
Weston Coyney Infant School
LNGTN ST3 ....**71** F2
Weston Coyney Junior School
LNGTN ST3 ....**71** E4
Westwood First School
LEEK ST13 ....**30** B4
Westwood High School
LEEK ST13 ....**30** A4
Whieldon Industrial Estate
STOKE ST4 ....**68** D1
Whitebridge Industrial Estate
STONE ST15 ....**90** B1
Whitfield Valley Primary School
BURS/TUN ST6 ....**37** F4
Willfield Community
Education Centre
BUCK/MIL ST2 ....**63** G4
Willfield Neighbourhood
College
BUCK/MIL ST2 ....**63** G5
The Willows Primary School
STOKE ST4 ....**60** D5
Wolstanton CE School
NEWUL ST5 ....**52** A4
Wolstanton Golf Club
NEWUL ST5 ....**51** G4
Wolstanton High School
NEWUL ST5 ....**52** A5
Wolstanton Retail Park
NEWUL ST5 ....**52** A5
Woodcocks Well CE
Primary School
ALS/KID ST7 ....**26** A2
Woodcroft First School
LEEK ST13 ....**30** B5
Woodhouse Middle School
BIDD ST8 ....**20** A3
Wood Lane Primary School
ALS/KID ST7 ....**41** H5

The Post Office is a registered trademark of Post Office Ltd. in the UK and other countries.

Schools address data provided by Education Direct.

Petrol station information supplied by Johnsons

One-way street data provided by © Tele Atlas N.V. Tele Atlas

Garden centre information provided by

Garden Centre Association   Britains best garden centres

Wyevale Garden Centres

The statement on the front cover of this atlas is sourced, selected and quoted from a reader comment and feedback form received in 2004

Notes